Trouble of Mind
and
the Disease of Melancholy

written for the use of such as are or have been exercised by the same

by

Timothy Rogers, M.A.,
(who was long afflicted with both)

Edited by Dr. Don Kistler

Soli Deo Gloria Publications
. . . for instruction in righteousness . . .

Soli Deo Gloria Publications
A division of Soli Deo Gloria Ministries, Inc.
P.O.Box 451, Morgan, PA 15064
(412) 221-1901/FAX 221-1902
www.SDGbooks.com

Trouble of Mind and the Disease of Melancholy was published in 1691 under the title *A Discourse on Trouble of Mind and the Disease of Melancholy*. This Soli Deo Gloria reprint, in which spelling, grammar, and formatting changes have been made, was retypeset from the second edition.

ISBN 1-57358-120-8

Second Printing 2004

Library of Congress Cataloging-in-Publication Data

Rogers, Timothy, 1658-1728.
Trouble of mind and the disease of melancholy / by Timothy Rogers;
edited by Don Kistler.
p. cm.
Originally published: 1691.
Includes bibliographical references.
ISBN 1-57358-120-8 (hardcover : alk. paper)
1. Depression, Mental–Religious aspects–Christianity.
2. Christian life–Puritan authors. I. Kistler, Don. II. Title.
BV4910.34 .R64 2002
248.8'6–dc21

2002012755

Contents

Part III

The Life of Timothy Rogers

(1658-1728)

Timothy Rogers, the son of John Rogers (a faithful and useful nonconformist minister in the diocese of Durham), was born at Barnard Castle, Yorkshire, on May 24, 1658. He received his grammar learning under a private tutor in Durham, or in Yorkshire, where his father resided. His father instructed him in the principles of religion and trained him up in the nurture and admonition of the Lord. When he was old enough, his father sent him to Glasgow University in Scotland, where he pursued his studies for the ministry. During this time he acquired a critical acquaintance with the languages, and after residing there for some years, earned the degree of Master of Arts. But before Rogers entered the ministry, he lived for sometime in the house of the learned Edward Veel, an eminent Puritan tutor. Veel, who resided in Wapping, held a dissenting academy for ministerial students. Veel had several pupils under his care and gave both his heart and life for their furtherance in Jesus Christ. Rogers felt a near kinship to Veel and never denied his mentor's patronage and advice.

His entrance into the ministry was as evening lecturer at Crosby Square, Bishopsgate-street. He held this position for several years in conjunction with Thomas Kentish, who afterwards ministered in a congregation in Southwark. Rogers acquired a considerable reputation as a preacher while lecturing at Crosby Square, which was supported by many merchants and other persons of respectability in the city. He was comfortable in the pulpit, clearly articulated his thoughts, and had a striking manner of address. His philosophy in the pulpit (exemplified in his published works) was to choose the best words he could find to express his thoughts. He believed that religion, which enlarges and beautifies the soul, was not the portion of the careless, but of the meek, humble, and devout.

His first appearance before the public as an author was in the year 1683, when his sermon "Early Religion, or, The Way for a Young Man to Remember His Creator," was published. The occasion of the sermon was the sudden death of Robert Linager, a fellow student training for the ministry in Veel's academy. Linager's friends not only urged Rogers to preach the funeral, but also pressed him to publish the sermon shortly thereafter. Rogers's only aim in printing the sermon (a discourse on Ecclesiastes 12:1: "Remember now the Creator in the days of thy youth") was "to show the necessity of a serious remembrance of God in youth." His words to those gathered at the funeral are sobering: "To you that were the acquaintances of the deceased, I shall only say this: now you have stronger engagements upon you to remember your Creator than you had before, for He has by the death of your companion sent you a near and a loud warning to prepare for your own. He had but a little, if any sickness at all, before that which proved his last. Flatter not then yourselves with the too great hopes of long life, because of your present health and strength."

About the year 1688 Rogers fell into a state of deep sickness and melancholy [depression] for nearly two years. The severity of his illness was to such an extent that he gave up all hope of the mercy of God and considered himself a vessel made for wrath. He described his mind as a land of darkness on which the sun never seemed to shine. The stress his mind produced gave him immeasurable grief. As John Colquhoun observed, "Melancholy . . . increases trouble of mind, and trouble of mind increases melancholy." Thus Rogers felt that he was in a worsening condition, driven from the light of God's countenance (as Adam was from paradise) and cast into utter darkness; he felt trapped with no way of escape.

Nothing seemed to comfort Rogers in this condition. Richard Baxter once said that "you may almost as easily keep the leaves of trees in quietness and order in a blustering wind as the thoughts of one in troubling passions."

The extremity of Rogers's illness may never be known as he himself could scarcely find words to describe it. "Who can describe that anguish and tribulation which such apprehensions [of God's displeasure] cause in a desolate and a mourning soul," he wrote. And in another place he said, "It is impossible to relate the whole [of my suffering], for my sorrows were beyond expression." The sufferings of his mind had so weakened his physical body that he could no longer attend the lecture. Many of his near relations suffered from similar infirmities, thus some have conjectured that his illness was "hereditary hypochondria." It is, perhaps, impossible to know whether his condition was prompted or aggravated by hereditary disease, but in either case it is certain that his ailment consisted of relentless fears concerning his soul's salvation.

His condition was well known to many pious ministers and people throughout the country, who were earnest and incessant in their supplications on his behalf. Rogers once told how his brother in the lecture, Thomas Kentish, had often prayed with him for his complete recovery, that he might be restored to God's service.

And these prayers were not ineffectual, for it pleased God to restore Rogers to a proper frame of mind. Darkness had clouded his mind for two years, but the light of God's countenance returned to him, and he could say, "God. . .hath wrought a double salvation for me."

In 1690, the year of his recovery, Rogers returned to the lecture and offered his grateful acknowledgements to the Divine Goodness for his wonderful restoration. In his first sermon, on Psalm 30:3:4 ("O Lord, Thou hast brought up my soul from the grave"), Rogers declared, "I come to you as one from the dead, to say no more." He subsequently preached four more sermons on the same text and published them as *Practical Discourses on Sickness and Recovery* in 1690. He included an epistle dedicatory to William Ashurst and Thomas Lane, with whom he had stayed in the country during "troubled and uneasy times."

In *Practical Discourses*, Rogers dealt primarily with the Christian's deportment under bodily ailments. He carefully warned the healthy not to exult in their temporal prosperity, for "he that is proud of his body is as foolish as if he should dote upon a flower, which in an unseen storm may deprive of all its glory." He also reminded the sick to be thankful for God:s sparing mercy: "How many are dead since you were first ill? How many excellent ministers whom you must never hear again?

How many of your dearest friends are now in the cold grave, with whom you cannot now discourse, and whose faces you shall never see till the Great Day? This should engage us to make suitable returns to that God who has spared us when he hath taken them away."

Due to the success of his *Practical Discourses,* Rogers published *A Discourse on Trouble of Mind and the Disease of Melancholy* the following year (which went through two subsequent editions in 1706 and 1808), in which he laid down many helps for the comfort and relief of dejected souls. In the preface, Rogers gives thirteen directions to the friends and relatives of melancholy persons, and discusses the best way of treating them (see pages 24 - 47 in the current reprint).

In addition, several ministerial letters introduced the book, either expressing gratitude for the author's recovery or strongly commending his work (these letters are not included in the present edition). In one of thes letters the celebrated Joseph Hussey wrote, "Doubtless God hath thus clothed you with the garment of salvation, that you may encourage others to put on Christ, though hell is naked before them, and destruction hath no covering from those that are not hid in Him."

Not long after his recovery, Rogers became an assistant to the eminent John Shower, minister of the Presbyterian congregation in Jewin Street, which subsequently moved to a larger and more convenient meeting-house in Old Jewry in 1701. Shower was a brilliant Puritan orator, who preached the funeral of Mary Doolittle, wife of Thomas Doolittle, in 1692. Shower highly regarded Rogers as a minister, and Rogers, similarly, esteemed his famous colleague.

For several years Rogers preached with great success

and shared in the affections of his people. He was known for his pious life and modest temper. In 1692 he preached "Fall Not Out by the Way, or, A Persuasion to a Friendly Correspondence between the Conformists and Non-Conformists," occasioned by the death of Anthony Dunwell. The discourse (consisting of two sermons on Genesis 45:24: "See that ye fall not out by the way") clearly envisions an ideal state that all Christians must strive for—unity in the bond of peace. Rogers confessed that the text he preached was chosen by Dunwell in his Last Will and Testament, and that Dunwell himself was known for his love of unity. Near the close of his second sermon, Rogers pleaded: "Oh, that we and all our acquaintance might meet in heaven above! And let us be sure not to fall out in our way thither. Let us while we live in a changeable and fading world, prepare for one what will never fade. Let us not be amazed at the grave, it now swallows us up and our friends, but it shall not keep us very long, for our Lord will shortly come and make our dust to live again, and make those bodies that were weakened by sickness and destroyed by death, to be like his own glorious body; and what we now believe, we shall see and know to be true."

In the same year, Rogers preached the funeral of Edmund Hill, on 1 Corinthians 7:31 ("For the fashion of this world passeth away"), and published it at the request of John Hill, Edmund's brother. It appeared in the summer of 1692 under the title, *The Changeableness of this World with Respect to Nations, Families, and Particular Persons, with a Practical Application thereof to the Various Conditions of this Mortal Life.* In the epistle dedicatory, addressed to Hill's relations, Rogers wrote: "The whole design of God in all His providence to us is to advance His own glory by drawing off our minds from the things which are seen, and which are temporal, to those that are invisible and eternal, and by all our earthly losses to teach us more the value of His own grace." The main emphasis of the sermon was to show the fleetingness of the present world and the reality of the world to come. Rogers's depiction of the unbeliever is strikingly descriptive of the modern world: "What is more inexcusable than for a man, for a sinner, to dread poverty and outward meanness, and contempt, and not to be afraid of hell, to live as if he were all body, and had no soul to save, to be fond of life, never to think of death, as if this would never perish, and that never come?"

The next appearance of Rogers in print was the funeral sermon of Edward Rede, a country man from Salisbury who had recently moved to London. The text chosen for the funeral was Psalm 27:13 ("I had fainted, unless I had believed to see the goodness of the Lord in the land of the living"). Apparently, Rede had expressed some inclination towards this text as it was the same text used for his mother's funeral in the country; Rogers recalled the tender moments with Rede discussing the sad event, and, accordingly, chose the text that was dear to his parishioner.

Rogers published two more funeral sermons in his lifetime, both at the request of others. "The Happiness of a Quiet Mind" appeared in 1696 (some sources erroneously place it in 1691), occasioned by the death of Martha Hasselborn, who died in her 95th year. And his last funeral sermon, "The Character of a Good Woman, both in a Single and a Married State," issued from the press in 1697. The sermon, on Proverbs 31:10 ("Who can find a virtuous woman, for her price is far above rubies"), was brought about by the death of Elizabeth Dunton, the daughter of the excellent Samuel Annesley. Rogers introduced the sermon with a lengthy history of notable women (calling them "lovely jewels" and "priceless rubies"), and finished it with an account Mrs. Dunton's life and death, including extracts from her diary. His only design for publishing Mrs. Dunton's funeral sermon was "that the world may not lose such an extraordinary instance of a good wife."

"The Character of a Good Woman" is full of practical insight for both the married and the unmarried. Two admonitions that Rogers gives are especially noteworthy: first, those who marry, Rogers says, must marry for love (he gives this counsel both to parents and to their children, observing, "where there is not an antecedent union of affection, there's no prospect of comfortable life"); secondly, one's prospective spouse must be judged by the understanding and the graces of the heart, not by physical attraction. "Many a fine face," wrote Rogers, "is spoiled by a little sickness; the small pox does often leave furrows there, where all the winning and conquering graces were before; in a little while all the sparkling vivacity of the eyes is gone, and a faint pale succeeds the lovely white and red."

Rogers was always afflicted, at least partially, in his mind, and prone to despondency. This trial rendered him a burden to himself and greatly hindered his usefulness. In 1707 his dejection of mind was so troublesome (he looked upon himself "as a lamp despised, a broken vessel, and, as a dead man out of mind") that he left the ministry and retired in Wantage, Berkshire.

Even though Rogers spent his last years in relative obscurity, he continued to bear witness to the splendor of Christ; in the midst of his darkness, he was enabled to justify God in all the dispensations of His providence. He entered triumphantly into his Father's arms in November 1728, and was buried in a Wantage churchyard on the 29th day of that month.

The Current Reprint

The present work, now thankfully published, last appeared in print in 1808. For almost two centuries, the author's work on melancholy has been out of print, destined for oblivion, as Archibald Alexander feared in his *Thoughts on Religious Experience*: "The writings of so many of our old English divines have recently been reprinted in London. But still, many valuable treatises are destined for oblivion." But this treatise, *A Discourse on Trouble of Mind and the Disease of Melancholy,* has seen a new day and will gain a new readership.

It is easy, perhaps, for many to dismiss this work as an oddity of historical interest. The reader should remember, however, that the author's ailment was primarily spiritual, even if it had hereditary overtones. This fact alone makes his work of tremendous import, and his cure all the more compelling. The editor to the 1808 edition wrote, "Those who are acquainted with the distressing circumstances in which the pious author was placed, previous to his writing the present treatise, will readily grant that he was the fittest person to write upon such a subject. He had nothing to do, but to detail his own experience. In so doing, he has recorded the experience of many thousand persons, who, in all periods of the church, have been afflicted more or less with a dejection of spirits, which has very properly been termed religious melancholy."

Rogers wrote from the depths of his heart; he expressed gratitude on every page, and gave witness to the beauty and grandeur of Christ (the best cure for all ailments). He had a sight and a sense that few equal, for he saw death face to face, as it were, and lived to tell others. He longed for the coming of his Deliverer, and yearned for the heavenly places in Christ Jesus. We would do well to imitate him in this way.

Rogers reminds us that in heaven "we shall feel the love of God in so sweet and transporting a manner that we shall never doubt whether He loves [us] or not." No longer will saints struggle with sin; no longer will they doubt their Savior's love; no longer will they despair of His mercy. "Even so, come Lord Jesus" (Revelation 22:20).

Randall Pederson
Grand Rapids, MI
March 2002

Dedication

To the very much honored and respected lady,
the Lady Mary Jane

Madam,

Your ladyship has a very just claim to this dedication, and under your patronage this book can, with good assurance, venture abroad. You, more than any other, have inquired of me concerning the following treatise, and more frequently urged me to print it. You were pleased to honor me, during my long affliction, with your kind visits. And though I was greatly afflicted, and in degrees beyond what are very common to me, yet you did not a little revive me by your compassionate and gentle words, and by the charitable hopes that you had of my deliverance, though you have often heard me say that I would never be delivered. I thought that I would never have any more ease in my pained body, nor every any more hope or quiet in my troubled soul.

But that God who is omnipotent, and who heard your prayers, and the prayers of many others on my behalf, has wrought a double salvation for me. He who is the Lord of nature has healed my body; and He who is the Father of mercies and the God of all grace has given rest to my weary soul. None have any cause to presume—when they consider what miseries I felt for a long time, and how I was overwhelmed with the deepest sorrows for many doleful months together—neither have any cause to despair, for they cannot be more low, more near to death and hell, than I thought myself to be. Yet I live, and am not without some refreshing hope of God's acceptance, and can say with the prophet, "Let Israel hope in the Lord, for with the Lord there is mercy, and with Him is plenteous redemption" (Psalm 130:7).

Your Ladyship has never indeed been afflicted with that distemper and those anxieties of soul whereof I treat in the following book; and I heartily pray that you never will. For melancholy is the worst of all distempers, and those sinking and guilty fears which it brings with it are inexpressibly dreadful. But I know that you have been in manifold afflictions, and you have had several very great losses. Some years ago you lost a father who was indeed, in all respects, for his holiness, his even temper, and his public and charitable spirit, worthy to be loved; and I am sure you greatly loved him, as he did you, to the very last. You lost a mother, whom all who knew her greatly valued for the skill and experience that she had in matters of religion, and especially for her admirable acquaintance with the Holy Scriptures. Though in the latter part of her life she did not see the light of this world, yet her soul was recreated with a spiritual and divine light. And the loss of her sight was abundantly recompensed to her by the clearer views she had of God and the life to come.

In addition to these losses, you have lost several children in whom was all the sweetness of youth, all that good temper and those blooming appearances of hopefulness which could make such little plants desirable. But you have borne even so great a loss with a submissive and Christian patience, knowing that you have not so much cause to mourn for those who are gone as to rejoice in those who are left, who are a very great comfort to you, and may they long be so.

As I have had for some time heretofore the honor to sojourn in your family, I always observed in you that meekness and good temper, that affability and condescension to your inferiors, which made your conversation very exemplary, and made it easy and pleasant for any persons to be in your house. If all the ladies and women in the world who are called "good" were of a temper so happy as your Ladyship's, what a quiet and peaceable world we would then have! The mutual love in which Sir Thomas and you live renders, indeed, the married state very excellent and honorable.

I thought, when I came to describe my inward troubles, that I should have described them at greater lengths; but I dared not review them too particularly lest the very thoughts of them would again, in some measure, overwhelm me. And, indeed, inward terrors are things that may be sadly felt, but cannot be fully expressed. To have the sense of tormenting, racking pain, the immediate prospect of death, and, together with these, an apprehension of God's displeasure, and the fear of being cast out of His favorable presence forever—these were all part of my case. And who can describe that anguish and tribulation which such apprehensions cause in a desolate and mourning soul!

I have, in the following treatise, said as much as will, I suppose, be believed by those who have never been in such a woeful state; and, if I had said more, it might perhaps sink some poor souls who are already low enough. If I cannot help them, which is my design, yet I will be sure, as much as in me lies, not to make them worse.

Madam, I could say a great many excellent things about your Ladyship, and which, in the opinion of all who have the happiness to be acquainted with you, would be no flattery; but I know your virtues are illustrious and evident enough in themselves, without my endeavoring to place them in a more open light. Excuse, I entreat you, the boldness of this dedication in which, to speak sincerely, I have a great deal of selfishness; for I question not but that by the means of your name this book will be more public, and so be more serviceable to people under long and sore afflictions, whereof this miserable world is very full. I wish you a continuance of those blessings of heaven with those of this earth, which you have in great abundance. May the candle of the Lord constantly shine on your tabernacle, on Sir Thomas, yourself, and all your children. And I desire you to be assured that there is none who more heartily prays for your present and eternal welfare than your Ladyship's most obliged servant,

Timothy Rogers
London
September 8, 1691

Preface

Containing several advices to the relatives and friends of melancholy people

There is a great difference between those who are only under trouble of conscience and those whose bodies are greatly diseased at the same time. A sense of sin and sorrow for it may, in some persons, not at all change their former state of health. And the mercy of God may so speedily relieve them that they suffer no visible decays in their constitution, but are so happy as to have a sound mind and body at once. It is not with relation to these that I write this preface, but for such as are under a deep and a rooted melancholy. And to the friends of such I think it is very necessary to give the following bits of advice:

1. Look upon your distressed friends as being under one of the worst distempers they can have in this miserable life. Melancholy seizes on the brain and spirits, and incapacitates them for thought or action; it confounds and disturbs all their thoughs, and unavoidably fills them with anguish and vexation, of which there is no resemblance in any other distemper, unless it is that of a raging fever. I take it for granted, and I verily believe, that I say nothing but what is true. When this ugly humor is deeply fixed and has spread its malignant influence over every part, it is as vain a thing to strive against it as to strive against a fever, a pleurisy, the gout, or the gallstone, which are very grievous to nature, but

which a man, by resolution and the force of briskness and courage, cannot help. One would be glad to be rid of such oppressing things, but all our striving will not make them go away.

Of all the inconveniences of melancholy, the lack of sleep, which it usually brings with it, is one of the worst. It is very reviving to a man who is in pain all the day to think that he shall sleep at night; but when he has no prospect nor hope of that for several nights together, oh, what confusion then seizes upon him! He is then like one upon a rack whose anguish will not allow him to rest; by this means the faculties of the soul are weakened and all its operations disturbed and clouded, and the poor body languishes and pines away at the same time.

And this disease is more formidable than any other because it commonly lasts very long. It is a long time before it has come to its height, and usually as long ere it declines again; and all this long season of its continuance is full of fear and torment, of horror and amazement. It is in every respect sad and overwhelming; it is a state of darkness that has no discernible beams of light. It is as a land of darkness on which no sun at all seems to shine. It generally begins first at the body, and then conveys its venom to the mind; and if anything cold be found that might keep the blood and spirits in their due temper and motion, this would obstruct its further progress and, in a great measure, keep the soul clear.

I do not pretend to tell you what medicines are proper to remove it, for I know of none. I leave you to consult with such as are learned in the profession of medicine, and especially to have recourse to such doctors as have themselves felt it; for it is impossible to fully understand the nature of it any other way than by experience. And that person is highly to be valued whose endeavors God will bless to the removal of this obstinate and violent disease. As Richard Greenham, in his *A Sweet Comfort for an Afflicted Conscience,* says, "There is a great deal of wisdom required to consider both the state of the body and the soul." He says that if a man who is troubled in conscience comes to a minister, he will likely look to the soul and not at all to the body; if that same man goes to a physician, he will likely consider the body and neglect the soul. For my part, I would never despise the physician's counsel nor neglect the minister's labor, because, the soul and body dwelling together, it is convenient that as the soul should be cured by the Word, prayer, fasting, or comforting, so the body must be brought into some temperature by medicine and diet, harmless diversions, and such like ways (providing always that it is so done in the fear of God as not to think by these ordinary means quite to smother or evade our troubles, but to use them as preparatives whereby our souls may be made more capable of the spiritual methods that are to follow afterwards).

2. Look upon those who are under this woeful disease of melancholy with great pity and compassion. And pity them the more by considering that you are in the body, and are liable to the very same trouble. For however brisk, however sanguine, and however cheerful you are, yet you may meet with those heavy crosses, those long and painful and sharp afflictions, which may sink your spirits. Many who are far from being naturally inclined to melancholy have been acciden-

tally overwhelmed with it by the loss of children, or by some sudden and unlooked-for disappointment that ruined all their former projects and designs. Oh, let every groan that you hear from persons thus afflicted deeply affect your hearts, and never look upon them but with a compassionate and concerned eye; never look upon them without making this application to yourselves: man at his best is altogether vanity. Let it wean you from the world when you see that by such a disease as this a man is quickly taken off from all his business, and is unfit to manage his affairs or pursue what was once delightful work.

Melancholy is a complication of violent and sore distresses. It is full of miseries; it is itself a sore affliction, and brings to our thoughts and bodies one evil upon another quickly. Any other distemper may trouble us, but this astonishes and amazes. Oh, look upon your friends who suffer from this with great tenderness, for they, alas, are wounded in both soul and body; and in all the world there are none, for that time, in so doleful an estate as they are. They are usually walking as if in the midst of fire and brimstone, and are most frequently under the very pangs of death and the pains of hell; they are in great bodily danger. Their burden is very often heavier than their groaning; their sighs are deep, their hearts are sunk, their minds are in a flame, and they are fallen very low. They are thinking on what is sad and frightful, and they cannot banish those ideas that are so terrible.

If you saw a wounded person, torn and mangled, on the highway, the sight of so deplorable an object would fill you with compassion; the sight of your friends under this disease of which I am now speaking ought to move you much more, for it is tearing them to pieces every moment. Every moment it preys upon their vitals, and they are continually dying, yet cannot die.

When you visit a melancholy person, make this reflection: "This friend of mine awhile ago rejoiced in the love of God as I do; he met with me in holy assemblies and sang the praises of the Most High with as pleasant a countenance, with as cheerful a heart, as I do. And now he is in despair, horror, and mourning; now his visage and his language are changed, and he is all dissolved in bitterness, tears, and woe. Oh, how vain a thing is man! How terrible it is to fall into the hands of the living God! My poor friend is under a sense of God's displeasure; he never eats or drinks with any pleasure. He is covered with sadness, while I rejoice in the blessings of providence. I will, by this example, learn to value my own mercies, and to have a great tenderness for such as are brought so very low."

If, as Mr. Peacock said in his distress, you did but feel their grief for one hour, you would have great compassion for them. Every one of their tears and sighs has this language, in which the poor, afflicted Job spoke to his hard-hearted visitors in Job 19:21: "Have pity upon me, have pity upon me, O ye my friends; for the hand of God hath touched me."

3. Do not use harsh speeches to your friends when they are under the disease of melancholy. Harsh words may fret and perplex, and enrage them more, but they will never do them the least good. Some indeed will advise you to chide and rebuke them upon all occasions, but I dare confidently say that such advisers never felt this disease, for, if they had, they would know that by such a method they merely pour oil on the flames, and

chafe and exasperate their wounds instead of healing them. Mr. [John] Dod, by reason of his mild, meek, and merciful spirit, was reckoned as one of the most fit persons to deal with people who were thus afflicted. Never was any minister more tender and compassionate, as those will find who read the account of Mr. Peacock and Mrs. Drake, who, by his assistance, were very much revived.

If you would be serviceable to such persons, you must not vex them with harsh and rigorous discourse. It causes many poor souls to cherish and conceal their troubles to their greater torment because they meet with very harsh entertainment from those to whom they have begun to explain their case. Our blessed Lord, our principal Physician, was meek and lowly, and would not break the bruised reed nor quench the smoking flax. The first visit that the aforementioned Mr. Dod made to Mr. Peacock, who was in anguish, was to put him in mind of God's kindness, of which Mr. Dod showed him four parts: (1) to take small things in good part; (2) to pass by infirmities; (3) to be easily entreated; and (4) to be entreated for the greatest things.

With such persons, you must use a great deal of prudence and gentleness, and not seek upon every occasion to thwart and contradict them; with love you may do them much good, but with anger you will do them none at all. If you are severe in your speeches, they will never be persuaded that it is in kindness, and so will not regard at all what you say. Nay, your sharp words pierce like so many daggers to their hearts, and make that inward fever that burns them more hot and scorching.

But of all persons, ministers are especially to be

blamed who, when they find poor sinners who are overwhelmed with a sense of guilt, with the terrors of the law, and who are slain by the law, still set the law more and more upon them. This indeed throws them down lower, but it is not the way to raise them up; it merely widens and enflames, but does not remove and heal their wounds. To such the words of the prophet in Ezekiel 34:4 may be justly applied: "The diseased have ye not strengthened, neither have ye healed that which was sick, neither have ye bound up that which was broken, neither have ye brought again that which was driven away, neither have ye sought that which was lost, but with force and with cruelty have ye ruled them."

And then the poor, distressed soul is more distressed by the harsh language, and is apt to conclude against itself and to say, "If the ministers of Christ speak so severely to me, what will Christ Himself do?" This is raking in the wounds that are already very sore and smarting. Such a minister is as an angel who troubles the waters more that were already troubled; but he is not an angel of peace to bring glad tidings to a weary soul. These people would not complain if they were not in violent anguish and perplexity. For, as Job 6:5 says, "Doth the wild ass bray when he hath grass? Or loweth the ox over his fodder?" And against the sharp expression of his friends, he says in Job 16:2–5: "Miserable comforters are ye all! Shall vain words have an end? I also could speak as ye do. If your soul were in my soul's stead, I could heap up words against you and shake my head at you. But I would strengthen you with mine mouth, and the moving of my lips should assuage your grief."

When the souls of afflicted persons are already full

of sorrow, a little more will make them overflow. When they are weakened with various assaults, a small stroke will throw them to the ground. And a sore that is continually rubbed and chafed cannot be cured.

4. You must be so kind to your friends who are under this disease as to believe what they say. Believe that their apprehensions are such as they tell you they are. Do not think that they are at ease when they say they are in pain. It is a foolish course which some take with their melancholy friends, to answer all their complaints and moans with this: "That is nothing but fancy, nothing but imagination and whimsy." This is a real disease, a real misery with which they are tormented! And even if it is but fancy, a diseased fancy is as great a disease as any other; it fills them with anguish and tribulation. But this so-called disordered fancy is the consequence of a greater evil, and is one of the sad effects that are produced by that black disposition that has vitiated all the natural spirits. These afflicted persons can never possibly believe that you pity them, or that you are heartily concerned for them, if you give no credit to what they say. And, truly, it often falls out that because melancholy persons do not always look very ill, or seem to have pretty good stomachs, and do not at first show much bodily decline, other persons who know nothing of the distemper are apt to think that they make themselves worse than they are, whereas, alas, they are so grieved that they do not need, nor will they counterfeit, any more grief.

In all other evils people take for granted what others say, and sympathize accordingly with them; but in this one people are apt to contradict and oppose those who are distressed—and as long as they do so, they cannot pity them as they ought. This makes the grief of such to overwhelm and strangle them within, because, when they disclose it, they find it is to no purpose. In this case, do as you would have others do unto you. Suppose that you have a toothache or a headache, and, when you complain of those ailments, people were to tell you that it was nothing but a fancy; would you not think their carriage to be full of cruelty? And would it not vex you to find out that you cannot be believed?

5. Do not urge your friends who are under the disease of melancholy to do things which they cannot do. They are as persons whose bones are broken, who are in great pain and anguish, and are consequently incapacitated for action. Their disease is full of perplexed, tormenting thoughts. If it were possible by any innocent means to divert them, you would do them a great kindness; but by no means should you press them to anything that requires more intense thinking, or that, by fixing their minds on their condition, will force them to muse and pore more; they are already very miserable. It puts them into a more anxious ferment when you are continually fretting them with doing this or that, for which they may have no more power than a man has to run who has broken his leg.

Do not be noisy or clamorous with them, but know that silence and quiet are most favorable to their condition. You know that they are overwhelmed with sorrows, and grief is a very unattractive, sluggish thing; the vehemence of this weakens the natural spirits, blunts the soul, and renders its conceptions very languishing and confused.

OBJECTION. But perhaps you will say, "Must we not urge these people to hear the Word of God?"

ANSWER. I answer, if they are so far gone in the disease as to be in continual, unbroken anguish, they are not capable of hearing because of the many great pains which they most frequently have at the same time. But if their distemper has not yet come to such a terrible height, you may indeed press them to hear; but at the same time you must use a great deal of prudence, and not persuade them with too much peremptoriness or vehemence. Strive to convince them of their duty by love and by good words. In cases like these, the pace Jacob kept with his flock is the best and safest way: drive them gently, especially seeing that they are overwhelmed with fear and perplexity. You may accomplish much by a mild, sweet, and affable demeanor.

If you imitate the friends of the aforementioned Mrs. Drake, you will not do amiss. And therefore I will mention their practice as I find it in the book about her life (*Mrs. Drake Revived*). Her friends wrote: "The burden with which she had overloaded herself was so great that we never dared add any thereunto, but fed her with all encouragements, she being too apt to overcharge herself, and to despair upon any addition of fuel unto that fire which was already kindled within her. And so wherever she went to hear, notice was still given so to manage the business that the minister might know that he had a hearer thus qualified; and by this means she received no discouragement in hearing the Word."

6. Do not attribute the effects of mere disease to the devil. I do not deny, though, that the devil has a hand in causing many diseases. The envy and rage that fill him prompt him to disturb the health and peace of men; and, by God's permission, no doubt, he brings a

great many sicknesses upon them. We know that in the case of Job he filled him all over with tormenting sores which brought the poor man into a very great melancholy, and woefully, by that means, perplexed him with spiritual terror and amazement. But notwithstanding all this, it is a very overwhelming thing to attribute nearly every action of a melancholy man to the devil when there are some unavoidable expressions of sorrow which are purely natural, and which he cannot help any more than any other sick man can forbear to groan and sigh.

Many persons will say to such people, "Why do you so pore and muse and gratify the devil?"—whereas it is the very nature of the disease to cause such fixed musings. They might as well say, "Why are you diseased? Why won't you get well?" Their so musing proceeds from a violent pressure on their spirits, which they are not able to remove. Some think that melancholy persons are pleased with their distemper, but I believe that they are as pleased as a man who is lying on thorns or briars, or as one who is thrown into a fiery furnace. It is vastly painful to them to be in this condition, and they cannot be supposed to hate themselves so much as to be fond of pain.

The devil indeed is very busy working during the darkness of a soul. He throws in his bombs and fiery darts to amaze us more. When we are compassed with the terrors of a dismal night, he is bold and undaunted in his assaults, and injects, with a quick and sudden malice, a thousand monstrous and abominable thoughts of God which, at the same time, seem to be the motions of our minds, and so most terribly grieve and trouble us. And, alas, we too often comply with the devil's designs; we are usually then under great unbelief, and too often think of God and of ourselves as he would have us think. Yet, if you think that every action of a melancholy person is from this evil spirit, you will, as it is easy to fix any sort of dire impressions on such as are overcome with fear, persuade them at length that they are possessed, and that all they do is from the devil, when, at the same time, they are pained in every part. And then they find themselves unable to get out of their distress, and your discourses simply plunge them even lower in their misery. I would not have you bring a railing accusation against the devil, so as to attribute to him a thousand things wherein he has no hand at all; neither must you falsely accuse your friends by saying that they gratify him, when they do not do so. Consider how ill you would take it to be so used, if you were in their case; or consider that to be without temptation is the greatest temptation.

7. Do not much wonder at anything they may say or do. What will people not do who are in despair! What will they not say who think themselves lost forever! What strange, extravagant actions do you see those do who are under the power of fear! And none are so afraid as these poor people are; they are afraid of God, of hell, and of their own sorrows. You need not much wonder at them when you know that even so great a man as Job cursed his day, and talked of God with much more freedom and boldness than he ought to have done. The Lord Himself said that Job darkened counsel by words without knowledge.

Do not think it strange if they complain very much, for their grief causes them to speak. You know the tongue will always be speaking of the aching tooth.

Their soul is sorely vexed, and though it is true that they get no good by complaining, yet they cannot but complain to find themselves in such a doleful case. And though they can say with David in Psalm 6:6, "I am weary with my groaning; all the night make I my bed to swim; I water my couch with my tears," yet they cannot forbear to groan and weep more till their very eyes are consumed with grief. Let no carriage of theirs provoke you to passion; let no sharp words of theirs make you talk sharply. Sick persons are generally peevish, and it will be a very great weakness in you not to bear with them when you see that a long and sore disease has deprived them of their former good temper. Do you not find in Scripture several instances of men who have uttered woeful complaints? who have said that their hope has perished, and that the wrath of God was laid hard upon them? that against them His terrors were set in array? that their prayers were shut out? that their iniquities had gone over their heads? that they were as spectacles of reproach, and the scorn and wonder of other men? Do not, therefore, wonder at anything that your friends say under their great trouble.

8. Do not mention to them any formidable things, nor tell any sad stories in their hearing, because they already meditate on terror, and by every sad thing they hear of they are much more terrified. Their troubled imagination is prepared to fix upon any mournful thing, and, by that means, will multiply its own sorrows. The hearing of sad things causes in them more violent agitations, and throws them into great disorders, having the same effects on them that storms and thunder have in nature, and which strike terror into men. You must know that they are very ingenious in heightening

every doleful thing, and they will argue thus: "If it is so dreadful to be so cruelly used, so tormented, so enslaved, how dreadful then is my condition when I have God against me and am likely to be in hell forever!"

Studiously avoid all discourse of what is grievous to them. And yet you must not be too merry before them either; for then they think that you are slighting their misery and have no pity for them. A mixture of affableness and gravity will suit their condition best. And, if I may so advise, I would desire parents not to set those children who are naturally melancholy to being scholars, or to any employment that requires much study; for that will engage them, perhaps, to think too much, and at last they will be overwhelmed with uneasy thoughts.

9. Do not think it altogether needless to talk with them; but when you do so, do not speak as if their troubles will be lengthy. It is the length of their trouble that amazes them, when, after a week or a month without sleep or hope, still the next week or month is as painful and as terrible to them as the former was. And this, many times, pushes them forward to seek to destroy themselves, because they see no end to their miseries, and their anguish is both tedious and insufferable. Some of the Platonists thought that a man might dislodge his soul by astract contemplation, and send it into the world of spirits by the mere force of thought. But this is nothing but so much talk, for if any could so die, none would more frequently do so than melancholy persons, whose disease is earnest, intense, undiverted thinking, and yet they cannot die for all that. Of itself, it rarely kills anyone. Revive them, therefore, by telling them that God can create deliverance for them in a moment; that He has often done so with others;

that He can quickly cure their disease and show them His reconciled, amiable face, though it has been hidden from them for a long season.

You will convey to them some little support by such discourse as this. Tell them that, it may be, in a little time their groans shall be turned into praises, and that God will satisfy them early with His mercies, and make them glad according to the days wherein He has afflicted them, and the years wherein they have seen evil. Though they are like the burning bush, yet they shall not be consumed; tell them that there shall be more sweetness in the deliverance than there was bitterness in the trial. Tell them that hereafter they may have cause to say with David (Psalm 43:4), "Then will I go unto the altar of God, unto God my exceeding joy." Tell them that it will make their joys more pleasant when they come after so long a sadness. For a man who has laid all night long in waking pain, the morning rest is very sweet. And help them to remember that the greatest mourner in Israel was the sweet singer of Israel.

Pain, indeed, makes the time seem to go on very slowly; an hour seems like a day and a day like a week. But if you can, by the blessing of God, give them any hope that they may one day be delivered, and that then they will be sensibly refreshed and will be enabled to pray and read—none of which they can do while they are in deep despair. But when you talk with them, you must, as I have said before, by no means thwart or contradict them, but allow for what they say. Take for granted that what they say is true, then proceed with whatever applications you think most proper to their case upon such a supposition. And if you think they were truly good people, and sincere in their conversation, before this woeful distemper seized upon them, let them know what you think, and that you have charitable hopes of their salvation, however it shall please God to deal with them as to temporal deliverance.

10. Tell them of others who have been in such anguish and under such a terrible distemper, and yet have been delivered. It is very hard indeed to persuade a person under great pain and anguish, and under a sense of the wrath of God and a fear of hell, that ever any has heretofore been so perplexed as he. Such persons generally think themselves worse than Cain or Judas, or any of the most wicked people in the world; they think that their sins have greater aggravations, and that consequently they shall be more miserable. But you may acquaint them with several instances of God's gracious dealings with others after they too had been afflicted for many months and years. I have known several who were long afflicted with trouble of mind and melancholy, such as Mr. Rosewell and Mr. Porter, both ministers, the latter who was oppressed for six years with this distemper; yet afterwards both rejoiced in the light of God's countenance. I myself was nearly two years in great pain of body, and greater pain of soul, and without any prospect of peace or help. Yet God has revived me in His sovereign grace and mercy.

There have been several heretofore sorely perplexed with great inward and outward trouble, whom God, after that, wonderfully refreshed. Mr. Robert Bruce, some time ago a minister in Edinburgh, was for twenty years in terrors of conscience, and was delivered afterwards. You may also direct them to the lives of Mrs. Brettergh, Mrs. Drake, Mr. Peacock, and Mrs. Wright, where they will see a very cheerful day returning after a black and stormy night. And the good that came from their afflictions was more glorious than their conflict was troublesome. They went forth weeping, they sowed in tears, but they reaped a harvest of wonderful joys afterwards.

You have in Mr. Foxe's *Book of Martyrs* an example of a Mr. Glover, who was worn and consumed with inward trouble for the space of five years, so much so that he had neither comfort in his food, quietness of sleep, nor any pleasure of life. He was as perplexed as if he had been in the deepest pit of hell. Yet at last, this good servant of God, after such sharp temptations and the strong buffetings of Satan, was freed from all his trouble, and was thereby framed to great mortification. He was afterwards like one already placed in heaven, and led a life altogether celestial, abhorring in his mind all profane things.

You also have a remarkable example of a minister, Mr. Holland, who, the day before he died, having meditated upon Romans 8, cried out, "Stop your reading! What brightness is that I see?" Those around him told him it was the sunshine. "No," he said, "it is my Savior's shine! Now, farewell, world, and welcome, heaven. The Daystar from on high has visited my heart. Oh, speak it when I am gone, and let it be preached at my funeral, that God deals gently with man. I feel His mercy; I see His majesty. Whether in the body or out of it, God knows, but I see things unutterable." And the next morning, he shut up his blessed life with these words: "Oh, what a happy change shall I make from night to day, from darkness to light, from death to life, from sorrow to solace, from a factious world to a heavenly being! O my dear friends, it pities me to leave you behind; yet remember what I now feel; for I hope you shall find it before you die. God does and will deal familiarly with men. And now, you fiery chariot that came down to fetch up Elijah, carry me to my happy home. And all you blessed angels who attended the soul of Lazarus, to bring it up to heaven, bear me. Oh, bear me into the bosom of my best Beloved. Amen. Amen. Come, Lord Jesus; come quickly." And so he fell asleep. You may see this story and several others like it in Robert Bolton's *Instructions for Comforting Afflicted Consciences* [published by Soli Deo Gloria].

11. The next kindness you are to show your melancholy friends is to pray heartily for them. Let your eyes weep for them in secret, and there let your souls melt in fervent, holy prayers. They are not able in a composed or lively manner to recommend their own case to God; you may use many arguments in your prayers that their forlorn state and the greatness of their miseries may be a very powerful motive to your supplications. You know that none but God Himself can help them. For, as Mr. Greenham says in his *A Sweet Comfort for an Afflicted Conscience,* "If our assistance were as a host of armed soldiers; if our friends were the princes and governors of the earth; if our possessions were as large as between the East and the West; if our meat were as manna from heaven; if our apparel were as costly as the Ephod of Aaron; if every day were as glorious as the day of Christ's resurrection; yet if our minds are appalled with the judgments of God, all these things would not yield us any help or consolation."

And you must wrestle with Him on behalf of these distressed persons. You may plead with Him that His power and goodness will be more illustrious if He saves those whom none but He can save, and that His grace will be more remarkable if He is pleased to create peace for those troubled souls in which none but He can make it calm. You do not know but that His light, at your request, may begin to shine on those who have bewailed His absence with many dreadful groans. And though your eyes are even weary with looking upward, yet continue still to wait and pray; for it shall not be in vain. Thus you will do them a great kindness, and perform your own duty, though, perhaps, they are ready to say to you, as Mr. Peacock said to his friends, "Do not take the name of God in vain by praying for a reprobate like me." When Mr. Peacock said that he could not pray, Mr. Dod said to him, "Though most sicknesses hinder prayer, and therefore the Apostle James said, 'If any man be sick, let him send for the elders,' yet if God stirs up your friends to pray for you, He will stir Himself up to hear their prayers."

Consider that nothing but prayer can do these people any good. It is an obstinate disease that nothing else will overcome. It is a very slight melancholy, one that is not deeply rooted, that can be drowned in wine or chased away with social diversions. Some indeed tell us that when they find themselves troubled, their way out is to bid their thoughts to battle with each other, and to oppose thoughts with thoughts, hoping to subdue this peevish distemper with the help of reason. But such must give me leave to say that they are not under the disease of melancholy; for that disease will hear neither faith nor reason till God Himself, by His almighty power, works salvation for them.

12. Not only must you pray for them, but get other serious Christians to pray for them also. When many good people join their requests together, the cry is

more acceptable and prevalent. When those people in Acts joined together to remember Peter in his chains, he was soon afterwards delivered, and that during the very time of their prayers. All believers have through Jesus Christ a great interest in heaven, and the Father is willing to grant what they beg in the name of His dear Son. I myself have been greatly helped by the prayers of others, and I heartily thank all those who kept any particular days wherein more solemnly to remember my distressed condition. Blessed be God who has not cast off their prayer, nor turned away His mercy from me.

Every day gives us several experiences of many who have been rescued from their diseases, their temptations, and their fears by the prayers of others. And, I might also add, you have great cause to pray for yourselves, that God may give you strength to bear so heavy a cross as you are afflicted with in the afflictions of your friends. Their doleful complaints, their repeated groans, and their long and sore trials are enough to sink you too, if God does not give you wonderful support. You need to beg for strong faith and great patience, so that you are not unhinged with their passionate or hasty speeches.

13. Put your poor friends in mind of the sovereign grace of God in Jesus Christ. Often put them in mind that He is merciful and gracious; that as far as the heavens are above the earth, so far are His thoughts above their thoughts; so far are His thoughts of mercy and love above their self-condemning, guilty thoughts. Teach them, as much as you can, to look up to God by the great Mediator for grace and strength, and not to pore too much on their own souls, where there is so much darkness and unbelief. Seek to divert them from

puzzling themselves too much with God's secret and unknown decrees. Instead, strive to help them to believe in Christ, which is their certain duty; show them what great sinners God has pardoned, and how He is merciful because He will be merciful. Find motives to help them from their very miseries, and from God's own gracious nature.

Thus I find they dealt with Mrs. Drake: she would write to various ministers, concealing her name, and asking whether such and such a person, who is without faith, hope, and love for God or man, hard-hearted, without natural affection, who had rejected all means nor could submit to any, yet might have any hope of going to heaven. And they all answered her that such persons, and many who were much worse (though even as bad as Manasseh), might, by the mercy of God, be received into favor, converted, and saved—and this greatly allayed her trouble. She later said, "The fountain of all my misery has been that I sought for that in the law which I should have found in the gospel; and I looked for that in myself which was only to be found in Christ."

This is what I thought necessary to say to you; and you will find that the course I have mentioned, being taken with your friends, will do them no prejudice. I do not speak only with borrowed expressions in this matter, nor without some experience. I know very well that the mild and gentle way of dealing you will find to be the best, and that the way of toughness and severity will but aggravate and increase their miseries. And I desire you who are still healthy and cheerful to improve your health; for if ever this distemper should seize upon you, you will be able to do nothing for your souls or bodies.

You may have time, but such will be your anguish that you will not be able to do anything of purpose in that time.

This book has a peculiar relation to the distress of the mind; for as to what concerns that bodily pain that I had met with in my inward trouble, I have largely showed what it was in my *Practical Discourses on Sickness and Recovery,* which was published about a year ago. And what a mercy it is to have our afflictions sanctified, and to bear the yoke in our youth, I have explained in my *Treatise of Early Religion,* which was recently published, and is peculiarly designed for young people. And if God blesses it to their good, it may help them to avoid those woeful terrors under which many have groaned. Since then I have also published *A Treatise on the Happiness of a Quiet Mind,* very necessary to those who have been under trouble. I also refer the reader of this book to another I have published, called *Consolation for the Afflicted, or The Way to Prevent Fainting.*

I think I could have used a little more exactness in composing this book, had I set myself studiously to do so; and by that means this book might have been more pleasant to the reader, but would not so well have served my design. I think of that old saying, "A physician who can remove the disease is more welcome to the sick than the one who can talk finely about it, but can do him no good." And if the cure is performed, it is no matter that the potion was not extremely sweet.

I purposely avoided all pretense to a regular smoothness of style, because the ears of people in great affliction are not so tender and delicate as the ones of those who are in good health. I know that the age in which we live is very curious and critical, and that the

English language has been greatly polished and improved in these last few years. And religion deserves the best words we can find wherewith to express our thoughts. Ecclesiastes 12:10 says that the preacher sought acceptable words, by which, I suppose, he means words that were gracious as well as profitable.

I hope the reader will find neither bombast or slovenliness in my expressions; and if there is not in them an accomplished beauty (and I do not pretend that there is), yet at least the words are not entirely deformed. Whatever some persons may say, I think it is my duty to express my thoughts not altogether in a neglected and careless manner, but with plainness and clarity, and such as may tend to edification. Though I have not given such a particular relation of my troubles as perhaps the reader expected, yet I desire the reader to take notice that, wherever I speak of inward distress as if I were speaking of a third person, I am there speaking of what I myself have felt.

It was an observation of the readers of St. Cyprian's writings that through them all nearly every word breathed martyrdom. His expressions are full of spirit and passion as if he had written them with his blood and conveyed the anguish of his sufferings into his writings. If I had had the judgment and the pen of so eloquent a person, I might have much better described the sadness of my case, but I am sure that nothing in the world could fully express it; it was so very terrible, and the greatness of the danger heightens the mercy of God my Deliverer, to whose grace and wonderful salvation I owe my present peace and hope, and to whom I will devote all my poor endeavors. That those which I have used in the following treatise may be serviceable to His glory, your advantage, and the relief of your melancholy friends, and many others as well, and also to my own good, is the prayer of your hearty adviser,

Timothy Rogers
September 10, 1691
London

Part I
Introduction

"For His anger endureth but a moment; in His favor is life. Weeping may endure for a night, but joy cometh in the morning." Psalm 30:5

The miseries under which the whole race of men have now for a long time groaned, and under which they still groan, are owing to the fall of man. The day on which our first parents complied with the temptation of the devil was a mournful day to them, and, in its effects, no less sad to us. It filled their once pure and quiet hearts with trouble and disorder, and made them unable to think of their Creator with delight. It intercepted those cheerful beams of His love which were more satisfying to them than all the glories of the lower paradise. For though it did, after the Fall, abound with all the same natural refreshments, with the same rivers, herbs, trees, and flowers, yet it was to them no longer a paradise. No music could delight their senses when they heard a terrible voice from God, summoning them to answer for their crime. No objects could please their eyes when they saw the clouds thickening over their heads, and dreadful frowns on the face of their mighty Judge. No creature can minister anything to his ease or safety when the great Creator is against him.

From their apostasy we derive all our miseries, both the pains and sicknesses that afflict our bodies and the fears and terrors that overwhelm our souls. Our bodies are liable to a thousand calamities that may be both long and sharp, but however long and sharp they are, they do not altogether give us such a sensible and lively grief as we have when we are under distresses of conscience, and when we are under a sense of the wrath of God that is due to us for sin.

There are many persons who endeavor, by all the rules of art, to give relief and help against the mischiefs that attend our bodies, which nevertheless, after all their art, will go into the grave. And there are as many who, by the duty of their office and the character they bear, are obliged to imitate their Savior: "To preach good tidings to the meek, and to bind up the brokenhearted; to proclaim liberty to the captives, and the opening of the prison to them that are bound" (Isaiah 61:1). But they are many times at a loss to know what remedies to apply to these inward and spiritual diseases, and they are always unable to make their applications successful unless God Himself, by His almighty power, creates peace and turns that chaos and confusion under which a poor, troubled soul is buried into the light of day.

It pleases the wise God, who may make us serve whatever uses He thinks most convenient for the good of the universe and the welfare of His Church, to suffer some of His servants to feel the bitterness of sin, and the terrors of His amazing wrath; to be overwhelmed with the fear of hell, and to be, for a long season, even as if in hell itself, so that, when they are delivered, they may warn those who are at ease to beware of sin lest it bring them also into a state so dreadful and so terrible; from their own experience, they may then, with tenderness and compassion, strive more earnestly to assist and help those whose consciences are in a flame, and who are full of anguish and tribulation. This is so that, when they have escaped out of the snare of the fowler, they may strive to disentangle those who are yet in trouble; being themselves cured of their horror and amazement, they may lead their still-wounded brethren to that kind Physician, that loving Jesus, with whose blood their wounds were cleansed and healed.

As for myself, having been in long affliction and great distress of conscience for many months, and under a continued fear and apprehension of God's displeasure, and being now, through His inexpressible grace, not without some hope of His acceptance, being delivered from violent and overwhelming sorrows, I would most readily give all the advice and help I can to those who are yet mourning under desertions, complaining that God has departed from them, and that He remembers them no more. After the many waves and billows that went over me, through the great goodness of God I now enjoy a calm. And I pity and would fain help those who are yet laboring in the depths. It is for them especially that I write this treatise, in which, though there are many things less exact than a critical reader may expect, yet there are some in which, I hope, a distressed soul may find relief.

In the first part, I intend to show:

1. What is meant by the anger of God, and why it is that He is angry with His own servants.

2. What obligations we are under to patience and humility, along with various other graces, when we are under a sense of His displeasure.

3. Why it is that His anger towards His own people is but for a short time.

Chapter 1

The anger of God, and why it is that He is sometimes angry with His own servants

We must know that the infinite majesty of heaven is not subject to those unquiet passions to which our weak and frail nature is vulnerable. He is not sometimes what He was not before. He is always in Himself the very same. His essence is unchangeable, but He is pleased to stoop to our weakness, and clothes His intentions in words that may most suitably convey to our minds the knowledge of what He designs.

In His most pure and blessed nature there is a perpetual calm and tranquility. Nor does He suffer any of those commotions and disorders that are in angry men. His anger is His resolution or His will to punish His sinning creatures; or sometimes it relates to the evils themselves which sinners endure, such as pain, fear, sorrow, wars, famine, pestilence, and similar calamities. He is said to be pleased with us when we are obedient, and when His face shines upon us in a comfortable and gracious manner; when He accepts our persons and our duties, and refreshes our hearts with the heart-reviving hopes of glory through Jesus Christ.

But He is angry when He withdraws the cheerful influences and quickening motions of His Holy Spirit; also when we pray, and He shuts out our prayers and leaves our poor souls to languish under despair or unbelief, and when we find no spiritual and heavenly life in ourselves. He may also be said to be angry when He sends long and sore afflictions and distresses on our bodies and our souls, and withholds His blessing from all the methods that are designed to help us. And when He proceeds to a terrible execution of His threats, this is called "vengeance," as in Psalm 99:8: "Thou wast a God that forgavest them, though Thou tookest vengeance of their inventions."

God is sometimes angry with His own people. It is indeed paternal castigatory wrath that He sends upon them, but not destroying fury. Thus He is said to be angry with Moses, Aaron, and Miriam. Psalm 74:1: "O God, why hast Thou cast us off forever? Why doth Thine anger smoke against the sheep of Thy pasture?" And so Heman complains in Psalm 88:7: "Thy wrath lieth hard upon me, and Thou hast afflicted me with all Thy waves." And so the Church complains in Lamentations 1:12, 2:1, and 3:1.

The reasons for this are these:

1. Because their sins are of a greater aggravation than the sins of others. They sin against Him when they have tasted of His goodness; when He has given them more clear light, more experience of His love than to the rest of men. When He is wounded in the house of His friends, He will resent such injuries and affronts. They usually sin against more frequent motions of His Holy Spirit, and after they have engaged to be His, they break their vows and forget their covenants; they loiter in His service when they have—by the peace of their souls and the hope of heaven that He has given to them—found His work to be a reward and that He is a very good master. And shall He not visit for

these things? What fitter methods can He take than to lash them for their ingratitude and unbecoming behavior to so kind a Friend, as He has been to them all along? He is at more cost and charge with the children of His family than with others; and, if they disobey Him, they must feel His displeasure and the smart of His rod. "You only have I known of all the families of the earth; therefore I will punish you for all your iniquities" (Amos 3:2).

2. To warn others, and to wipe off all aspersions that might be cast upon His holiness. He is angry with His own to let the profane world see that He is no respecter of persons, and that sin, wherever it is, shall not go unpunished. He puts some into the fiery furnace to let those who are at ease know what they have also deserved, and what they may expect if they do not speedily repent and return. Some ages feel the weightier blows of His hand, and are visited with severe judgments, to teach future generations to be more careful to observe His laws and do His will. Deuteronomy 29:22, 24: "The generation to come of your children that shall rise up after you, and the stranger that shall come from a far land, shall say when they see the plagues of that land, and the sicknesses which the Lord hath laid upon it . . . even all nations shall say, 'Wherefore hath the Lord done thus unto this land? What meaneth the heat of this great anger?' "

He lays some countries desolate so that their desolations may more effectually show the evil of sin, and preach repentance to their neighbors round about. He sets some on fire so that they may serve as beacons to warn the rest of approaching danger. He is sometimes angry so that He may maintain the honor of His laws and the justice of His government. He throws some upon sickbeds so that others may learn by them to know their own frailty, and prepare for similar trials. Some He leaves in darkness, anguish, and tribulation so that others may learn to prize the light, lest they come to the very same calamity.

He shoots His arrows into the souls of some of His servants so that all who behold His severe and righteous proceedings may tremble at it, and learn to fear Him who is so holy and so just a God; that they may not dare to venture upon those sins under the woeful effects of which they see their fellow creatures groan so very much. And he must be a hardened malefactor indeed who practices his old crimes when he sees another whipped or executed for those of the very same kind.

Thus the view and report of His judgments have a natural tendency to reform the world, to purify and make it better, as thunder and lightning clean the air and make it more healthy. How wicked is this present world, notwithstanding the manifold examples of His justice! And how much more wicked would it be if He allowed sin to always go unpunished! His best servants are too secure and careless, too forgetful of Him and of themselves, till He awakens them by some severe stroke upon themselves or others. It makes them more diligent and serious when they see the clouds gather and the night drawing on; and by His anger He designs to teach us all to put a higher value on the love of Christ, and makes us know of how high a nature our offense was, seeing that His only Son endured so much of His wrath before we could obtain a pardon. And when we smart ourselves under His displeasure, it makes us increasingly admire the kindness of our Savior, who freely suffered so much smart and pain for us.

He is angry with His own to teach them to value His favor more than they ever did. If we did not feel the bitterness of His anger, we would not so sweetly relish His love. If He did not sometimes withdraw Himself, we would not think His presence as comfortable as it is. If in winter we did not have stormy or frosty weather, we would not take such great pleasure in the summer season. Oh, how pleasant are the smiles of God when we have long lain under the terror of His frowns! How pleasant it is to find Him to be our Friend when we have long thought Him to be our enemy. How pleasant it is to have the hope of heaven when a man has long trembled at the very gate of hell. When we have been long wandering for our follies, as in a strange land, how pleasant it is to come home again. After we have been among our enemies, how pleasant it is to come to our heavenly Father, to have Him meet us with encouraging words and embrace us in His arms, to feast at His table, to have Him call us His children, to forget all our former injuries, and to have Him be at peace with us.

How shall we run under His wing for shelter when we have found that innumerable dangers overtook us while He withdrew His care! How shall we wait upon Him with love and obedience, and yield Him faithful service in all that He commands, when we remember what griefs our former disobedience brought upon us! He is angry with us to cure our luxuries and pride; and when our follies have brought us low, we shall give a most hearty welcome to the first dawning of the day, to the first shining of His face. And though before we prized His highest favors and His largest entertainments at a small rate, we shall now value one glimpse of light as much as we did the whole sun before; and to partake, though but of the crumbs that fall from His table, will seem to us to be both an honor and a privilege. After many days of storm and darkness, it is more pleasant to see the sun; even the very birds sing with a sweeter note when there is a clear sky. The furrows of the fields rejoice after a long drought to be refreshed with the former and the latter rain. When a country has been long harassed with confusions, tumults, and bloody wars, how delightful is the return of peace! When a soul has mourned a great while in fear and trouble, how delightful it is to hear the voice of God saying, "Be of good comfort"! How His promises, like dew from the womb of the morning, cause His poor, drooping spirits to revive (Isaiah 12:1).

Chapter 2

The anger of God towards His people is but for a short season; and why He is pleased to order it to be so

His anger is but for a moment, if compared with the eternity of happiness which He designs for them. Their troubles and afflictions shall have a period, but their glory shall never have an end. They weep for a while, but they shall rejoice forever; they are disconsolate for a few years on earth, but how little and inconsiderable are these to the vast durations of eternity!

His anger is but for a moment if compared with the continuance of His love. In His favor is life; that is, the greater portions of our life are usually laden with His benefits. We have more pledges of His love than messengers of His wrath; we have more mercies than crosses; we have a thousand easy blessings for one sharp affliction. His displeasure brings a storm, but His favor shines when that is past and gone. We have many a fair season to one dark and gloomy day. The reasons why His anger is but for a moment are these:

1. His anger is but for a moment because He remembers the frame of His poor people; for if His wrath should be long continued, they would utterly sink and perish. Psalm 103:14: "For He knoweth our frame; He remembereth that we are but dust." One frown causes us to sink and tremble; what, then, would His multiplied frowns and displeasures do? He knows our tenderness, with what evil inclinations our nature is

corrupted, how prone we are to sin, and how, if He should be so strict as to mark what we do amiss, He must continually destroy the works of His own hands and have no one left to serve Him here on earth. He remembers with what frailties we are daily beset, and He pities us as a father does the weakness of his child.

He could kill us in a minute, and take away our breath. How soon can He scatter a little dust, and pull in pieces our frail constitution! For we are as unable to resist His anger as the dust is to resist the wind. He knows that we are so weak that if He were to let us alone we would soon decay. There need not be the force of His arm and the greatness of His power to crush such worms as we are. David said, "Is the King of Israel come out after a flea?" (1 Samuel 24:14), and so we may say to God in our distresses, "Why dost Thou arm Thyself with wrath against us, whom one word of Thy mouth can throw upon the ground or send into the grave?" It is not with Him as with the great oppressors of the world who use their greater power to trample upon those who are of unequal strength. No, He delights to bind up the broken, to heal the wounded, and to comfort those who mourn. Isaiah 57:16: "For I will not contend forever, neither will I be always wroth; for the spirit should fail before Me, and the souls which I have made."

Such are the impatience, the unbelief, and the unsuitable behavior of His people that they give Him cause enough to always be angry; but He does not proceed with the utmost rigor of His justice. He freely pardons what with right He might exact. Psalm 78:36–39 tells of those whose hearts were not right with Him: "They did flatter Him with their mouth . . . but He, being full of compassion, forgave their iniquity, and destroyed them not; yea, many a time turned He His anger away, and did not stir up all His wrath. For He remembered that they were but flesh, a wind that passeth away and cometh not again." And when our extremities are so great, and our sense of His displeasure is so very pressing that we do not know what to do, we may desire Him to remember His own greatness and our frailty; that we are His own handiwork, and that we are no more able to resist His power than we are to change our own natures and to be His equals. Job 13:25 and 10:9: "Wilt Thou break a leaf driven to and fro? Wilt Thou pursue the dry stubble? Remember, I beseech Thee, that Thou hast made me as the clay."

2. God's anger towards His people is but for a moment because He is obligated to it by His covenant. Psalm 89:31–33: "If they break My statutes . . . then will I visit their transgression with the rod, and their iniquity with stripes; nevertheless, My lovingkindness will I not utterly take from them, nor suffer My faithfulness to fail." He is obligated by the covenant of grace to be their God, to use all the methods that His infinite wisdom sees necessary for their final happiness; and if His anger and their own afflictions will contribute to this, though their flesh is pained and their bodies smart, He will not fail to use those severities. His dearest servants may, by temptation and their unwatchfulness, be overtaken by their spiritual enemies; they may wound and harm themselves, and occasion His departure. And to excite them to a due consideration of their folly, He will leave them for a season.

Their sins are the object of His abhorrence, and He may send very sore troubles upon them, though they shall even then come upon a gracious errand and promote their future welfare when, in the anguish of their souls, they may conclude them to be the mark of His eternal wrath. He will not spare His rods, nor by a fond indulgence suffer them to take their own course. A parent, you know, will correct his own child, though he does not concern himself with those who are strangers to the family.

The anger of God for your sin may deprive you of your dearest comforts, your most kind relations, your most beloved children, your estate, your health, and your ease, and yet, in all these, He may have a design to make you more full of holiness, and to bring you nearer to Himself. This is an ordinary discipline, wherewith He trains up all those whom He will convey to glory, though their own reason and their gloomy thoughts may judge that it is for quite contrary purposes. He has promised that all things shall work together for our good, and He is faithful when He lays upon us the most severe strokes, because they stir up our sleeping grace and purge away our sin.

3. His anger towards His people is but for a moment because, whatever His present dispensations are, He will never throw off the relation of a Father to them. They do not make void the kindness and grace by which He did at first adopt them to be His own. When a father frowns and corrects, he is still a father; and his bowels yearn within him when the rebellion and undutifulness of his child cause him to be severe. Though we groan and weep through the bitterness of our grief, yet He does not change His paternal care. When Christ was a man of sorrows, he was pronounced by God to be His beloved son. Psalm 103:13: "Like as a father pitieth his children, so the Lord pitieth them that fear Him."

None of our earthly friends can be more tender-hearted than He is, except for this difference: they would heal our wounds when they first begin to smart, and He, being more skillful, makes our cure advance by slow degrees. He bereaves us of this or that enjoyment, which we dearly love, because He sees it as necessary many times for our salvation—as it is many times expedient to cut off a gangrenous part of the body to save our life. He will separate us from our iniquities rather than that they should separate us from Him. And there is nothing but the most tender love in all of this. Jeremiah 31:20: " 'Is Ephraim My dear son? Is he a pleasant child? For since I spake against him, I do earnestly remember him still; therefore My bowels are troubled for him. I will surely have mercy upon him,' saith the Lord."

When we wander, His goodness and His love will not allow Him to see us run to misery. His anger will overtake us, stop us in our hasty course, and put us on the right way. He never strikes but for just reasons, though they may be, for the present time, very much wrapped up in His own decrees. There are many people with whom we are angry and whom we reprove, whom we, notwithstanding, in the meantime love most sincerely. And Christ has told us in Revelation 3:19, "As many as I love, I rebuke and chasten."

4. The anger of God is but for a moment because He delights in mercy. Psalm 103:8–9: "The Lord is merciful and gracious, slow to anger and plenteous in mercy. He will not always chide, neither will He keep His anger forever." It is long before He punishes, and it is with haste that He comes to our help when we repent—and many times even before that. In the midst of wrath He

remembers mercy. He does not always inflict what we have deserved, but considers what is most proper for Him to lay upon us, and what we are able to bear. And therefore He gives to us some mitigations with our most bitter cup. He is called the "Father of mercies and the God of all comfort" (2 Corinthians 1:3). And though punishment does proceed from Him, as well as tenderness and affection, He is nowhere called the Father of judgments.

Mercy arises from His very nature, and He delights in it. Micah 7:18: "He retaineth not His anger forever, because He delighteth in mercy." His wrath is said to be reserved in golden vials (Revelation 15:17), that is, it does not flow forth all at once, but by degrees. But His mercy is compared to a river and a flowing stream (Isaiah 66:12), to the oil of gladness, to the smell of myrrh, aloes, and cassia. It is a glory to this God to relieve the miserable, and to help His servants when all their power and might are gone. And He ends the controversy with them when there is enough cause on their side that He should pursue the quarrel further.

When He leads us into a wilderness, yet He provides some water, some refreshments for us there. It is one of the great wonders of His providence that He supports those poor souls who have no light of evidence, no sense of His love, no hope, nothing but the fears of wrath and desolation. And yet the matter of fact and our own experience plainly tell us that it is so. His everlasting arms are underneath, and His power maintains our life, when we say that He has forgotten to be gracious. He bottles our tears when we weep, hears our groans when we lament, and proportions the troubles that He sends so that they shall not be too long or too violent. Jeremiah 30:11: "I will not make a full end of thee. I will correct thee in measure, and will not leave thee altogether unpunished." And those afflictions which His people suffer are not in all respects proper punishments, because His anger is mixed with mildness and mitigated by the intercessions of a Mediator. Lamentations 3:31–32: "The Lord will not cast off forever; but though He cause grief, yet will He have compassion according to the multitude of His tender mercies."

5. That His anger is but for a moment is for His own name's sake. His nature is most inclined to do us good. Therefore the prophet said to those idolaters mentioned in 1 Kings 18:24, "The God that answereth by fire, let Him be God." He chose that element above the rest to signify how soon we shall have mercy. It comes as upon the wings of the wind; it is as swift as the rays of light. Hosea 11:9: "I will not execute the fierceness of Mine anger, I will not return to destroy Ephraim; for I am God and not man." When a man is greatly provoked by his enemy, he is not satisfied with having once made him feel his anger, but carries on his revenge to further degrees, and ceases the pursuit only when his enemy dies. But the great God, though He is able to conquer those who oppose Him with a total defeat and ruin, yet allows them to breathe and live so that they may repent, and that He may cause His goodness to shine before the world with a greater brightness. He could follow them with one blow after another, with a succession of new and greater miseries, but He restrains His anger for His own sake.

It may be a great consolation to poor, afflicted people to consider that they have to deal with God and not with men when they have sinned. They do not have to deal with men who are full of rage and cruelty, but with a God who is gracious and full of mercy; not with men who may caress them today and hate them tomorrow, but with a God who is unchangeable. And even when they are in the fire or in the water, His love for them is still the very same. Men think it is a dishonor to spare their inferiors if they do not, by the lowest submissions, testify their sorrow for their crimes; but the great God is so far above all His creatures that He may, when He will, think them below His indignation, and magnify His goodness in sparing and forgiving them when they most deserve to die. Isaiah 48:9: "For My name's sake will I defer Mine anger, and for My praise will I refrain for thee, that I cut thee not off."

It is His power that moderates His anger. Those persons who have the least strength, either of reason or of courage, are the most passionate and inclined to revenge. In punishments He shows His dominion over His creatures, but His power over Himself is most shown when He forgives great injuries and is slow to punish great affronts. His power in those acts of grace is very great and illustrious.

He is God and not man; there is more compassion and real pity in Him than in the most compassionate or tender-hearted man we ever knew. He is God and not man. He whom we have offended, and who can destroy us, is the first to begin to seek reconciliation with us. This is not the manner and way of men, who think that those who have offended them ought to be the first to make advances towards repairing the breach. There is no attribute in the displaying of which the great God glories so much as in this one of mercy; and it is by this that He would be known (Exodus 34:6–7).

6. His anger is but for a moment because He would make a difference between the righteous and the wicked. The afflictions that He sends upon the righteous are to prepare them for heaven and glory; but those scourges that He uses on the wicked and impenitent are but the beginning of their sorrows, the flashes of those flames that will consume them forever. The distresses of the righteous are short, and so are the properties of the wicked. The righteous are weeping here, but they shall rejoice hereafter. The wicked now have their heaven, such as it is, and hereafter they go to an eternal hell; and there they must weep and wail while the good and holy shall have all their tears wiped away. The one shall find Him to be a loving Father, and to have been so in all their trials and calamities. The other shall find Him to be an enemy, and to have been so though they had many good things in the time of their temporal life. The righteous have sweetness and mercy mingled with their sorrows here, but the wicked shall have pure, unmingled, and intolerable wrath there. Here, in the heaviest strokes, the servants of God find now and then some little comfort; but His enemies, in the next world, will have no drop to cool their tongues, no refreshment nor support forever. The same sun that will cherish the righteous with His everlasting beams will scorch the wicked, and fill them with an inexpressible rage and fury. God will throw them from all their heights, silence all their lofty speeches, and ruin all their vainglorious designs (Daniel 4:17).

Stephen Charnock, in his treatise on *God's Dominion,* wrote: "The demand is by the word of the Holy One, to the intent that the living may know that the Most High ruleth in the kingdoms of men," that is, by the petition of angels, who cannot endure that the empire of God should be obscured by the pride of men. Besides the tender respect that He has to His own glory, He is constantly presented with the solicitations of the angels to punish the proud of the earth who darken the glory of His majesty. It is necessary for the rescue of His honor, and necessary for the satisfaction of His illustrious attendants, who would think it a shame to serve a Lord who was always unconcerned with the rebellion of His creatures, and would tamely suffer those who spurn His throne. His wrath toward His servants is with mercy and but for a moment; but to His enemies it will be severe and abiding wrath.

Chapter 3

The several advantages that are designed by God for His servants in His being angry with them only for a moment, together with the obligations they are under from so merciful a dispensation of His providence, and the various improvements we are to make of it

1. None of the people of God have cause to conclude that, because He is angry with them at present, therefore they are in a state of wrath. Our sense and feeling of things that are very bitter, joined with the knowledge that we have of our guilt and our innumerable sins, frequently corrupts our reason and obscures our faith. And from the severity of His present dispensations, we are apt to say that He has forgotten to be gracious. "If the Lord be with us, then why is all this befallen us? And where be all His miracles which our fathers told us of?" (Judges 6:13). We think that He will be gracious no more. But this is the language of our mistaken unbelief. Isaiah 49:14–15: " 'The Lord hath forsaken me, and my Lord hath forgotten me.' Can a woman forget her sucking child? Yea, they may forget, yet will I not forget thee." Isaiah 40:27: "Why sayest thou, O Jacob, and speakest, thou, O Israel, 'My way is hid from the Lord, and my judgment is passed over from my God'?"

Our sins may indeed cause Him to withdraw the manifestations of His love, so that we shall feel no comfort in our prayers, none in His ordinances, none in His Word; every threat shall pierce us to the quick, and no promise shall yield us any comfort. Yet, for all this, He may, with His vital influences, return again; and though we have not seen the sun, moon, or stars for many days and nights, yet a glorious light may succeed afterwards.

In sore afflictions, our grieved sense and the fear that attends our guilt, and the malice of the devil, may put us upon desperate and unwarranted conclusions. And then the deserted person may say, "I am abhorred by the Lord. He counts me as His enemy. He is cruel to me, and has departed from me. He does not answer me. I go to His ministers and they give me no relief. I go to His Word and it is bitter to my taste; it fills me with gall and wormwood. I seek Him in my solitudes and in the assemblies of His people, but I do not find Him. He has left me, and He has thrown me off. The comforter who should relieve my soul is far from me. He hath built against me. He hath hedged me about, that I cannot get out. He hath made my chain heavy. Also, when I cry and shout, He shutteth out my prayer. He is unto me as a bear lying in wait, and as a lion in secret places' (Lamentations 3:5–10)."

This is a sad and doleful case, and yet one who suffers all this ought not to say that there is no future help; for God may be gracious, and His wrath, though very terrible and perplexing, is but for a moment. No believer ought to conclude that, because he is under the displeasure of God at present, he is therefore a child of wrath; nor ought he, from his present feeling, dare to assert his being in a state of reprobation. It is a usurping of that judgment which does not belong to men, and a positive determination of that which we cannot know. We may as well conclude that when the sun sets it will never rise again, or that when thick clouds darken the air it will never again be fair weather.

We ought never to forget the case of Job. Never was any man covered with a greater heap of miseries, never was any man more seemingly left by God and harassed by the devil than he was; never did any man make more doleful complaints than what we hear from this poor man in his heavy trial. Job 10:16–17: "Thou huntest me as a fierce lion; and again Thou showest Thyself marvelous upon me. Thou renewest Thy witness against me, and increasest Thine indignation upon me." Job 19:6, 10–11: "Know now that God hath overthrown me, and compassed me with His net; He hath destroyed me on every side, and I am gone; and mine hope hath He removed like a tree. He hath also kindled His wrath against me, and He counteth me unto Him as one of His enemies."

And yet what a glorious deliverance this poor man had after all this! We ought not to say that because we are so miserable at present we shall always be so, or that, because God is now angry, He will never be pleased again. No, we ought rather to remember that it is but for a moment; and though the kind hand of our Friend may put us to pain, yet He is but searching our wounds in order to find a cure. He will not poison our stores, nor, as an enemy, take pleasure in our torments.

2. We have great cause to be patient in all those sufferings that are the effects of God's displeasure, seeing that it is but for a moment. Micah 7:9: "I will bear the indignation of the Lord, because I have sinned against Him, until He plead my cause." There is nothing to which we are more vulnerable under the sense of God's displeasure than fretfulness and discontent. Thus it was

with David in Psalm 31:22: "I said in my haste, 'I am cut off from before Thine eyes.' " And we should, with all imaginable care, be fortified against it. This grace of patience is that for which we shall all have great occasion during the manifold evils of this miserable world; for this we shall have occasion since we are men, and, as such, are born to trouble. And much more shall we need it if we are true Christians, for, as such, we must expect more trouble from the corruptions of our hearts, from the world, and from the devil. For if he sees us going to that haven from whence he is forever excluded, his rage will prompt him to give us a continual molestation on our way there.

So that we may therefore be prepared to resist his subtle and violent assaults, and to bear those long and sore trials that may be our lot, let us keep these things before our eyes:

(1) When God is angry with us, if we are impatient, we will provoke Him to further wrath, and cause Him to double the blows of His arm, which are at present heavy enough for us to bear. If the first corrections do not bring us to a malleable and tender frame, He will, if He intends our good, be forced to send many more upon us; and thus that which was at first but a single stroke will multiply to many more, and by this we shall make the evil of our afflictions, which was designed for our good, become our sin, and so carry that inconvenience to our souls which, if we had kept a quiet and submissive frame, would only have hurt our bodies. And by this means we lose all the comfortable blessings of a sanctified and well-improved cross, and cause that yoke to gall us which otherwise might lie with ease upon our necks.

(2) Let us remember that we are in no way injured when we are under long afflictions, and that, whatever comes of us, God is always very just. "He will not lay upon man more than right" (Job 34:23). An earthly parent, in the warmth and heat of anger, may correct the follies of his child in an overly severe manner; but the God who knows our frame, who knows what is fitting for Him to do, and who knows what we are able to bear will proportion His corrections to the necessities of our case, and will not allow our troubles to stay a day longer than is needful to accomplish those excellent ends for which they were designed. He may in His anger pull us down and make us desolate, but we do not know what a comely structure He intends to build from those ruins. It may be that the darkness that frightens us is to usher in an eternal and glorious day.

His ways are far above our ways. There is so much greatness, wisdom, and goodness in Him that it should produce in our hearts a patience and resignation, though we do not know what a period He intends to put to His present dark and unsearchable designs. Though we are pained, He is still faithful; and though He does not gratify our curiosity or suffer our blind eyes to pierce into the depths of His counsel, yet let us hold this as a certain truth: the Lord is righteous and just in all His ways. He may say to us as Christ said to Peter, "What I do thou knowest not now, but thou shalt know hereafter" (John 13:7).

His justice should silence our murmuring complaints, and His faithfulness our discouragements and faintings. He never afflicts us without a good reason. He never does it but with a design of our final good. The sword that wounds us brings a balsam with it; it opens a passage to let out our corruptions, and then it heals and closes that wound again. Isaiah 30:18: "Therefore will the Lord wait that He may be gracious unto you, and therefore will He be exalted that He may have mercy upon you; for the Lord is a God of judgment. Blessed are all they that wait for Him."

(3) That we may bear His anger with patience, let us consider what mercies He has given us, and how much worse we might be than we now are. It may be that He frowns on us, but those frowns might have been our final sentences, and that anger which is now kindled against us might have been everlasting burnings. Though He speaks to us by terrible things, yet He might have said, "Depart from Me, ye cursed." The drops that fall upon us might have been a deluge and a storm of wrath, and the fiery furnace whereunto we are now thrown, to consume our dross, might have been hell. Why do living, sinful men complain, who might have been deprived of both hope and life long ago?

Oh, how does our gracious God, even in our sorest trials, deal much better with us than we have deserved! We multiply our sorrows to a vast account; but if we compared them with our sins, their number would appear to be very small. If we put our crosses and our iniquities into the same balance, we would quickly see what a mighty difference there is between them. It will be a considerable motive to patience to consider what we have deserved. We bewail the sense of the loss of the love of God, and, alas, we did not value it as we should have done! We complain that He has forsaken us, but who among us valued His presence to the extent that we should have? We say that He does not hear our prayers, that He is deaf to our request; and how often did we pray as if we prayed not? How often did He seek to enter into our hearts and we rebuffed Him? How often did He call and invite us to come to Him, and we did not obey His call? Have we reason then to be impatient that He is a stranger to us when we remember how He would have dealt with us if we had not shut Him out? It was our ignorance that betrayed us, and we do not know what we did.

We reckon up our nights of darkness, how long and how dismal they are, but we forget that He has given us many a bright and clear day, many an hour of peace and joy, for each one of grief and trouble. We have deserved to be miserable all the days of our lives for every day that we sin; we have many healthy seasons as well as times of sickness, whereas He might have made our passage uneasy and troublesome in the deep waters from the womb unto the grave. “Know therefore that God exacteth of thee less than thine iniquity deserveth” (Job 11:6).

We suffer justly for our sins. If God should inquire into the multitude, the heinousness, and all the aggravations of our sins, we would have a greater multitude of crosses. Let us cease, then, being impatient, for He deals in great tenderness and mercy with us. Our troubles have been sharp and long, it may be, but they might have been more stinging, more bitter, more violent, and drawn out to a more formidable length. But now, because it is not so, “He hath visited in His anger, yet he knoweth it not in great extremity” (Job 35:15). God has not stirred up all His wrath, nor amazed us with all the thunder of His power. Let us not be like the Israelites, who provoked Him and did not remember the multitude of His mercies.

(4) Consider that He uses no other method when He is angry with you than He has used with His dearest servants heretofore, and this may tend to compose your spirits under long and sore trials. Are you better than Moses, than Job, than Heman, than David and Asaph, and many other excellent and holy men with whom He was displeased, and who felt His wrath, though it was but for a moment? Are we more dutiful and obedient than they were? Do we not merit the chastisements of our heavenly Father as much as they did? Yea, and much more. If we have the Spirit and the privileges of children, we ought not to murmur if we have our share in the discipline of the family.

Would we have the course of providence inverted and changed for us? Can we imagine that we shall always be spared when so many great saints have smarted under the pleasure of God for their sin? We are apt to think that there is no "sorrow like to our sorrow wherewith the Lord hath afflicted us" (Lamentations 1:12). But we do not wisely inquire concerning this matter; for if we trace the steps of holy men of old, we shall find that innumerable and extremely grievous calamities were their portion as well as ours. We have heard of the distresses and the patience of Job, of the pains of his body and the troubles of his soul; and when either our bodies or our souls are more afflicted than his was, then it will be soon enough for us to begin to murmur. And if we do not do it until then, we shall be as remarkable for our patience as he was.

1 Peter 4:12: "Think it not strange concerning the fiery trial which is to try you, as though some strange thing happened to you." And 1 Peter 5:9: "The same afflictionss are accomplished in your brethren which

are in the world." These verses ought to be duly contemplated, for there is nothing of which Satan makes a greater use to perplex us in our hour of temptation than the length and the sharpness of our trials—as if God were our enemy because He afflicts, or as if we are not children because we are afflicted so very long.

Thus will that evil spirit say: "If you were a friend of God, who is so compassionate and so slow to wrath, would He follow you with breach after breach, with one stroke after another, and let His hand be heavy upon you day and night? He supports, comforts, and refreshes all His servants, but you have no refreshment, nothing but anguish and vexation; therefore you are none of His."

But by faith we must quench this fiery dart, and know that the fruit of our affliction may be very sweet, though for the present it is very bitter; we must know that we are under the conduct of that wisdom which can order even this cross for good. And whatever mists that envious spirit may raise before our eyes, let us still remember that His anger is but for a moment; that others, whom we are sure that He loved, have undergone similar troubles; that His own dear Son was still a Son even when He was a man of sorrows, and that His afflictions were of a great length, even from the manger to the cross.

And if God will have us be so far conformable to this blessed Person that we have no rest from trials till we are quiet in the grave, we should not distrust His goodness nor murmur at it.

(5) Let us compare our present sufferings and afflictions with that happiness which is to come. God's

anger is but for a moment, but His love will be forever. He frowns for a moment, but He will show them His pleased face forever. He corrects them and they weep for a moment, but He will embrace them and they shall rejoice forever. "Weeping may endure for a night, but joy cometh in the morning" (Psalm 30:5). And do we not find our hearts begin to spring within us when we consider that we are in pain for a moment, but shall be at ease forever? Is this not good news to those who fear God, and are yet afflicted? Lift up your heads, you mourners, you prisoners of hope; it is but for a little season. Do not let your hearts faint.

But you will say, "Oh, I could bear anything but the wrath of God! He is angry with my soul. He denies me answers to my prayers. He does not speak one comfortable word to me. I look up to His heavens and they are like brass. I run to His ordinances and I hear His Word in the assemblies of His people; but while others are wet with the dew of heaven, I remain as dry and neglected as I was before. I seem to be as the mountains of Gilboa: there is no dew nor rain falling upon me. I seem to be under the curse of God. And because I have not formerly improved the means of grace, He seems to say of me as He did of the barren fig tree, 'Never let fruit grow upon thee more.' Can you tell me where I shall go or what I should do in such a case as this?"

You must still, in humble submission, wait upon the Lord. He does not send immediate help upon a very gracious design. He bottles your tears and is acquainted with your griefs; and that anger that now bows you to the ground shall in a little while be removed, and your faith and hope will not be in vain. There are thousands of joys prepared to meet you when you are a little more purified and prepared for them. Isaiah 54:7–8: " 'For a small moment have I forsaken thee, but with great mercies will I gather thee. In a little wrath I hid My face from thee for a moment, but with everlasting kindness will I have mercy on thee,' saith the Lord thy Redeemer."

Nothing can be less than a moment; it is the least part of time. And yet, so small a thing as that is are all our troubles here, compared to that endless eternity which is to come. So if your outward afflictions and your spiritual fears should last for life, and none can give you assurance to the contrary, yet all this life is but as a moment, as nothing compared to the state of blessedness that comes afterward.

Nor are the degrees of your sorrows here proportional to the degrees of your approaching glory. "For our light affliction, which is but for a moment, worketh for us a far more exceeding and eternal weight of glory" (2 Corinthians 4:17). This great apostle called his afflictions "light," and yet never did anyone suffer more troubles from the malice of the world than did he, as you may see in 2 Corinthians 11:23–27. What is a moment to a day, or a day to a year? And yet such, and infinitely less, are our longest afflictions here to that eternity. What is one grain of sand to all those vast heaps of sand that are in all the seas? What is one drop of water to the vast collections of it that are in the large oceans? What is a little gnat to the whole universe? So are all the afflictions of this life, which pass away, when compared with the glory which is to come.

Yet a grain of sand is something in comparison to the whole earth, and a drop is not altogether nothing though it is compared to the ocean; for by a continual heaping of grain upon grain, it would be possible to make a globe as great as the earth. And the ocean might be emptied of its water, but eternity cannot be diminished. It suffers no changes; after millions of years in happiness, it will be as sweet and as comfortable as it was the first moment.

It is the length of our troubles and pain that makes them more grievous. And when we do not sleep the night seems very long, and the doleful hours of our sickness seem to move with a much slower pace than those of our pleasant health. Thus Job discoursed as if his time, being clogged with miseries, seemed like an eternity. Job 7:15–16: "My soul chooseth strangling, and death rather than my life. I loathe it, I would not live always; let me alone, for my days are vanity." He was weary of being long in pain, and thought that his afflicted life would never have an end. Yet all "the sufferings of this present time are not worthy to be compared with the glory which shall be revealed" (Romans 8:18). We are near to a blessed change, and who would not undergo the dangers of a troublesome voyage for a month if he knew that he would return home laden with great treasures, and live in splendor ever after?

What a pleasure it is to such as are besieged to know that they shall certainly be relieved in a little time. It causes them, though pressed very close by their enemies, to resume a new courage and to hearten one another. So it should be with all believers. The day of their Lord's coming draws near, and then He will put all their enemies to the flight, and reward His people's diligence and perseverance. The enemy of our souls is full of rage, but that which fills him with fury may yield us comfort, because we know that his time is short.

"The God of peace shall bruise Satan under your feet shortly" (Romans 16:20). Oh, what comfortable words these are! That enemy of ours, who fills us with vexation, and whose malice is both great and constant, shall, in a little time, not molest nor interrupt our satisfactions any more.

The tears that you shed for your offenses now are very just; it is what we owe to God for having sinned so much against Him. But shortly we shall be with Him, and never complain of His absence from us any more. When a man is tossed by storms and sees no prospect of reaching the shore, it is very dismal; but it is not so with us who have our haven in view. What if our troubles should continue for twenty or thirty years? This would be overwhelming to our senses, and yet it is nothing when compared with an eternity of joys above. How soon will this be over, but how long will that remain! It casts a great damp on all things under the sun, that they are unsatisfying, and that they are very short. However pleasant they are to us, they will depart. Our friends and all the delight of their conversation; our riches and all the respect and service they procure for us, will fade away. Our beloved bodies, which we maintain with great expense and care, will leave us, and must go into the grave. But our happiness will be forever; it is eternal happiness, and what that is our thoughts cannot comprehend nor our words express. We shall know what it is when we are in actual possession of it. To be forever with the Lord, what an encouragement this affords to patience and resignation! To be with Him who is our portion and our all; to be with Him, and to be without the sin that provoked Him to wrath, and made our spirits sad—what a heaven this will be!

As this life, by its tedious afflictions, seems to those who are in distress to be as an eternity, so the pleasures of that undecaying life will seem but a moment to us, it will be so very pleasant. And we are near to it. Though the pains that precede our departure prove to be very sharp, yet in a moment death, whenever it comes, will be past; in a moment we shall see the face of God that was hidden from us here. We shall be changed as in the twinkling of an eye; and when we are in that eternity, shall we then say that we cleansed our hearts in vain? Shall we not then see that we had no cause to murmur or repine? All our faculties will be gratified with proper objects and with suitable employment; they will all be overspread and swallowed up with a quick and lively joy. Oh, how blessed are the tears that will lead us to such a joy! Blessed is the cross that will yield us such fruit as this, and blessed be that God who will bestow such a reward upon us!

When we come there, we shall sing in the consideration of those very afflictions that, while we were here on earth, made us sigh and groan. It is good to be there, and how freely should we allow our thoughts to always dwell upon the pleasant subject. But our worldly business, and the necessary affairs of life, often call us away from the mountain of our transfiguration. However, let us not forget that these things are the truth of God which He has shown to His servants, and which shall shortly come to pass and will have a suitable influence upon us. How did the martyrs of old rejoice when they saw the day wherein they were to suffer! How they embraced and encouraged one another, saying, "We lack but an hour or two before we arrive at heaven. We have but one combat more to finish and we shall be with Christ. We dine upon bitter herbs, but we shall sup with Him. Before the crowd that came to see us die is dispersed, we shall be with God, and with innumerable angels and the spirits of the just."

With what calmness have the blessed sufferers bid this world adieu, saying, "Farewell, sun, moon, and stars; and welcome, better lights. Farewell, wives, children, friends, and acquaintances. Farewell, you deceiving pleasures of the world, and welcome, you joys of paradise. Welcome, you sweet cross of Christ, and welcome, death, that will convey us there."

And thus their souls were driven in chariots of fire to their Father's house. Whether there is music in the revolution of the celestial spheres, as some of the philosophers have imagined, we do not know; but it is very likely that the separated soul of the patient and triumphant Christian will have those angels that rejoiced at its conversion, that wait to carry it to its blessed home, to present it to the throne of God with joyful praises and united hallelujahs. Thus we should admire and imitate the patience of the saints, whose life was begun with darkness and sorrow, but ended with light and pleasure; whose life began with a combat, but concluded with a victory.

And then shall the soul, which a few moments before was disconsolate, have cause to say in that day, "O Lord, I will praise Thee; though Thou wast angry with me, Thine anger is turned away, and Thou comfortest me. Behold, God is my salvation . . . the Lord Jehovah is my strength and my song. He also is become my salvation" (Isaiah 12:1–2).

Chapter 4

The great love of Christ in suffering the wrath of God in His soul, which is all the more to be admired in that He bore it for us, and not for the fallen angels; and because of that He is now, from His own experience, more qualified to relieve us under all our temptations

How great cause do we have to value Jesus Christ, who, by suffering the wrath of God in His own person, has procured this privilege for believers: the anger of God towards them shall be only for a moment. Had it not been for His spotless satisfaction, the divine justice would have perpetually flamed out against us, and He would not only have been angry with us now, but forever. He has delivered us from the wrath to come.

That which comes easy to us (upon our faith) was purchased by Him at a very dear price. He shed His own blood to obtain peace and mercy for us. Oh, how great was the burden of that heavy cross which He bore for us! How terrible and amazing was that wrath which He felt in His bitter and doleful agonies, when He saw not one smile on His Father's face; when it was with Him an hour of thick darkness; when, under the smart of what He felt and the view of what He was to feel, He said, "My soul is exceeding sorrowful, even unto death"; when the agonies of His soul affected His body, and caused it, even in a cold season, to sweat, as it were, great drops of blood! What a gloomy time it was when

He fell upon His face, and, in a sorrowful posture, with strong cries and tears, prayed, "O My Father, if it be possible, let this cup pass from Me!" What flaming wrath that was which scorched Him when He uttered those dreadful words, "My God, My God, why hast Thou forsaken Me!" The angel told Mary that a sword would pierce through her soul (Luke 2:35), when she would see what injurious usage her Son met with; but how much sharper was the sword that pierced the soul of Christ Himself! The wrath that He bore would have totally overwhelmed and destroyed angels and men, had they joined their strength together. None but He was able to sustain such a combat, and to bear such a load.

Oh, where would we guilty creatures have been had He not died for us! God would have been our enemy and hell our portion. His holiness would not allow Him to be gracious to us without any satisfaction; and there was none who was able to make it but His own dearly beloved Son—and this excellent Person freely did it.

What cause we have to admire the breadth, length, depth, and height of this love which passes knowledge! Angels in heaven wonder at it, it was so great in itself, and accomplished in such a painful and costly way. And we may be justly filled with a wondering joy, for we are more concerned, and our sin and guilt make us need it more than they do. There was nothing in us to move Him to begin, or to finish the blessed work of our redemption—nothing but misery. He saw us lost and came to find us. He saw us perishing, His bowels yearned within Him, and His own pity and compassion made Him come and save us.

What punishment we had deserved for our manifold

transgressions! And He came and bore the punishment that was our due, and discharged that debt which we were never able to pay. How kind was He, who thought His own life and His own blood not too much for us! Whoever exposed his person and life for an enemy? And yet He died for us when we were so, which is as marvelous an act of mercy as if a prince's son should lay his head upon the block to save one who had rebelled against the crown and government of his own father.

And what does He require from us for all that He has done? He asks nothing but our love, and shall we not give Him our best affections, our highest thoughts, and our hearts, which He has so dearly bought? Have ever any of those things to which we give our love done so much for us as He has done? He has the best title, and will prove to be our best friend in the end; had it not been for Him, we could never have prayed to God with hope, nor lived without a fearful expectation of vengeance. We were children of wrath, and must, but for Him, have been the heirs of wrath too. Who would not love such a Benefactor? Who would not give Him all, who gave Himself for us?

It is by His death that God is appeased, and that is why His anger is but for a moment to those who receive His Son. God has smelled a sweet savor in this sacrifice, and is highly pleased with it. And it is upon this account that He is pleased. He does not follow us with wrath, but invites us to Himself in mercy. He has sheathed His flaming sword and is ready to embrace us in His arms. And though He sees nothing in us to excite His goodness, yet every time He looks upon our blessed Lord, He sees one who has entirely pleased

Him, who has done His will, and who is the beloved of His soul. And it is for His sake that His anger towards us is so long delayed, and that, when it comes, it is but for a moment. Let us love this Redeemer with all our hearts, remembering that terrible sentence of our apostle, "If any man love not the Lord Jesus Christ, let him be Anathema, Maranatha" (1 Corinthians 16:22), or cursed till He comes again.

There are two things that should engage us to love Him for bearing the wrath of God for us: that He bore it for us, and not for the fallen angels, and that, from His own experience, He is able to help us under all our temptations, and when we are under the sense of God's displeasure.

1. Christ did not bear the wrath of God for the fallen angels; they fell from Him as we did, but He did not design to raise them again. They groaned under the wrath of the mighty Judge, and they must always groan under it. No beam of cheerful light will shine into their dungeons; no messenger will be dispatched to give them the glad tidings of salvation. The anger of God threw them out of heaven, and the door is forever shut; they know this to be their woeful case, and therefore they rage against Him and His servants, and against His interest in the world.

What could move Christ to take the nature of man and not of angels (Hebrews 2:16), to say to us, "Live," and to allow them to die? To visit our sinning world, to set us at liberty, to open the prison doors, while He allows them to roar in chains of wrath? As they have greater capacities, and natures more knowing than ours, so they might have honored their Creator more than we, had they been redeemed. But they must mourn forever, and never sing His praises; they must grieve while we rejoice; while we look for our Lord, they tremble in the fear of His coming; while we have the sweetness of hope, they are in anguish and vexation, in despair and horror. We have our sabbaths, but they have no days of rest; we can, through Jesus Christ, call God our Father, but they do not know Him by such a comfortable name; they feel His power, but they do not taste His love; they tremble under His vengeance, but all comfort and joy have fled away from them forever. Why are we in the light and they in the darkness? Why is Christ a Physician to us while He is a Judge to them? Truly nothing makes the difference but His own love, and what manner of love this is!

2. It was great love in Christ to bear the anger of God because now His poor, tempted servants have one to whom they may repair in all their straits. Hebrews 2:18: "For in that He Himself hath suffered, being tempted, He is able to succor them that are tempted." It is a great relief to the miserable and afflicted to be pitied by others. Job 19:21: "Have pity upon me, have pity upon me, O ye my friends, for the hand of God hath touched me." It is some relief when others, though they cannot help us, yet seem to be truly concerned for the sadness of our case, when by the kindness of their words and their actions they smooth the wound a little that they cannot heal. But it is an unspeakable addition to the cross, when a man is brought low under the sense of God's displeasure, to have men mock at his calamity, revile him, or speak roughly to him. This merely inflames and exasperates the wound that was big enough before; and it is a hard thing, when one has a dreadful sound in his ears, to have every friend become a son of thun-

der. It is a small matter for people who are at ease to deal severely with such as are afflicted; but they little know how their severe speeches and their angry words pierce them to the very soul.

It is easy to blame others for complaining, but if such had felt what it is to be under the fear of God's anger for even a little while, they would find they could not *but* complain. It cannot but make any person very restless and uneasy when he apprehends that God is his enemy. It is no wonder if he makes everyone whom he sees, and every place that he is in, a witness of his grief. But it is a comfort in our temptations and in our fears that we have so compassionate a friend as Christ is, to whom we may repair. Hebrews 4:15: "For we have not a High Priest which cannot be touched with the feeling of our infirmities, but was in all points tempted like as we are, yet without sin. Let us therefore come boldly to the throne of grace, that we may obtain mercy, and find grace to help in time of need." Had it not been for His mediation, the absolute and pure Deity would have been too glorious and inaccessible to us. But He is clothed with our nature, and though it has undergone several alterations (since He is now exalted), yet we are sure that He retains a tender sense of our miseries. And though He is very high, He does not think it beneath Him to regard the most troubled and sorrowful believer. While on earth, He was acquainted with grief (Isaiah 53:3). And He has carried to heaven with Him a remembrance of what He felt in His own temptations, and of what He felt when His Father frowned upon Him. Thus His own experience renders Him more capable of helping us; it makes Him full of pity when He sees us mourn, knowing well what was His own case.

As God has fashioned the hearts of all men, and given some naturally more mercy and pity than others; and as then the Holy Spirit, by its renewing grace, carries their good dispositions to greater degrees, and proceeds and works usually according to their tempers—so it is certain that He tempered the heart of Christ and made it of a softer mold than all the tenderness of all the men in the world put together would have made it. He had such a human nature that might be more merciful than all men and angels put together (see Thomas Goodwin's work *Christ's Heart in Heaven*). Our groans and sighs reach His heart above; and though He does not come with help just when we desire it, yet He is providing for our welfare. He sends us some inward supports when we do not have an immediate deliverance. He will not allow us totally to sink, though He may leave us for a while to try our faith, or to let us understand our own weakness. We may think that our vessel will be covered with waves when He is guiding us to shore, even when we think that He is asleep and has forgotten us, and does not care if we are cast away. Only let us never cease to say, "Master, save us, or else we perish."

Chapter 5

The unreasonableness of long-continued anger among good people; also that the temporary effects of God's displeasure are more eligible than the wrath of men; the excellence of religion, and that the enemies of the Church have no cause to gloat over it because of its certain deliverance, and the dismal conclusion of their own wickedness; upon which account Christians have no reason to envy the prosperity of the wicked

Seeing that God is angry for but a moment, how unreasonable long-continued anger among good people is! "Let not the sun go down upon your wrath; neither give place to the devil" (Ephesians 4:26–27). In other words, he who has injured or provoked another must control his temper and sue for reconciliation speedily, or else before the time of solemn praying to God, which was always at evening. And this exhortation is consistent with Matthew 5:23–24: "If thou bring thy gift unto the altar, and there remembrest that thy brother hath ought against thee, leave there thy gift . . . first be reconciled to thy brother."

It is a strange thing that any good people should be so passionate and hasty as some are. They are quickly enraged, and hard to be reconciled; and there are many who will keep their anger for several months and, it may be, years at a time. Oh, how this is unlike that God whom they call their Father in heaven, who is slow to wrath, and whose anger towards them is but for a moment! And what an honor and a privilege would it be to resemble Him! If He were not more patient with His creatures and His children than they are with one another, what confusions, what woeful punishments would the world be filled with! "Anger resteth in the bosom of fools" (Ecclesiastes 7:9).

Hasty, passionate people are commonly the weaker sort of Christians; and though the strong must pity their weakness and bear with them, yet they must not bear with it in themselves, but pray and strive against it, and not coin excuses to defend that which is inexcusable, that which is a reproach to religion and is in itself a great sin. A good man may be surprised suddenly and put into a fret, but to always be fretting and uneasy, and displeased with those who have injured you, is very unsuitable to the example of your blessed and meek Savior. What pleasure can such take in hearing that their enemies abroad lose the day when they have a worse enemy in their own breasts that leads them captive, and takes them at the first assault? The worst enemies, in this sense, are those of a man's own house. And it is a wonder that those persons who appear to be very conscientious in other things yet indulge themselves in this: they give place to the devil, and he casts a mist before their eyes. And though he cannot keep them from fearing other sins, yet he so cheats them with false pretenses that they do not believe rash anger to be a sin, or are easily drawn to commit it.

What differences have been kept up in churches, in families, among acquaintances and friends, for a long period of time, whose anger should have been like that of God, but for a moment! They do not consider aright their own duty, nor the infirmity of mankind, and how most of their errors are to be cured in a loving and a gentle manner. We are unwilling to pardon our enemies, or the injuries of our friends; and God is most ready to forgive us all. Ephesians 4:32: "Be ye kind one to another, tender-hearted, forgiving one another, even as God for Christ's sake hath forgiven you."

There are, it may be, angers that have lasted ten or twelve years, and what estrangement, what distance, what shyness is there among such! It may be spoken to their shame, how seldom will men who have received an injury speak well of the persons who may have only given them a slight provocation. They'll have no commerce nor familiarity with them; but is this a blessing for those who curse us, or praying for those who despitefully use us? Is this an imitation of our gracious God who has forgiven us all our innumerable provocations?

I am not speaking here of those bold fellows who, upon every small affront, are for challenging another to give them satisfaction; who are so weak that they cannot agree without a duel; whom a false notion of honor pushes forward to those rash enterprises that are condemned by both the laws of God and the laws of men. And is he not a stout man who has the courage to trample upon the authority of his Maker and his rulers too; who dares venture his damnation to preserve his reputation, and hazards sending his own soul, or that of his friend, to hell to keep himself from being called a coward here on earth? What a low value these persons have of their lives who throw them away merely to satisfy their own passions! And in what posture or preparation is that man for dying who dies to satisfy his own revenge? It would be more honorable to forgive a fault than to pursue it after such a bloody manner. James 1:19–20: "Wherefore, my beloved brethren, let every man be swift to hear, slow to speak, slow to wrath, for the wrath of man worketh not the righteousness of God."

Seeing that the anger of God is but for a moment, then it is better, as for the temporal effects of it, to fall into the hands of God than into the hands of men. We may say of all wicked men what Jacob said of Simeon and Levi in Genesis 49:5–7: "Instruments of cruelty are in their habitations. O my soul, come not thou into their secret; unto their assembly, mine honor, be not thou united. Cursed be their anger, for it was fierce, and their wrath, for it was cruel." Their tender mercies are cruelty (Proverbs 12:10).

Wicked men are soon transported into violent passions, and, when they are armed with a power suitable to their rage, what horrible effects does it then produce! They are inspired with barbarous principles and designs by an evil spirit that delights in mischief. And he communicates to them of his own fury; and what is it that they then scruple? Nothing softens or makes impressions on their cruel hearts.

The various massacres that have occured in Ireland, Piedmont, and France have been sad examples of these kinds of passions. The perpetrators did not spare the aged, the feeble, the sick, or the young; no age or sex but felt the woeful effects of their wrath and rage; they have torn poor, harmless infants from their mother's breasts; others they have killed in the womb; some they have cut in pieces, others they have put to long tortures and lingering deaths. They were not moved at all by the hideous cries of parents who died several deaths in beholding their children die; and then, when their eyes had beheld the sad spectacle, they had their own blood shed.

Oh, what a vast difference is there between the temporary anger of God, as to outward evils, and that of men! He no sooner sees us at His feet and His bowels yearn over us; and then He raises up His hand and bids us be of good cheer. But cruel men delight to trample on the poor and desolate. He hears our cries when we pray, but they are deaf to all the entreaties and supplications of afflicted and miserable people. They set themselves to invent methods of torture to make those who are within their power die with greater pain and sorrow; but God does not willingly grieve nor afflict the children of men. Their wrath is unruly; it assigns itself no bounds; they know no moderation; they forbear nothing that tends to gratify their lusts. But it is a comfort that our God is of great power, and His mercies are infinite. Men go about that work which God sometimes permits them to do, with cruel intentions to ruin and destroy; but God has a design in all His corrections to purify and reform, and to do us good in the final end. 2 Samuel 24:13–14: "Gad came to David and told him, 'Shall seven years of famine come unto thee in thy land? Or wilt thou flee three months before thine enemies, while they pursue thee? Or that there be three days' pestilence in thy land? Now advise, and see what answer I shall return to him that sent me.' And David said unto God, 'I am in a great strait; let us fall now into the hand of the Lord, for His mercies are great, and let me not fall into the hand of man.' "

What a good Master God is, whose anger is but for a

moment. Other masters may be hasty, froward, and hard to please, but God is patient and slow to wrath. He is never angry till we disobey His voice, and, by our laziness in His work, force Him to it—and even then His nature inclines Him to moderate our stripes. He adds no more than what is necessary to promote our good. He does not treat us as slaves, but exercises toward us a mild and a favorable government. He threatens for a long while before He punishes. The clouds gather blackness to give us notice of a coming storm; and the thunder of God's wrath, as well as that of nature, roars before it falls. He threatens, advises, persuades, and uses various affectionate expostulations with us before we feel the rod. And when, in vindicating His own right, He seems to be very just, He does not cease at the same time to be very good.

We frequently provoke Him, and He is most ready to forgive. He does not seek advantages against us, nor does He wait for our halting; it grieves Him when we sin, and He is angry only so that we may repent. He delights in peace, not in war; in the manifestations of His mercy and love more than in the terrible displays of His wrath. He whets His sword before He strikes that, in the preparations of His judgments, we may see what we may expect, and seek to prevent them. He summons us to surrender ourselves before He begins to make us, by sharper methods, sensible of our follies; and while His rod is in His hand, He waits to see if we will even then return. He is unwilling to punish even when He is forced to do it, just as a tender judge, with sorrow and regret, pronounces the sentence upon a malefactor. Hosea 11:8: "How shall I give thee up, Ephraim! How shall I deliver thee, Israel?" Psalm 78:38: "Many a time turned He His anger away." He recalled His anger, or ordered it to return, as one interprets it, as if He were unresolved what to do. He recalled His anger as a man does his servant, several times, when he is sending him upon an unwelcome message, or as a tender-hearted prince trembles when he is to sign a writ for the death of a rebel who had been his favorite heretofore. He blots out his name again and flings away the pen.

So God singles out here and there some of His servants when He might punish all for their sins. He makes one smart so as to be a warning to the rest. And, according to the scholars, He recompenses good works far above their merit, but punishes crimes far below their demerit. He makes His mercy triumph over judgment. He punishes with regret, and retains a great deal of His wrath when He corrects; but He keeps no measure when He rewards. Thus the miseries of the miserable are no greater than the joy and happiness of the blessed.

Oh, who would not serve so gracious and so good a Master as God is, who is patient before He is angry, and who is soon appeased again! Are the cruel commands of Satan, the slavery of the world, or the defilements of sin to be preferred to the gentle and pure commands of God? How many curse their folly in adhering to these! But none repent that they have been employed in His service. His most aged servants find the greatest honor and delight in having served Him very long, and would not quit their experienced and kind Master for all the world. They know that His corrections are short, but His love is everlasting; they know that His wrath is but for a moment, but their heaven will be forever.

The enemies of the Church of God have no reason

to gloat over those in it who are afflicted; for though God is angry for their sins, yet His anger is but for a moment. Thus they treated David in Psalm 41:7–8: "All that hate me whisper together against me . . . an evil disease, say they, cleaveth fast unto him, and now that he lieth he shall rise up no more." And Psalm 42:3: "My tears have been my meat day and night, while they continually say unto me, 'Where is thy God?' " They thought that he was entirely forsaken and abandoned forever, so they put these questions to him: "What has now become of your God, in whom you were wont to boast? Where is He whom you once called your refuge and your hiding place? Where is His power and His goodness, considering that He leaves you to such a deep and violent affliction?"

The allusion in that passage is of Shimei in 2 Samuel 16:7–8: "Thus said Shimei, when he cursed, 'Come out, come out, thou bloody man, and thou man of Belial. The Lord hath returned upon thee all the blood of the house of Saul, in whose stead thou hast reigned, and the Lord hath delivered thy kingdom into the hand of Absalom thy son. And behold, thou art taken in thy mischief because thou art a bloody man.' "

This bold man put a wicked interpretation on the providence of God, and because David met with so many troubles, and such interruption in his affairs, ere the kingdom was well-settled in his hand, he thought that God was against him. But he lived to sit with prosperity on the throne for many years together; and Shimei had enough leisure wherein to repent of his foolish and extravagant reproaches of so good a king.

Thus the barbarians thought that Paul had been a murderer because a viper fixed upon his hand; they thought that vengeance had pursued him for some great offense, till he shook the viper off and taught them how ill-grounded their opinion was, and that the God they thought was his enemy assisted him to work miracles.

When you see any who are greatly afflicted and groaning under a sense of the wrath of God, you ought to tremble rather than rejoice, to weep rather than to laugh, to consider how holy and just God is, seeing that He will not even spare His own; for all His elect shall, at one time or another, taste the bitterness of sin. You who were never serious have reason to humble yourselves, and to think what you may expect when His children are corrected after so severe a manner. If His own family suffers such afflictions, what does He have in store then for His open enemies? If the righteous scarcely are saved, where shall the ungodly and the sinner appear? Proverbs 24:17–18: "Rejoice not when thine enemy falleth, and let not thine heart be glad when he stumbleth, lest the Lord see it, and it displease Him, and He turn away His wrath from him." Do not entertain some secret pleasure in the downfall and distress of any man whatsoever; for these inhuman affections are so displeasing to God that they may provoke Him to translate the calamity from your enemy to you, and thereby dampen your sinful joy with a double sorrow, first to see him delivered from his trouble, and then to find yourself involved in it.

Do not triumph over any in affliction lest the cup be taken out of their hand and put into yours. Do not, with the friends of Job, censure them as being greater sinners than any in the world because their trials are greater, as if you were acquainted with the secrets of the decrees of God and could pierce, with your shallow reason, into the bottom of His unfathomable judgments. Those who are under an apprehension of the divine displeasure know that it is for sin; it is that which troubles and afflicts them more than anything else besides. But you ought not to conclude that they are sinners beyond the rest of men, but rather wonder at the goodness of God, that He is gracious and favorable to anyone, when they all deserve to die.

Do not add affliction to those who are afflicted by reproachful language. Zechariah 1:15: "I am very sore displeased with the heathen that are at ease, for I was but a little displeased and they helped forward the affliction." It was cruel gloating of wicked men over her miseries which made the Church say in Micah 7:8, "Rejoice not against me, O mine enemy; when I fall, I shall arise; when I sit in darkness, the Lord shall be a light unto me."

How much happier is the condition of a good man than that of one who shall remain impenitent in his wickedness! God is angry with the one for a moment, but with the other He will be so forever. The servants of God have never so much cause to mourn under the sense of the heinousness and aggravation of their sins as they have cause to rejoice in the riches and freeness of His grace. They have never so much cause to be troubled at their own distress as to sing at the remembrance of His holiness. They have cause to weep indeed because they have provoked so good a God to wrath, and to be glad that His anger is but for a moment. They have cause to be concerned that they have made Him frown, but cause to rejoice that He will smile on them forever.

The righteous have a bitter cup, but since it is here mingled with love, so it prepares them for a sweeter taste of heavenly pleasure. Psalm 75:8: "In the hand of the Lord there is a cup, and the wine is red. It is full of mixture, and He poureth out of the same; but the dregs thereof, all the wicked of the earth shall wring them out, and drink them." God does correct His own here with measure, but His punishments of the wicked will know no bounds. Wrath shall come upon them to the uttermost; and how low they must sink, and what a load they must bear, who have this God to punish them, whose being is eternal and whose power is omnipotent.

On His own people, He frowns for a season, and He does it to bring them to their duty; but on His obstinate, unrelenting enemies He will frown forever. He will abhor them. He will cast them out of His presence, trample upon them in His fury, and leave them to be the brands of hell and the prey of devils.

Now, indeed, we cannot, even with all the terrors of the Lord, which are terrible beyond expression, persuade men to repent. Though we tell them that death and destruction are at hand, though we show them the threats of the Scriptures and the examples of their evil predecessors who have gone to their own place, they slumber on. Though we tell them of the danger ahead, of a pit that is opening its mouth to swallow them up; though we see wrath gathering and the clouds ready to burst, and bid them make haste to get shelter before the storm comes; though we bid them fly for their lives out of Sodom—they still linger and delay.

But after death, they cannot, even if they would, be secure. They will then have no pillows whereon to rest their head, no water to quench their thirst, no friend to help them, no God to hear their cries; they cannot then stop their ears at the roaring wrath of God; they cannot then stupefy their consciences, nor put off the evil day.

Now they make shifts to stifle the checks of their own consciences; they mock at the threats of God, and deride His message; but, sinners, you shall sadly know what a dreadful and terrible God you provoke to wrath. All your entertainments and diversions, all your mirth and laughter, all your carnal comforts and jolly company will be gone, and be gone forever! And what will then remain? Nothing but consternation, amazement, and woe; nothing but anguish and tribulation. Who shall speak comfortably to you? Who shall deliver you once you have fallen into the hands of the living God? What will you do when you find that God, who is a gracious Father to the saints, is a severe judge to you; when He who is the joy of their hearts shall depart from you, and He who refreshes them with the smiles of His face shall kill you with His frowns? What will you do when the full wrath of God shall be poured on your guilty souls? Where will you turn when it shall scorch and burn you, and set you all on fire? How will it overwhelm you when you find that all your hideous cries, all your lamentations and groans, are to no purpose; when you are in the power of cruel devils, and meet with no pity from God, and none from His angels or His saints?

We think it long to be in pain for a month or two, or a whole year; but how long will they think it to be who are in pain throughout all the duration of a sad eternity? We think it long when we do not sleep in the night, and wish for the light of day; but, oh, what a long night that will be, and how uncomfortable, that will have no morning, and that will not be followed with a beam of daylight ever! Men now think that an hour or two attending upon God is a great while; they think that fast-days and sabbaths are long; but if they come to that misery of which I am now speaking, oh, how long and how tedious they will find hell to be! How insupportable and unavoidable!

Hear, therefore, all you who live in sin; hear and live. Oh, do not throw yourselves down that precipice, under which there is a sea of wrath and a lake of fire. Oh, do not wound or destroy or torment your own souls; do not carry fuel to that fire which will never be quenched; do not run into the furnace out of which there is no escape. For the Lord's sake, for your own sake, and for the sake of your friends who would fain see you become religious, awake and call, every one of you, upon your God; seek Him while He may be found; hear His voice while it is called today, lest the God who alone can help you laugh at your calamity, and lest He who is now so merciful hereafter take pleasure in your punishment. If you will forget your danger and sleep on, know that when you are in hell you will then be forced to open your eyes, and they will never be closed again.

Oh, what a dreadful and amazing sight you will then see, when you see the great God to be your enemy, the devil to be your tormentor, damned souls to be your companions, and everlasting fire to be your own portion! God will not then repent of the evil; He will not then send His messengers with glad tidings any more. What will you do in the day of the Lord? Nahum 1:5–6: "The mountains quake at Him, the hills melt, and the earth is burned at His presence; yea, the world and all that dwell therein. Who can stand before His indignation? And who can abide in the fierceness of His anger? His fury is poured out like fire, and the rocks are thrown down by Him."

Have we not some representation of the terror of that great day in some of the great thunders that make us tremble, that with their noise and lightning make the inhabitants of this earth astonished? Psalm 29:4, 7: "The voice of the Lord is powerful, and full of majesty; the voice of the Lord rends the air, and sends out flames of fire." But what a more terrible season will that be when you shall hear the voice of the last trumpet saying, "Arise, ye dead, and come into judgment"; when the elements shall melt with fervent heat, when the sun shall be turned into darkness and the moon into blood! When the stars shall fall from heaven, and this admired earth shall be full of convulsions and violent agitations! When the seas shall roar and the graves open, and the Judge appears in the clouds! When you shall hear the cracks and groans of this dissolving world! Where will you sinners hide your heads? What will you then think of the wrath of God on that great and terrible day?

You will then wish that you had never been born. Oh, how happy would you then reckon yourselves if you could but go into the grave again! Oh, how happy if you could but die; but death will fly from you. This is that hell where the wicked must live, and live forever, though it is in misery. Oh, little do you think what you do when you sin. You are like a man who is drinking at the edge of a furnace, into which he will be thrown when he has had a few drinks; you are like a malefactor who is jolly and merry the night before he is to be executed. Then you shall see that it shall be well with the righteous, though it goes ill with you. Judge things now as they will appear to be on that day; join yourselves to that society among which you would then want to be found.

Judge religion as it will then appear. Here it seems, through the many afflictions and sorrows that attend it, not to be such a lovely thing; but then it will appear in its true luster and its fullest beauty. Here you see many times a true servant of God brought very low, complaining of his iniquities. Now you hear his groans, but a moment from now you shall hear his praises and hallelujahs. It is night with him now, but a moment hence you shall see him triumph in eternal day. He is now in a strange land, but shortly he will be with God at rest in heaven. And happy is he who gets to such a blessedness, though he goes out with a sad heart and weeping eyes, and meets with broken bones and many a trembling dispensation on his way there.

Which course will you take? Which pattern will you choose? Will you serve God or your own lusts? Will you come to have your portion here or in the world to come? Will you be content with the present afflictions of religion in hope of eternal joy? Consider that they are not to be judged the happiest men who fare well for a moment, but those who do so forever. If you serve your sin, you will have pleasure, it may be, for a while, but bitterness and sorrows in the latter end; your farewell will be very terrible. Will you please yourselves for a moment and venture eternal wrath? Or will you not rather yield yourselves to a gracious and loving God? And then you shall sow in tears, but you shall reap in joy; you may feel His anger for a moment, but He will entertain you in His own kingdom forever.

We have no cause to be offended with the prosperity of the wicked. It is true, the righteous are now sowing in tears, but they shall reap in joy. In a little while it shall be the portion of the ungodly to mourn and to be sorrowful. Would you envy a malefactor who is jovial and pleasant one night, when you know he is to be led to execution the next day? His approaching punishment might justly spoil the relish of his own dainties, but it gives the spectators no occasion to begrudge him his drunken joys, seeing that they are the last ones that the poor man is ever likely to have; and a little time obscures all the gaiety of his looks with an everlasting cloud.

It is no just objection against the wisdom of divine providence that the good are afflicted while the rod of God is not upon the bad. For He gives to the one the blessings of the right hand, the knowledge of Himself and their duty, while to the other He gives only the blessings of the left hand, riches and honor and the like goods; these, being only outward and for this present world, are not of such great value as those which are spiritual and relate to the life to come. We think it fares well with the wicked because we do not, for the present, see them shed so many tears, nor complain after so doleful a manner, as the good are often forced to do. But we do not see in what chains they are held, nor with how many stinging thoughts their minds are harassed all the while they forget God. We do not see the perplexities to which they are reduced by the contrary commands of divers lusts. If we consider that God is angry with them every day (Psalm 7:11), and that we do not know but that in a day or two they shall be cut off and perish, we shall have no cause to murmur at their present undisturbed case and their seeming welfare; for their happiness is not real but apparent, and all the goods that are bestowed upon them are but mean and low in themselves, though our erroneous and blind judgments think them to be somewhat great and considerable. Considering of what little moment the present goods and evils are which good men suffer and bad men enjoy, they ought rather to be looked on as an argument of God's wisdom than as any objection against His providence; for He understands the just value of things, and knows that the best of these worldly goods are bad enough to be thrown away upon the worst of men. And so He expresses His just scorn of these admired vanities by scattering them abroad with a careless hand; for why should He partake of the error of vulgar opinion, and express Himself as so very regardful of these trifles as to put them in gold scales and weigh them out to mankind by grains and scruples? When we see, therefore, bad men rejoicing and good men mourning, let us not censure, but adore that providence that will assign to them both different portions in another world. Those who are healthy are not more beloved for that; nor are the sick and weak more hateful to God for those outward troubles that they now suffer. There are many who have their paradise in this world and who shall have none hereafter; and there is many a one who has been torn and mangled with the thorns and briars of the wilderness but for whom God reserves a throne above.

We see many a vessel on which the sun shines, and which sails with a fair gale, that yet, by splitting on a rock or upon the sand, never reaches the port. And we see others who that with nothing but high waves and contrary winds, and though they have an unpleasant voyage, yet for all that they land very safe and attended with comfort in the end.

The wicked do not always prosper in this life. God sometimes makes them examples of His justice, and if He does not usually do so to those who are very bad, it affords us a certain ground for the belief which we have in a judgment that is to come, wherein punishments and rewards will be distributed after another manner than now they are.

This maxim of Christian theology—that God sometimes afflicts very severely those whom He tenderly loves, even when they well perform their duty, even when He is well-pleased with them—was unknown to the ancient Israelites. This was a lesson above their understanding. God did not afflict them except when they had provoked Him by some particular transgression; when they did not do so, they always had a peaceable and happy life. It is not so with us. Our afflictions are sometimes indeed not the marks of His anger, but of His favor. An example is when He calls His own to endure things that are very bitter and unpleasant for the trial of their patience and faith. None of the prophets reckoned suffering among the gifts of God, but the apostle esteems them to be so in Philippians 1. We find no writer in the New Testament, which gives us a clearer discovery of another world, saying as they did heretofore, "Why doth the way of the wicked prosper?" But now it is, "Count it all joy when ye fall into divers temptations" (James 1:2).

Chapter 6

The duty of such as have never been under a sense of God's wrath and terror; and what the doleful condition of a soul is that apprehends itself to be under His hot displeasure

1. Seeing that God is often angry with His own servants, what cause have those of you who fear Him to bless Him that He is not angry with you, and that you do not feel His displeasure! He sets up others as His mark against which He shoots His arrows. You hear others groaning for His departure, and yet your hearts are not saddened as theirs are; your eyes can look up towards heaven with hope, while theirs are clouded with a veil of sorrows. He speaks roughly to them, but comfortable words to you. He seems to set Himself against them as His enemies, while He deals with you as a loving Friend. You see a reviving smile in His face, and they discern nothing there but one continual and dreadful frown.

Oh, admire and forever wonder at the sovereign, distinguishing grace of God! Are you who are at ease better than many of His people who are now thrown into a fiery furnace? Have you less dross than they? Have they sinned at a higher rate than you have ever done? He is angry with them for their lukewarmness, for their backsliding, and have your hearts always burned with love? Have your feet never wandered? Have you never turned aside to the right hand or to the left?

Surely you have, and therefore what a mercy it is that He is not angry with you as well as with them!

You see many whose consciences are all turned into flame, horror and perplexity, full of accusations, full of guilty fears, for their sinning against light, knowledge, mercy, and love; and have you never sinned? Have not your consciences also been defiled? Have you never done what was evil when you knew it to be so? Have you not kindly entertained God after you have run away from Him? Have you not, after great transgressions, met with joy and pleasure in the sense of His pardoning, healing grace, while others who have been more dutiful, perhaps, did not fare as well, nor have ever had a fatted calf killed for them, nor such feasts to refresh their souls as have been prepared for you?

You can never sufficiently bless God for His mercy. Every day you deserve His anger, and yet you have not been under the terrible apprehensions of it for a moment. Why are you sitting at His table? Why are you honored with His presence in all your duties, in all your sufferings, while He is a stranger to them, and as a wayfaring man who tarries for only a night? What is it that makes Him bless some children of the family with greater peace and comfort than He does the rest? Nothing but His own grace and mercy. Some are drawn with cords of love, and some have their iniquities constantly visited with stripes. Some are glad with the hopes of heaven, and some are afraid that they shall never go there; they know not by experience what joy and pleasure mean.

Some have their spirits overwhelmed, their entire souls covered with thick darkness and their bones broken, while others are at ease; they see the light of His countenance and have an unchanged health. Some travel with weary steps and make their pilgrimage with their own sorrows as a vale of tears, while others run in the way of His commandments with enlarged hearts. Some families are filled with lamentations, and some with songs of praise.

And all this gives us still greater occasions to magnify His grace and love, that we have a moment's ease. That we can observe one sabbath, or make one prayer with hope—these things deserve our highest thanks and admiration.

2. Do not presume for all this, however, for though He is not angry yet with you, He may one day be. This was the fault of David in Psalm 30:6: "In my prosperity I said, 'I shall never be moved.' " But verse 7 immediately follows with, "Thou didst hide Thy face, and I was troubled." The sun now shines upon you, and the candle of the Lord refreshes your tabernacle, but you may meet with many storms, clouds, and darkness before you come to your journey's end. The disciples were once greatly pleased with the glory of the transfiguration; and during the delightful interview among Christ, Moses, and Elijah, they though that they were in heaven. But a cloud came and obscured the preceding glory, and then the poor men were afraid.

It is true the anger of God endures but for a moment, but even that moment is very sad, terrible beyond expression. Weeping endures but for a night, but it may be a very bitter and doleful night for all that. It is a night such as the Egyptians had, when they arose and saw all their firstborn slain, and then there was a hideous, universal cry and mourning throughout all the land. So this night of the anger of the Lord may destroy all our comforts, and make the firstborn of our strength, the confidence and the pleasure of our hopes, give up the ghost. Psalm 77:2–4: "My sore ran in the night, and ceased not; my soul refused to be comforted. I complained, and my spirit was overwhelmed. Thou holdest mine eyes waking. I am so troubled that I cannot speak."

Though you are at ease today, and feel no trouble or disquiet, are you sure that it will be so tomorrow? Are you sure that you shall never see any frowns on the face of God? Do not presume on the strength of your grace, nor the brightness of your evidence for salvation; for that may languish and this may be obscured. And those of you who now think yourselves to be at the door of heaven may be brought, for all you know to the contrary, to the very gates of hell.

Though God is pleased at present to deal gently with you, yet your sins may cause Him to send His dreadful rebukes upon you. Your souls lie open and naked to Him (Hebrews 4:15), and He can make whatever impressions He pleases there, either of His goodness or of His severity. Do not be secure, for it is a dreadful thing to fall into the hands of the living God. Who can stand when He is angry? Who can bear His blows? Or what hand can strike so hard a stroke as His? There are these things in the sense of His anger that may prevent your security, and I will tell you not only what I have seen and heard, but what I have experienced in my own soul.

(1) Once you have a serious and fixed apprehension of the displeasure of God, no creature can yield you the least comfort. Though you are never so rich, all your gold cannot purchase one hour's peace and joy.

You may complain to your friends, and you cannot but complain, but alas, they can give you no relief. Their language is, "Unless the Lord helps, we cannot help." You may go to your ministers, and they may speak kindly to you, but they cannot make their words have any effect. If the heavens above you are as brass, they cannot give you rain, nor make the dew of God fall upon your branches as they used to do. Your friends can mourn with you, but they cannot wipe your tears away. Once you apprehend that God is angry with you, in vain you shall seek for rest in pleasures, diversions, or changes in your company, for such a stinging thought as this will always pierce you to the quick: "God is my enemy, and what will these avail?"

The sense of His anger will put even your natural spirits into a strange, unquiet agitation; and after this you will not find your very bodies at ease, as they used to be. Psalm 38:2–3: "Thine arrows stick fast in me, and Thy hand presseth me sore; there is no soundness in my flesh because of Thine anger, neither is there any rest in my bones because of my sin." "When I say, 'My bed shall comfort me, my couch shall ease my complaint,' then Thou scarest me with dreams, and terrifiest me through visions" (Job 7:13–14).

All the fountains on earth will never quench your thirst if the Fountain of living waters is shut up. Your bed will not be a place of rest then, nor your meat delightful to your taste; your sorrows will keep you waking all the night, and your fears will haunt and pursue you in the day. "My sighing cometh before I eat, and my roarings are poured out like waters" (Job 3:24). Your soul will then abhor all dainty meat, and your life will draw nigh unto the grave. And when you have tired yourselves in seeking rest among the creatures, and yet have found none, you must then sit down and say, by sad experience, "You all are miserable comforters." For though you run to never so many crowds of quiet people, you meet with no quiet. It is just as with the wounded hart: though she runs into the common herd, yet by that means she does not lose her pain, but carries her wound with her wherever she goes.

(2) While you are under the sense of God's displeasure, you will find no comfort in His ordinances; every part of His blessed Word will be as a sword cutting to your very soul. You will find every threat to be as a dart thrown at you, and every promise that is full of consolation to others will be dry to you. That Scripture which was once your delight will fill you with gall and wormwood; that which you once reckoned to be the Book of Life will then seem to be the book of death, and you will be afraid to read it for fear of reading your own condemnation—so great a change does the sense of God's displeasure make.

Those assemblies that were once your joy will then be terrible to you. The troubled soul says, "I do not go here to meet a Friend, as I used to do, but to see an Enemy; to see others joyfully serving God and singing His praise while I am silent with deep affliction, and can only mourn while they rejoice. What pleasure is it to see others feasting at His table while my sins have destroyed my appetite, and there is not one crumb of the bread of life that belongs to me? I pray, and He shuts out my cries. He does not regard my entreaties or ease my distresses, nor does He seem to relent with all my groans. I have sinned against Him, and I dare not say 'My God, and my Father" any more. I have lost all my fervor and my confidence, and all my hope in prayer. I go around the streets to seek Him who was once my Beloved. Help me, all you servants of the Lord, to find my God again. For my former undervaluing of His presence, He has now departed, and I cannot find Him. Woe, woe is me! What have I done? Woe is me that I have lost Him, whom to lose is hell."

(3) All this will be attended with great anguish of spirit and with great tribulation. Job 16:12: "I was at ease, but He hath broken me asunder. He hath also taken me by my neck, and shaken me to pieces, and set me up for His mark." Then all our sins are brought fresh into our mind with a new and a cutting remembrance, as if they had all been committed but yesterday. They rank themselves in order. Every one of them being set before us gives us a new stab and a wound, to increase the sore and the pain of our former wounds. They present themselves with all their hideous aggravations of that mercy, that goodness, those checks of conscience, those warnings and motions of the blessed Spirit against which they were committed. And who can bear so terrible a sight as this? Job 13:26: "Thou writest bitter things against me, and makest me to possess the iniquities of my youth." That is, He causes me always to think upon them, to feel pain and smart in that remembrance, and to be astonished with my guilt and fears.

Then all our thoughts of God Himself are uneasy. We can think of nothing but His greatness, His majesty, His justice, and His holiness. How it overwhelms us to think what a powerful God we have against us. It troubles us to think that He is displeased, and yet we know that He is justly so. "If God were for me," says the troubled soul, "I would bear any pains, and wait and hope. But He who alone can help me has gone away. He who alone could speak peace seems to take no notice of the sadness of my case. My sins have taken my God away, and what more do I have?"

And when we are set on fire with the sense of His wrath, the more we think, the more we are distressed; every thought returns with sad tidings and pours oil into the flame. And what anguish that is which we feel, when we continually think of a displeased God! There is nothing on earth that resembles it; neither are there any words capable of expressing it. We then smell the fire and brimstone of the infernal pit. Then a man may say with David, "The sorrows of death compass me, and the pains of hell get hold upon me" (Psalm 116:3).

I think that these spiritual terrors are of the same kind as those who are now in hell feel. They differ only in degree and duration. A sinner under the sense of God's displeasure, and in terror for his sin, is as if he were in a burning oven or in scalding oil. He is in every way beset and in every way tormented. Trouble of conscience, indeed, is a slighter thing; but the sense of wrath kindled there is vastly terrible. It is the suburbs of destruction; it is the noisome smell of the bottomless pit. Job 6:4: "The arrows of the Almighty are within me, the poison whereof drinketh up my spirit." The terrors of God set themselves against him. Whatever He thought of, whichever way he turned himself, he saw nothing but what filled him with amazement. Psalm 88:16: "Thy fierce wrath goeth over me; Thy terrors have cut me off."

(4) That which afflicts these troubled souls is the fear they have that this displeasure will be eternal. This

is implied in Psalm 77:7–8: "Will He be favorable no more? Is His mercy clean gone forever?" So it is with the Church in Lamentations 3:18: "My strength and my hope is perished from the Lord." Psalm 88:5: "I am free among the dead, like the slain that lie in the grave, whom thou rememberest no more." Sickness is grievous to us when we have no hope of being better. That wrath is not to be borne which we think to be the forerunner of eternal wrath.

Thus it is that the troubled soul argues: "God has withdrawn Himself, and, it may be, will never return again. I have lost Him for the present. And, oh, what will become of me if I lose God forever? I have now no beams of light, and what if I go hence into outer darkness? What if my lot and portion should fall among those who are abhorred by the Lord? Have I once tasted how good He was, and must I lose henceforth all the pleasant sense of His mercy? Must Christ not be my Savior, nor heaven my home after all this? Oh, what shall I do? Where shall I appear if He should say at the end, 'Depart from Me, for I know you not'? Shall I be placed at the left hand of Christ? Shall I, after all that I have read and heard, after all my prayers, be shut out of that kingdom while others enter in? How shall I bear so great a disappointment? How shall I dwell with everlasting burnings?"

3. If you have not yet been under the apprehension of God's displeasure, take warning from those who are so; do not dare to venture upon any sin when you behold their grief and their sorrows for their iniquities. You see their tears; you hear their lamentable groans; you see that nothing in this world is refreshing or com-

fortable for them. And will you hug the serpent that has stung them, and has made them cry out in the bitterness of their souls? Oh, stop where you are; go no farther, lest you fall into the depths, lest the fire that scorches them begin to seize you, lest the God whom they account their enemy begin also to frown on you. Learn obedience by their strokes lest you also be made to feel the smarting rod.

You see how those who were once as cheerful, as pleasant, and as unafraid as you are now cast down, troubled and perplexed, and cannot be merry as they used to be. The sense of God's displeasure has untuned their harps so that they cannot sing the songs of Zion. You see how their pleasure and their hope is shipwrecked; beware lest you run upon the same rock, for doing so, after seeing their examples, will make you guilty of a double crime: first, of doing ill, and then in doing it after such a warning as their sorrows gave you.

Job said that he was "set up as a mark" in Job 7:20. And so are others in the like case. They now receive the shots of that justice which they have provoked; but if their punishment does not make us humble ourselves and repent, we may be set in their place. And it will render the wounds that we shall then receive more poisonous and malignant, for not having taken and improved the warning that was given to us by them before.

Be drawn by His goodness and His gentle methods, so that you may never know what His severe displeasure is. For God has further ends in long and terrible afflictions than the correction or the good of the person so afflicted. They are a part of His government of the world, and He has a regard to the welfare of the public in that which seems only to relate to us. Deuteronomy 17:13: "All the people shall hear and fear, and do no more presumptuously."

4. Beware of provoking God; dread the beginnings of His wrath. "When His wrath be kindled but a little, blessed are all they that put their trust in Him" (Psalm 2:12). "Whoso provoketh Him to anger sinneth against his own soul" (Proverbs 20:2). And in such a case, the evil spirits have a power given to them to molest and trouble us with their impure suggestions, and with strange and unaccountable fears. Psalm 78:49: "He cast upon them the fierceness of His anger, wrath, and indignation, and trouble, by sending evil angels among them." And in that unhappy moment, when our sin has stirred up His wrath, there is nothing in heaven or on earth but what will range itself on the part of God against us. The devil himself will then take the same part, not out of love for God, but out of revenge to us, to execute the designs of His justice. And all the world will be so far from yielding us the least shelter from His wrath that it will tremble at it (Psalm 18:13–15). Psalm 104:32: "He looketh on the earth, and it trembleth. He toucheth the hills and they smoke." And Job 9:13 says, "The proud helpers do stoop under Him."

What minister can speak peace to such a soul when the God of peace will not? His ambassadors cannot go with a reviving message unless they are charged with it by their Lord and Master. If He makes the heavens be as brass, all the fountains of waters will be dried up. The spirit of a man will indeed bear his infirmities, i. e., his bodily weakness and pain, for a little while; but if he is followed with breach upon breach, and more heavy crosses press upon the former lighter evils, then his spirit and his courage will begin to fail. But no briskness of temper, no strength of nature, no liveliness of spirit can stand before one spark of the wrath of God. None can shut their eyes so that they do not see it; they cannot sleep that they may forget it; they cannot lose the sting that afflicts them by all the diversions and pleasures in the world. The sense of guilt will haunt and pursue them wherever they go.

5. Strive to be safe from the eternal wrath of God, from that wrath which will not be for a moment, but forever. If His wrath here makes His servants a terror to themselves and others, what terror will the damned have when they are compassed about with pure and unmingled wrath that is more hot and scorching than all the eruptions of it here on earth? While you see but a small cloud, the least intimations of His displeasure, seek to make your peace with God through Jesus Christ, lest all of a sudden ruin and desolation fall upon your heads—lest, if you stay a little longer, you have no time, no space wherein to repent.

Oh, how can you fold your arms and be at ease if the great God of all the world is your enemy, and if you do not know but that the next day, the next hour, or the next minute His arrows may be shot against you? Job 36:18: "Because there is wrath, beware lest he take thee away with His stroke; then a great ransom cannot deliver thee." The withdrawing of the favor and love of God, the least eclipses of His shining light, are very terrible; but, oh, how much more dreadful would it be if you should fall into the terrors of an eternal night! You can in no way escape His justice (Psalm 139:8). Take yourselves to God while He is entreating with you for your good. And though His justice frightens you for your guilt, yet, upon your humble submissions, His mercy will relieve you.

It is He alone, through Christ, with whom you have chiefly to do. His anger will pursue you wherever you go, unless you meet Him with humble and repenting tears and plead the blood of Jesus; and this will quench that fire that has already begun to flame. Your salvation is concerned and your souls are in danger; therefore make the most earnest applications to God so that He may be merciful to you before it is too late. If I could tell you that there is a person who designs to burn down the house in which you live, and gave you clear information of the time, I need not after this persuade you to be watchful. The love that you have for your own safety would oblige you to prevent his purpose. This is not what I can acquaint you with, but I can tell you of that which is more formidable: the devil is laying a train to destroy your peace, your comfort, and your hope. Seek to counter his malicious designs lest he betray you to danger while you think there is nothing at all.

6. Speak kindly and compassionately to those whom you perceive to be under the sense of God's anger. Job complains in Job 19:2, "How long will ye vex my soul, and break me in pieces?" And as men who have been long used to poring over their troubles, he tells them how often they had vexed him in verse 3: "These ten times have ye reproached me; ye are not ashamed that ye make yourselves strange to me." It is very likely that they did not vex him with their words purposely, for, being good men, they could not be so extremely barbarous. They made good sermons, but very sorry and mistaken application. It is easy to trample upon those with sharp and cutting speeches whom God and their

sorrows have already thrown into the mire. It is easy for those who are in no trouble to silence and upbraid those who are. As Job says to Eliphaz, "Shall vain words have an end? I also could speak as ye do, if your soul were in my soul's stead. I could heap up words against you, and shake mine head at you. But I would strengthen you with my mouth, and the moving of my lips should assuage your griefs" (Job 16:3–5).

When any of your friends are under spiritual trouble, you must carefully abstain from any passionate or sour word or action that may increase their grief; it will be some small help to them to see that you pity them, though you cannot give them relief. Use all the compassionate and kind words to them that you can, and seek to bind up their sores with a gentle hand. Beware of using any expression that savors of sharpness, reproach, or scorn, for these will, as they did to Job, vex their souls more, and they will be evil in you as well as unpleasant to them. Hence is that complaint in Psalm 69:20–21: "Reproach hath broken my heart, and I am full of heaviness; and I looked for some to take pity, but there was none, and for comforters, but I found none. They gave me also gall for my meat, and in my thirst they gave me vinegar to drink." And Psalm 123:4: "Our soul is exceedingly filled with the scorning of those that are at ease, and with the contempt of the proud."

But above all, abhor the thought of delighting in their miseries. Obadiah 12: "Thou shouldest not have looked on the day of thy brother, in the day that he became a stranger; neither shouldest thou have rejoiced over the children of Judah in the day of their destruction; neither shouldest thou have spoken proudly in the day of distress." And Job 19:28: "Ye should say, 'Why persecute we him, seeing the root of the matter is found in me?' " Roughness and severity are not the ways to help such as are troubled and cast down. He must be learned who speaks a word in season to the weary (Isaiah 50:4). The rarity of such a one is expressed in Job 33:23: "If there be . . . an interpreter, one among a thousand, to show unto man his uprightness."

Those who, under the character of being ambassadors of the gospel of peace, do nothing but thunder out the law to a wounded and troubled soul show that they are unlike the Jesus whom they would seem to represent; and they show that they have, in such matters, very little skill and no experience at all. Neither do such do as others would have done to them in the like case. There is a sort of balsam in compassionate and gentle words; though they do not fully perform a cure upon our wounds, yet they make the pain and the smart less, whereas a rough and sour carriage exasperates and heightens them, and is but pouring oil onto the flame.

Chapter 7

Showing what is to be done by those who think God is angry with them: the first thing is prayer, as a principal help against their troubles; with some objections of tempted persons answered

I am now to make application to those who are under an apprehension of God's anger. There are no people in the world whose case requires a greater pity, and to whose relief we should be more forward to contribute all that we are able. While we are at liberty, their poor souls are under the bondage of an overwhelming fear. That God whom we serve with hope is terrible to them; in those ordinances, and in that sabbath, which yield sweetness and refreshment to us, they find no delight, because the Comforter who should uphold their souls has departed from them. If on a journey we saw a person who was wounded and mourning under his bleeding wounds, crying out for help, the compassion that is fixed in human nature would move us to assist him, and not to pass by and allow him to groan under the smart of so deplorable a condition. And much more should we be ready to help our fellow creatures in a case that is far more sad and dreadful, such as this one which is now before us.

There are a great many at this time who are complaining that they have no hope, no prospect of deliverance from their present miseries and afflictions; who tell us that they are cast off by God, that their sins are set in order before them, and that they are afraid the God whom they once thought to be their own God will be favorable no more. Oh, how little do we know what we are doing when we sin! It is easy for a moment; it yields us a little superficial, transient delight; but it leaves a woeful sting and a lasting bitterness behind.

Oh, what would such poor creatures give to make it so that they had never sinned! Or that they had never sinned so willfully, so frequently, against that God whom they once experienced to be very good and gracious, but whom they now find to be very severe and terrible! They cannot look below without thinking that hell is opening its mouth to swallow them up; they cannot look above without seeing the great Creator of heaven and earth as an enemy against them. And who can stand before thoughts so cutting and overwhelming as these are?

Now this was a condition which I was in myself not long ago, and from which the mighty grace of God has been pleased to save me. And therefore I desire to give all the help I can to such dejected and trembling souls. There are none among us but perhaps may, at one time or another, fall into such depths as those; therefore I hope the following directions may be of some use. I beg of you who are now at ease to regard these things; for if you fall so low, the anguish and bitterness of your spirits will not allow you to give such a distinct and careful attention to what shall be spoken to you then, as now you may.

DIRECTION 1. If you are under the sense of God's anger for your sin, pray earnestly to Him to turn His wrath away. We usually deprecate war, famine, and the plague, and those other mischiefs which by the evils they bring upon our bodies are very formidable to us; but this sense of the divine displeasure has something in it that is more formidable, for it brings an unspeakable load of trouble on the soul, and wounds that part of ourselves which is capable of having either a very pure and noble joy or a very piercing grief and sadness. A man who is sunk under a burden that is too heavy for him to bear cannot but groan to be at ease. Thus Psalm 6:1–4: "O Lord, rebuke me not in Thine anger, neither chasten me in Thy hot displeasure; have mercy upon me, O Lord, for I am weak. O Lord, heal me, for my bones are vexed. My soul is also sore vexed; but Thou, O Lord, how long? Return, O Lord, deliver my soul. Oh, save me for Thy mercies' sake."

These are the breathings of one who is sensible of a great and violent distress; and they tell us that even our weakness and our helpless condition are arguments that we may plead with God. So it was in the text just quoted: "Have mercy upon me, for I am weak." In other words, "Thy goodness, Thy glory, and Thy power will be rendered more illustrious in giving some relief to someone as desolate and as low as I am."

OBJECTION. But I hear some poor, trembling souls replying, "Alas, I cannot pray! The Spirit that should warm my soul and kindle my desires does not move upon me as He used to do. I grieved and vexed Him heretofore, and now He has left me to grieve and to vex alone. I am so troubled that I do not know what to speak; and, when I endeavor to speak, I find no fervor or life at all. My prayers have grown very troublesome and uneasy to me."

ANSWER. I grant you, this is a case that is sad enough. It is sad for creatures as miserable and as full of wants as we are to not be able to pour out our supplications before the Lord; and it is more sad when our sins have caused the Spirit, who alone can teach us how to pray, to retire. But there are some considerations that may support us even in so sad a case as this:

1. Our distress teaches us the folly of our sin, and causes us to hate that which has cost us so very dearly. And it is well for us that we see the odiousness of it, though it is smart and pain that opens our eyes. It is better to be wounded in order to find a cure than to die at ease, and so perish forever.

2. The Spirit is not so withdrawn but He will return upon our earnest addresses for His grace. He hovers still about us, and though we did ill to shut Him out before, yet this blessed Guest does but wait for a favorable opportunity to do us good again. He is not quite gone, for that sense which we have of sin is His own work.

3. Our indisposition to the duty of prayer is no sign that we are void of life. A bedridden person lives as well as one who is in firm and pleasant health; a groan is a sign of life as well as laughter and a merry song. It is very undesirable indeed to have such a feeble and decaying life, but the way to make it stronger is to keep our souls exercising; and the weak and creeping motion wherewith we stirred at first, being continued, will enable us to tread with a more steady foot, and we shall get several paces further in a very little while.

By praying, though in a very poor manner, we shall learn to pray. Though we may only sigh after God, yet even a sigh may ease us a little, and, by frequent use, be turned into a loud and prevailing cry. God is still your Creator, and He who hears the ravens and the young lions when they roar for meat will not be deaf to you.

4. It is a more excellent state of soul to pray to God, and to persevere in it, when you have no more comfort than what you have. Sensible consolation is a very desirable thing; it is as the dew of heaven, as manna coming thence, or like honey and the honeycomb, very pleasant to the taste. But a dependence and trust in God, when He is a withdrawing God, is one of the most glorious acts of faith. And if He is not treated with feasts and splendid entertainments here, I can assure you, nay, God Himself has assured you that it shall not fare very well in the next world.

Sensible consolation may be in the inferior nature, as the mystics call it; it may be occasioned by the temper of the body, by the harmony of the passions, or by the agreeable dispositions of the natural spirits; but those other less pleasant acts are seated in the highest region of the soul, in the understanding and the will, and upon that account are more truly spiritual and more abiding.

5. Those poor, troubled people who complain of their deadness and incapacity to manage the duty of prayer ought to consider what an influence their fears have had upon their bodies; fear naturally contracts and dulls the heart. The motions of it are weak and languid; despairing thoughts and apprehensions about our everlasting state dry up our moisture and, by cutting off our hopes, make everything that was pleasant to us wither away. And it is a very hard matter for the soul to retain its heat and warmth when its dear companion, the body, does not assist it as it used to do—when the spirits with which it serves itself in so many various actions are stagnated into a feeble and almost undiscerned motion.

There have been some great saints who, by a sort of holy resistance, have glowed in their hearts with a quicker flame to God when all has been cold and stormy about them. There have been some who have never had more inward health than when their outward man decayed, and whose souls seemed manifestly to thrive when their bodies were molding away. But generally speaking, the nearness of a sickly body proves to be a great clog and hindrance to the mind; and there is no question but that God will make allowances for our weakness. In fact, the groaning after Him by one who is under the grip of a disease may be as grateful to Him as the long-continued prayer of one who is in good health. Pray, therefore, to God; though it is with heaviness, though it is mingled with many a bitter sigh, yet it will be a payment of that homage which you owe to God. And you do not know how soon you may meet with a gracious return. You may kneel down in sorrow, and He may lift you up with joy and say, "Be of good comfort; thy sins are forgiven thee." I know that would be very welcome and pleasant news to you; the news of a kingdom given you to be your own would not be half as refreshing.

OBJECTION. "It is not for me to pray. I am sinner enough already, God knows; and would you have me aggravate my guilt? For I have wandering thoughts and an unbelieving heart. I am a wicked person, and the prayer of the wicked is an abomination to the Lord (Proverbs 28:9). And therefore, to what purpose would I pray?"

ANSWER. If any man indeed breaks the laws of God with contempt, and then thinks to make satisfaction by his prayers, or by an outward and pompous devotion, he offers an affront to the all-knowing God. God's holy eye cannot look upon so criminal an action without the greatest disdain and scorn. If a man will swear, curse, and damn himself with one breath, and then desire God to bless him with the next, this would be a ridiculous pretense to religion; and such are likely to find severe punishment from that God whom they abuse with so shameless a confidence, and of whom they speak with so little reverence. If a man should desire God to help him to rob, plunder, or wrong his neighbors, this would be, as far as he could, to make the Holy One of Israel a partner in his crimes. If a man should kill another man unjustly, and glut himself with revenge, and then, as some have expressed it, say grace over his bloody banquet, this would be to commit a double wickedness.

It was an abominable thing, when so many harmless Protestants were so barbarously butchered in France, to sing *Te Deum* in Rome for the massacre of so many poor creatures, as if the God of mercy had been cruel as well as they—as if the rage that came from hell had descended from the God of love. This is as if a man who lives at the prince's charge, and is maintained at his table, should break the most venerable laws of his kingdom, and then thank the prince for giving him a power to do that which he knows the prince detests and hates.

There is no question but that it is the duty of a wicked man to pray to God. I suppose there is no one who thinks Simon Magus was a very good man, and yet he was exhorted, even when he was in the gall of bitterness and the bond of iniquity, to pray, "if perhaps the thought of thine heart may be forgiven thee"

(Acts 8:22). If you think yourselves wicked, there is nothing that is more your duty than to beg for the grace of God—to strive, to knock, and to call upon Him while He may be found. But beware that you do not think that some failings, even in some considerable duties, are a sign of your total apostasy. Unbelief is in the best of people, but not indeed in its reigning power. Strive as much as you can, and then bewail your weakness. Implore the help of God, and He will be favorable to you.

OBJECTION. "It is true, I know that it is my duty to pray. But I have prayed for several months and for several years, and I still have the same diseases and fears that I ever had. I have no less pain in my body, no less disquiet in my soul, than I had the first moment I began to pray. 'He hath hedged me about that I cannot get out. He hath made my chain heavy; also, when I cry and shout, He shutteth out my prayer' (Lamentations 3:7–8). I am just like Saul when he inquired of the Lord in 1 Samuel 28:6: 'The Lord answered him not, neither by dreams, nor by Urim, nor by prophets.' God would have no communication with him, or take notice of what he did. Even in such a case am I. I inquire after Him in His ordinances, but have no news of His gracious presence there; in tears I pour out my soul day and night, and pray, but the prayers that I send up to heaven bring to my poor, weary soul no tidings of comfort or of peace. My eyes fail with looking up; my heart faints, and I can hold out no longer in a duty wherein I find no delight, and which brings me no advantage. Why should I wait upon the Lord any longer?"

ANSWER. I think that this is one of the greatest temptations wherewith Satan assaults troubled souls.

He well knows that if they once quit their hold of God, they fall into his hands; they lengthen out his chain, whet his malice, and come within his reach. And there is no duty which the devil hates more than prayer; for it has many a time defeated his designs and made his kingdom shake. Therefore, I earnestly desire that—if you love your souls, and if you would not dishonor God nor gratify the devil—you never give up praying. Though you only chatter like a crane, yet it is better than being altogether silent; though you only mourn after God, it is better than to resolve to let Him go. Though you can only say, "Lord, be merciful to me a sinner"; though you can only smite your breast and look up to heaven; though you can only creep on in His ways—it is better than to leave them; though you can only speak a word or two in prayer, it is much better than not to pray at all.

Oh, what a terrible thing it is to stop calling upon God, to give ourselves up for lost, to say it is vain, when nothing is too hard for almighty power to do, or for infinite goodness. And woe to us when we quit the Rock of Ages and commit ourselves to the waves. What sorrows we will meet with, and how low we will sink!

How intolerable it is to have the rebukes of our conscience, the upbraiding of Satan, the guilt of sin, and the fear of hell, and to have no God to whom we can go with hope! Do not allow the greatness of your evils to deprive you of that support which is to be found in the performance of this duty. Though you do not have an immediate answer to what you desire, it in no way follows that your prayers are not heard. God knows better than you what will be the most proper season in which to bestow the mercy that you think to be most necessary. His delays in this case are no sign of His abhorrence. He may allow us to fall into very great agonies so that, like our Lord in the garden, we may pray more earnestly. Our requests are not vain, though we have no dawnings of a near and immediate deliverance. The prayers of the primitive church for kings and all in authority were answered many years afterwards when Constantine was converted to the faith.

Beware of fainting under the hand of God. And yet, when we look upon Him only as an enemy, it is almost impossible not to faint. Under smart and sore troubles, we must frequently look up to God and beg for His strength. Seeing that in such a case we cannot perform any long or regular duties, we must often renew, though it is the very same desires (Psalm 142:4–5; Ephesians 6:18). And to this purpose, consider:

1. There is none besides God Himself who can help you. This should cause you to persevere in prayer: His hand alone can heal the wounds. It is common for the troubled soul to say, "Oh, what I would give for one beam of hope! I would give all the world, if I had it, for one pleasant sight of the face of God."

This sight of God is not obtained by bare wishes, nor by the purchase of anything that is so low and contemptible as is all that which is in the world. When the heavens are brass, none can cause the rain to fall; when the sun has set, all the artificial fires which the skill of man can make will not yield so large and so pleasant a light to the earth as He does. His return chases the darkness, and brings to us the welcome day. In a distrust of your own weariness, have recourse to this God and say with David in Psalm 51:12 and 17: "Restore unto me the joy of Thy salvation, and uphold me with Thy free spirit." "The sacrifices of God are a broken spirit; a broken and contrite heart, O God, Thou wilt not despise." It must be the act of a power that is omnipotent to give you comfort; all the angels in heaven, and all the men on earth, cannot help you unless God is pleased to do it. You contribute nothing to your first regeneration. The created thing does nothing to bring itself into being; it only receives from the Creator's power and goodness that which He is pleased to give. Do not expect too much from the most knowing ministers, or from your dearest friends; they are but cisterns who can yield no water to quench your thirst unless they are filled with water by the clouds of heaven.

As for the satisfaction and the quiet of a troubled soul, all men are vanity; and it is an incommunicable prerogative of the divine nature, certainly and infallibly, to relieve the miserable (Isaiah 57:19). Other friends either do not know your wants or, by their own poverty or distance, are not in a capacity to supply them. But God is always near, always full of goodness, and is acquainted with whatsoever we need or expect.

If all the people in the world were your friends and God was your enemy, the gaiety of their looks and the pleasure of their smiles would not take away the terror of His frowns. The threatening cloud would hang over your heads and frighten you with its dreadful presages wherever you went. And, on the contrary, if all the people in the world were your enemies and God was your Friend, His love would sweeten all their hatred, His voice would still all their clamors, His arm would fend off all their blows, and under the wings of His providence you might lie down and sleep in peace. He can save you when you have destroyed yourselves; when you have run to the very door and gates of hell, He can pull you back; when you are even dying, He can strengthen and revive you.

It is with Him that you have principally to do; to Him you must therefore pray, because from Him alone can come your help. When Adam had committed sin, he was afraid, and took no pleasure even in his paradise, even though the sun shone upon his head with gentle and refreshing beams, the rivers ran as clear as before, the birds sang with as melodious a voice, the flowers had as fragrant a smell, the herbs were clothed with as fresh a verdure, and all the fruits flourished as before. But from that poor man peace and innocence had fled away. All without was calm, but he found a tempest rising in his own breast, which he did not know how to allay.

Those of us who, by woeful experience, have felt the terrors of the Lord know that all the advice of our friends, all their arguing and discoursing, all their entreaties and prayers gave us no manner of ease until God Himself was pleased to command salvation for us. Job 34:29: "When He giveth quietness, who then can make trouble? And when He hideth His face, who then can behold Him, whether it be done against a nation or against a man only?" The greater our distresses are, the more fervent our prayers should be; and when the winds are highest, when the storms increase and threaten us with shipwreck and ruin, the nearness and the greatness of our danger must cause us to arise and call upon our God with more speed. Therefore, though you have the sense of His displeasure, yet say, "None can help me but God Himself; there is none who can heal my diseases or forgive my sins but He. Therefore, as long as I live, I will pray, and will call upon Him until He has mercy upon me."

DIRECTION 2. Though you are under the sense of God's anger, you have encouragement to pray from many promises, and from the office and the name of Christ. That Mediator, who well remembers what He felt when He groaned under His Father's wrath, also knows with what flames your souls are scorched. With a most compassionate eye He looks upon you, and will awake to promote your safety if you will but say, as did the frightened disciples, "Master, save us or else we perish."

It is true, He is attended with illustrious spirits, some of whom were never thus sick, and others whom He has fully cured; but in the throng of His admiring courtiers, in the midst of their cheerful and pleasant hallelujahs, His heart is concerned for you and His ears will be open to your cry. His intercession gives you good ground of hope. He ever lives to manage that glorious and honorable work; and, having an unchangeable priesthood, "He is able to save them to the uttermost that come unto God by Him" (Hebrews 7:25).

Thomas Goodwin, in his work entitled *The Triumph of Faith from Christ's Intercession,* observes that the phrase "to the uttermost" is a good one, and put there for our comfort. He goes on to say, "Let your soul be set upon the highest mountain that ever any creature was yet set upon; and let it be enlarged to take in and view the most spacious prospect, both of sin and misery, and the difficulties of being saved, that ever yet any poor, humbled soul cast within itself; yea, join to all these the objections and hindrances of your salvation that the heart of man can suppose or invent against itself; lift up your eyes and look to the utmost that you can see—and Christ, by His intercession, is able to save you beyond the horizon and furthest compass of your thoughts, even to the utmost and the worst case that the heart of man can suppose."

Cry often to God, "Oh, pity me, a poor, helpless sinner, for the sake of Christ. He bore Thy wrath; turn it away from me, for I am not able to bear it." The name of Jesus carries comfort and salvation with it. He is a perfect Savior in every time of need. The name of Jesus Christ tells you that His office is to do good to the miserable, to heal the diseased, to open the eyes of the blind, "to preach good tidings to the meek, to bind up the broken-hearted, to proclaim liberty to the captives, and the opening of the prison to them that are bound" (Isaiah 61:1).

You are to pray in that name which was celebrated by all the patriarchs and holy men of old, by the prophets and by the priests under the law, though it was then wrapped up in obscure types and representations; that name in which God Himself delights, at which the angels bow with reverence and at which the devils tremble; that name which is great in heaven and earth, in which you were baptized and in which you must place all your hopes.

In this name you may implore assistance with all your wants. And this may furnish you with a holy confidence, for it is the name of the Son of God, of His entirely beloved Son. And it would be a reproach to this great and venerable name to pray with distrustful thoughts.

Oh, let this be a support to you: you have access to God by this name, which has been dear to all the faithful and must be so to you. This name has been the refuge of many a poor, trembling soul. This is the name which the saints of God have mentioned in all their difficulties with great delight; the name of which they were pleased frequently to hear and to speak, which was the joy of their hearts, and for which they did not refuse to suffer death. Some have taken the pains to observe that it is mentioned in the epistles of Paul 220 times, and often in the gospel of John, so sweet, so dear to them was the name of Jesus.

This is the first general way of relief that those who are under the sense of God's anger ought to take, that is, to pray to Him. Jeremiah 10:24: "O Lord, correct me, but with judgment; not in Thine anger, lest Thou bring me to nothing." Psalm 39:10: "Remove Thy stroke away from me, for I am consumed by the blow of Thine hand." See also Psalm 38:21–22, 85:4–7, 138:3, and 143:2.

Chapter 8

Faith in Christ as another help under the sense of God's displeasure, and the various tendencies it has to calm an afflicted soul under long and sore trials

When you are under the sense of God's anger for your sins, act faith upon God and Christ. Faith, I may well say, is the mother of all the graces; it conceives and brings them forth, and takes care to promote their growth; it contributes life to them at first, and causes them to thrive and flourish afterwards. With faith our meaner services meet with a cheerful and favorable acceptance; and without it, all the most pompous devotions and all the most tedious and painful mortifications that we could ever practice would be of no value in the sight of God.

What mighty things has faith produced! What miraculous triumphs has it gained! No history can furnish us with an account of so many great and illustrious heroes, of so many difficulties and such great victories, as Hebrews 11 furnishes us with. No one is mentioned there but who met with great troubles, and no one is mentioned there but who overcame them; and it is always expressed that they did this or that "by faith."

To most, faith appears to be an easy thing, because they have not seen their sins in their odiousness and aggravations, since they have not thought much of the holiness, justice, and majesty of God, and of the spiritual law that pierces into all the depths and recesses of the soul. They think it is a small matter. But to a poor sinner who is under the rebukes of God and of his own conscience, who is awakened with terrible threats and amazing fears, who sees vast multitudes of sins within and hell without, there is nothing more difficult. For thus he argues: "Can a holy God bear with so vile a sinner? Can He forgive so many and such great iniquities? Will He be gracious to one who has been so much His enemy as I have been? Will that love ever be shown to me which I have so much slighted and undervalued, and for my contempt of which, God knows, I now pay very dearly? Will the great ruler of heaven and earth be favorable to a worm? Will He admit a rebel into His presence and glory?"

It is not easy to satisfy a mind that is struggling with those manifold objections which carnal reason and sense, and a man's own heart, set forth with so much seeming strength and force. But now there are several ways by which this much-opposed faith prevails, and obtains a conquest over so subtle and plausible enemies as these are.

1. Faith quiets the soul by directing it to consider the nature, the promise, and the Word of God. It takes away the sourness of our thoughts, whereby we are apt to conclude that God is of a furious and implacable nature; that He will never be reconciled, or have anything to do with creatures as lowly and sinful as we are. This reveals to us the terms of His covenant, the free offers of His mercy. Isaiah 27:4–5: "Fury is not in Me; who would set the briars and thorns against Me in battle? I would go through them, I would burn them together. Or let him take hold of My strength, that he may make peace with Me, and he shall make peace with Me."

When God speaks of His strength, He means the holy properties of His nature—His goodness, His unchangeableness, and His faithfulness—which He has graciously revealed with a design thereby to support our hearts. Faith guides us to the view of His promises, to the truth and authority of the Promiser, to His all-sufficiency and His readiness to pardon and to save.

It is hard indeed to entertain the thought that, when we are under the apprehensions of His wrath, He is ready to forgive. For, if I may judge others by myself, it is not so much His power that we then question as His goodness; not so much whether He *can* help, for that we well know, but whether He *will* give us help. Now faith leads our trembling souls to the promises, which are the voluntary engagements of God, whereby He has obliged Himself to do us good, which are the product of His love, and which convey a quickening power and virtue to the soul. Faith shows us also the foundation on which all these promises rely, even Jesus Christ, in whom they are all "yea and amen," i.e., very certain and very true. Hebrews 13:8: "Jesus Christ is the same yesterday, and today, and forever."

Faith makes us humble and, consequently, patient; it empties the soul of all proud and lofty thoughts; it sees that it has nothing of its own whereon to trust, and therefore it depends on God alone. Faith discovers His relations as a Creator and as a Father, and produces acts in the mind suitable to these comforting titles. Psalm 42:11: "Why art thou cast down, O my soul? And why art thou disquieted within me? Hope thou in God, for I shall yet praise Him, who is the health of my countenance, and my God." Suitable also is Isaiah 50:10: "Who is among you that walketh in darkness, and hath no light? Let him trust in the name of the Lord, and stay upon his God"—that is, if he is without any reviving sense of the love of God, any sight of his own grace, and, I may add, without any hope of deliverance and salvation; for the least hope carries with it some light, though it may be very feeble and almost indiscernible.

Now for a man to cast his anchor in the dark, and to trust when he has no visible foundation for his faith, is a work of labor and difficulty. The name of God in this case is a great relief; and that name is proclaimed in Exodus 34:6–7: "The Lord God merciful, and gracious, long-suffering, and abundant," and so on. Thomas Goodwin, in his work entitled *A Child of Light Walking in Darkness,* says, "A poor soul in distress is not able to say, 'I see such or such signs, or any evidence in myself whereby I can conclude that God is my God, or Christ is my Savior; though I know nothing by myself whereby I can claim any present interest, yet, because "Grace and Mercy" is His name, and "Our Righteousness" is His Son's name, therefore I cast myself upon both for pardon and favor. Thereupon my soul relies, stays, and abides, and from these it will not be moved. Two things concur with this trust: first, that there is free grace, good will, and mercy in God, and that Jesus Christ is appointed and made to be my righteousness; and, second, that I am capable of, and may come to have an interest in, both of these. Though there is nothing in me which may claim an interest in them, yet neither is there anything that excludes me; whereupon I cast myself upon God for both, and there rest.' "

2. Faith will greatly help us, as it gives a right understanding of the nature of those long and severe afflictions whereby we are apt to conclude that God is angry

with us. It will show us that there is nothing in them that is new or strange; it will carry our minds beyond the present pain and show light beyond the darkest clouds. It will teach us to judge God not by that which is present, but by that which is to come; not by what we feel, but according to His own promise. Faith will show us by a delightful manifestation the period and conclusion of God's design, and cause us not to judge His works by the first rough and less amiable draft.

Faith will show us that anger and love may very well consist together, and that the ruder blows that make us groan and sigh may be to polish and fit us for His heavenly temple. Faith will hold us up when our sense is puzzled and our feet are likely to slide; it sets before our eyes not only the first corrections, which are painful to the flesh, but the end of the Lord, and that He is "pitiful, and of tender mercy" (James 5:11). It shows us the justice and equity of God's proceedings, that there is nothing in them but what is highly reasonable and necessary, even when they seem to be severe; that they are needful to keep us from wandering, and to prevent our sleeping the sleep of death; that those heavy crosses that tire and weary our spirits may be sent to promote our eternal rest, and that the deepness of our groans here may cause us to hereafter sing louder hallelujahs.

3. Faith will greatly help us as it reveals, and then fortifies us against, the power of Satan and his wiles, though these designs of his are invisible and very little known, and are yet the more dangerous because they are so. In those doleful troubles that I myself have experienced, in all those terrible reflections and overwhelming fears, I was not sensible of any agency of evil

spirits, but thought that all my thoughts and fears were the product of my own mind. Now, however, I am apt to believe that some of those strange thoughts that I had of God now and then, and those sudden terrors that pierced my soul, must have had something in them of the cruelty and malice of Satan, they were so very terrible.

I verily believe that people greatly wrong both the devil and melancholy people by calling the unavoidable effects of their disease "the temptations of Satan," and the language of that disease a compliance with them. They ascribe to the devil a greater power than he has, and vex the diseased person more than they need to do. For though I do not question that an evil spirit, through the permission of God, is the cause of many sicknesses that come upon our bodies, yet there are also many such that are the result of a disordered motion of the natural spirits, and in which the devil has nothing at all to do. But as it is the common custom of cruel and barbarous persons to set upon the weak, and to trample on those who are already thrown down, so it is very common for the devil to take occasion from our bodily indispositions to attack and molest our spirits, which are bereaved even of that force which they used to have when the house in which they dwelt was at ease, and free from those that they are always under at such seasons. For then it is night with us, and in the night those beasts of prey range abroad that stay in their dens during the brightness of the day.

But however it is, whatsoever agency there is of evil spirits in our troubles, either upon our understandings, our passions, or our imaginations, this grace of faith will unveil their designs and baffle all their strategies.

Ephesians 6:16: "Above all, take the shield of faith, wherewith ye shall be able to quench all the fiery darts of the wicked." And that this is so very necessary appears from Luke 22:31–32: "Satan hath desired to winnow you as wheat; but I have prayed that thy faith fail not." There is nothing against which that engineer of hell levels his batteries with a greater fury; there is nothing that can lay us open to greater danger than either downright unbelief or the weakness of our faith. Faith that is not exercised is like weapons of war lying beside us: they rust and are in no way serviceable. For while faith remains in exercise, we persevere in our watch, and the God whom it shows us looking upon comes to our assistance in every time of need, as does that Redeemer who has conquered the devil by His death and resurrection, and at whose glorious name those evil spirits tremble and are afraid.

4. Faith will greatly help us under the apprehensions of God's displeasure, since it leads us to the consideration of Christ as crucified (see John Owen's work on Psalm 130). It is easy indeed to learn the notion of faith, but it is much more difficult to experience the efficacy and power of it. For a man to have a sight of that within him that would condemn him, and for which he is troubled, and at the same time to have a discovery of that outside him which will justify him, and to rejoice therein, is something that he will not be led to except by faith in the mystery of the gospel. If we pore upon our own qualifications, duties, evidences, and the like, we shall, by a continued circulation of easy thoughts, merely increase our own trouble; the imperfection and faultiness of all that we have done, or are able to do, will fill our minds with perplexity and distress; the ho-

liness and the spirituality of the law of God will kill our most forward hopes.

Our best way, therefore, is not to sit still, bewailing our miseries and the sadness of our case, but to arise and to run to the city of refuge that is before us. When we are wounded with the sense of sin, with weeping eyes and grieved hearts, we must look up to Christ, of whom the brazen serpent was a type; when the burden of our iniquities sinks us down and makes us groan, we must go to Him in whom the weary and the heavy-laden find rest. We must go to that gospel, which, as it reveals and manifests the abundance of sin in us, at the same time manifests the righteousness that is in Christ; while the one terrifies us with the fear of hell, the other will refresh us with the hope of heaven.

The blood of Jesus extinguishes the wrath of God, and as it makes us safe, it also makes us holy; for it cleanses us from all iniquity. This is the shelter and the healing of a soul that is in danger and is diseased. How many souls have cast their anchor in the dark when all comfort has failed them for many days, and have obtained support and relief by saying that if they perish, they will perish at the feet of Christ. And He who is the Lamb of God, so full of meekness and pity, is too gracious to let any perish there. As a Priest, He died for His enemies.

He is a meek King; though He is upon a throne of majesty, and in a place of joy and glory, yet He will admit mourners into His presence. He is a King of poor and afflicted persons, and a Prince of peace; and as He has beams of majesty, so He has bowels of compassion. What mercy may we not expect from so gracious a Mediator, who took our nature on Himself that He might be gracious? Let us therefore go to God by Christ, who has satisfied His justice by His death, and who, without Him, is to us sinners as a consuming fire. Let us go boldly to His throne, in the name of Jesus, and we shall find that the God of whom we were afraid will become our Friend; we shall experience Him to be better to us than we ever thought He would have been.

Our unbelieving hearts, while they are such, will be full of darkness and full of trouble; but upon our faith, the storm will cease, and the morning will begin to dawn upon us. And then, instead of that wrath which we feared, and had deserved, we shall find there is mercy with the Lord, and plenteous redemption (Psalm 130:7).

The first thing that a convinced, awakened sinner thinks of is his own danger, how he may avoid the wrath of God, and what it is that he must do in order to avoid it. Now it is not to be accomplished by pompous, ceremonial services, nor by external mortifications, nor by offering the fruits of the body for the sin of his own soul, but by faith in Jesus Christ and His death, by the means of which God has become propitious and favorable to us.

And the first view that a humble soul is to take of Christ is that of His being a Savior, as being made sin and a curse, and obeying to the death. Christ must be considered not only with respect to the excellencies of His person, but as clothed with His garments of blood, and the qualifications of a Mediator and Reconciler. This renders Him the fit object of a sinner's faith. If we think of God without thinking of Christ, He is vastly terrible and amazing to us; but in and through Him, those otherwise overwhelming apprehensions become very pleasant and comfortable to us.

Let us honor the love that God has shown in Christ with admiring thoughts, and never have low or mean apprehensions of His grace. Christ is near to God and full of pity to us, able to help us and most willing to do so. And those who come unto Him, He will in no way cast out. He will not upbraid us for our former follies. He will not increase our grief, but when He sees us lying at His feet, and washing them with the tears of an unfeigned humiliation, He will raise us up and bid us be of good cheer.

5. Faith will remove the troubles that we have from the sense of God's displeasure by conveying to us that life and strength from Christ which will enable us to subdue all our spiritual enemies (Philippians 4:13). It will bring Him to us; and, when He is in our vessel, let the waves threaten us with never so formidable a noise, we are surely not going to be cast away. All the specters that frighten us will vanish if we can once hear Him say, as He did to His disciples, "It is I, be not afraid." This grace will unite us to Christ, and communicate His power to us in the various measures that we need. And without His assistance, long and sore afflictions will tire our spirits and destroy our hope. He is necessary for us, for He has a perfect knowledge of our enemies—of their force, their policies, and their designs. He has, by His own combat, learned to fight; and by His experience He can teach us how to get the victory. Neither the multitude, nor the violence, nor the obstinacy of our enemies can hinder the success and the glory of His triumph. In Colossians 1:11, Paul prayed that we might be "strengthened with all might," because, as we have to deal with divers enemies, and are

sick of divers infirmities, we need to receive not one or two kinds of strength, but many different kinds.

In nature, you see the strength of bodies is different, one resisting one thing and yielding to another; one has the virtue to repulse the force of one element, but not to guard itself against another. It is so with the souls of men: such a man will free himself from the temptation of one sin who will not be able to defend himself from another; such a man will resist the temptations of prosperity whom adversity will overthrow; such a one will bear troubles for a while whom the length or tediousness of them will overcome—and if one of our spiritual enemies succeeds against us, we are undone forever. Therefore, as the apostle says, we need to have recourse to Christ, who can furnish us with skill and strength to defeat whatsoever stands in the way of our peace or our salvation.

To have someone on our side who has returned from the field of battle as a conqueror is a mighty encouragement and privilege. Such is our Lord: He is a victorious and triumphant Savior. He will not leave His conquests incomplete, for He goes on conquering and to conquer. And the glory of His enterprises has not filled Him with disdain or contempt for the poor and needy; for He who is King of Zion is, as I said before, a meek and lowly King.

By faith in Christ we obtain His Spirit, which, by opening our eyes, will show us that fountain of living waters where we may both quench our thirst and wash away our filth. This Spirit will take away the sting of guilt and sweeten the cross that was very bitter to us; and when our Lord has come to help us, when we know that He is afflicted in our affliction, that yoke which galled us before will become as an ornament around our necks. When we have the pardon of our sins and the hope of God's acceptance, that affliction that we thought was a burden too heavy for us to bear will become light and easy to us. "Out of the devourer shall come forth sweetness." From those very tears that overwhelmed us shall spring glorious hopes; those hearts which a slavish fear of wrath had contracted shall be enlarged with a sense of His goodness and love, and we shall not look upon Him as an enemy, but as a Friend; not as a judge, but as a Father. Isaiah 33:24: "The inhabitant shall not say, 'I am sick.' The people that dwell therein shall be forgiven their iniquity."

Alas! When God leaves us, the smallest danger terrifies us; the least dart of Satan makes an impression on our spirits; the least trouble sinks us, such inconsiderable creatures are we. But if the Lord is with us, if Christ is on our side, neither the law, nor sin, nor death can hide us from being defiant to all that is against us (2 Corinthians 15:56–57).

6. Faith will give us relief under the apprehensions of God's displeasure for our sin, as it will show us the period and conclusion of those miseries which we are now groaning under. Our sense will tell us that our troubles are very tedious and long; but our faith will rectify our judgment and show us that, though we have been in heaviness, it is but for a season. Our sense makes us think that our night of weeping was very long, but faith sets the morning before our eyes. And indeed, when that comes, the time of sorrow will appear to have been very short; our weeping will bear no proportion to our joy, nor our groans with our hallelujahs. The luster of our crown and the glories of our tri-

umph will make us forget the blood, sweat, and labor of the combat, though while we were here below we thought them very hard.

Faith will wipe away our tears and cause us to take a further prospect, and to see where they now are who were mourners as well as we. Job is no longer wondered at upon a dunghill by his friends, but shines with glory in the highest heaven. Heman is no more distracted with terrors, but is infinitely pleased with the sight and enjoyment of His God. Asaph is also singing praises to God, though He thought and was afraid that His mercies were clean gone, and that He would be favorable no more.

Faith will solace your drooping spirits by causing you to remember frequently that, though God is angry, it is but for a moment, and that, though you now have sour grapes, they are only to prepare you to better relish the joys above. It is this that sets our feet upon a Rock, and produces in our fainting souls a secret support and hope that, though it is night with us for the present, it will not always be so. Revelation 3:21: "To him that overcometh will I grant to sit with Me on My throne, even as I also overcame, and am set down with My Father on His throne."

The dangers and distresses on our way will make us like our home better. All the years of our life, though spent in sore afflictions and anxieties, will appear to have been very short when we land at our haven of joy and immortality.

Chapter 9

The direct acts of faith, as the most suitable to a distressed soul, as also of waiting upon God; with several considerations to enforce it. And a person in great affliction ought to hope that it may be better with him

Look forward to Jesus Christ when you find things perplexed and troubled in your own souls; and indeed, in the direct acts of faith, we have nobler objects to converse with than when we look and pore upon our guilty selves. When we look into our troubled hearts we can see nothing besides confusion and disorder there; but we may at the same time discern an all-sufficient fullness in God and Christ to relieve our wants. It is a long and tedious work to consider the several steps by which we are to proceed in such a case, whether we have believed or not; our duty is, at this very instant, to believe—that is, under a penitent sense of what we have done amiss, to look unto Christ for help.

We must carefully distinguish between justification and sanctification, between those habits and those holy actions that are the effects of faith and faith itself. Our sanctification is full of imperfection, but that righteousness of Christ, wherein alone we are to trust for acceptance with God, is complete and perfect. These are things to be considered by people under spiritual distress; but if you are under the disease of melancholy to any great degree, I am sensible that neither this nor any other direction will be altogether available. It is such a stubborn and obstinate disease that it is not to be overcome by rational methods and persuasion any more than a broken bone can be set again by words and talk. Only God is fully acquainted with the nature and violence of this worst of distempers. His power and His grace alone can chase it away; and all those things that depend upon consideration, and that may succeed in other cases, do not have the same tendency to do good in this one, because it is our disease always to pore and think, and it is our misery that we cannot think to any purpose.

I beseech you to remember that the foundation of all our peace and comfort is Christ alone, and faith in Him. Mortification, self-denial, and other graces are the superstructure that is laid upon it, but truly all that we can do in great and deep affliction, and in sore distresses of soul, is only to look up to Christ as a poor, wounded, bleeding man looks and cries to one who passes on the road for help. And our Savior and Physician is so compassionate that He will regard us, though we are able to say little more than, "Have mercy on us, Thou Son of David."

Under the prospect of our great infirmities and the manifold imperfections of our duties, and under the sense of our own nothingness and unworthiness, let us humbly take ourselves to Christ. He will not disdain nor slight our approaches to Him, nor will He leave them unattended without some manifestations of reviving grace and mercy.

When you have done all this, you must wait till the Lord appears to give you relief and help. Psalm 123:2: "Behold, as the eyes of servants look unto the hands of their masters, and as the eyes of a maiden unto the hands of her mistress; so our eyes wait upon the Lord our God, until that He have mercy upon us." Though His strokes are very smart, yet we are sure that we have deserved them; though His delays of help are tedious, yet we have merited at His hands a much longer delay. We are as so many poor slaves indeed, under the bondage of our fears and our troubles; but, alas, we have brought ourselves to that slavery, and we must look unto God till He sets us free again. And though our Master is angry with us, yet He is a Master still; and that relation that we have to Him, that interest which we have in His covenant, may be somewhat supporting and comfortable to us.

It is an easier thing to bear any trouble that continues for a week or a month, and then passes away; but the trial of our faith will be if we can maintain our dependence and trust in God when He afflicts us sorely for many months or years together. If we see no sign of help, no prospect of deliverance, we are still to wait till the time, even the set time, to favor us has come. And this must be done with patience, with a silent resignation to His will. It is the product of a calm and quiet soul that is satisfied in the justice of providence, though it is severe, except with this limitation: that you have the freedom and the command of your natural spirits; for if they are put into a hurry and confusion by a disease, then indeed you can neither perform this nor any other spiritual action with calmness and liberation. But in other cases, where the disorder of the spirits is not so great and violent, "he that believeth shall not make haste" (Isaiah 28:16). In other words, he is not furious and precipitant.

It is our common fault that we would have the help of God come just when we want it, to be eased as soon as we find ourselves in pain, to get to heaven immediately when we find ourselves no longer fit for service here on earth, and to have a pain-free and easy passage there. But God, who is not as concerned with our flesh as with our spirits, will allow us to be long in trouble so that all may know by their own feeling how evil and bitter a thing it is to sin, and that by the methods that please us least He may do us the most good, and by our temporal inconveniences promote our eternal welfare.

In patience, we ought, in a humble silence, to possess our souls, and to approve of all the dispensations and works of God; for how it is possible for us not to manifest our sense of grief in doleful expressions, I do not know. When a man is under a burden he cannot bear, or when he is in sharp pain, it is natural for him to groan and to sigh; that is a thing he cannot help. It would be, as I have intimated before, a needless labor to advise people under great affliction and spiritual distress not to complain; for, say what we will, they cannot but complain. Can a man think that God is his enemy, that his soul is in danger, and that hell is likely to be his portion; can he see his comforts wither, his hopes expire, and others at ease while he is in woe and trouble, and not be greatly concerned? Can he be so and not express his concern for the sadness of his case? Do not blame people who are under the terrors of the Lord for complaining; if your souls were embittered with wormwood and gall, you would complain as much as they. Can they be silent when they think that God has departed from them, and, as they fear, departed forever? Can they be, in such terrible calamity, as quiet and unmoved as when they were at ease?

Our blessed Lord Himself, in the days of His flesh, when His suffering increased, offered up prayers with strong crying and tears (Hebrews 5:7). And in the pain of His inexpressible agonies on the cross, He cried out with a loud voice, "My God, My God, why hast Thou forsaken Me?" (Matthew 27:46). And Psalm 32:3: "When I kept silence, my bones waxed old through my roaring all the day long." And he assigned the reason for it in verse 4: "For day and night Thy hand was heavy upon me; my moisture is turned into the drought of summer."

There are some natural, unavoidable expressions of grief and sorrow which are consistent with that waiting and dependence upon God which I have mentioned before. Nor is it contrary to this waiting to desire a speedy and a quick deliverance; you may lawfully pray for such. Of this we have several instances, such as Psalm 22:19: "Be Thou not far from me, O Lord. O my Strength, haste Thee to help me." Psalm 31:2: "Bow down Thine ear to me; deliver me speedily." Psalm 69:17: "Hide not Thy face from Thy servant, for I am in trouble; hear me speedily" (so also Psalm 102:2). And Psalm 40:17: "Make no tarrying, O my God." You may, in imitation of such great examples, frame your requests after this or the like manner; but if when you have done so relief does not immediately come, if your distress and your anguish remain, you must be content to wait still, and to justify your Maker in His delays and proceedings towards you, though they are very terrible. Psalm 22:1–3: "My God, my God, why hast Thou forsaken me? Why art Thou so far from helping me, and from the words of my roaring? O my God, I cry in the daytime, but Thou hearest not; and in the night season, and am not silent. But Thou art holy, O Thou that inhabitest the praises of Israel."

Those who claim religion to be in all respects an easy thing do not know what they say. If they know what it was to be under the sense of God's displeasure, and under violent, painful distempers for many months at a time, and yet to wait and be satisfied with that providence which sees fit to continue on them long pains and terrible fears, they would find that it is not such an easy matter to be truly religious. But that you who are exercised with severe and sharp trials may arrive at this excellent disposition of being able to wait still upon God, consider these four things:

1. Consider how long God has waited upon you. How long did He knock at your doors! How did He entreat, beseech, and call out to you before you let Him in! How He followed you from day to day and from sabbath to sabbath! How He waited for your repentance year after year, doubling and renewing His expostulations with you, saying, as He did to Jerusalem in Jeremiah 13:27, "Wilt thou not be made clean? When shall it once be?"

And if you have refused to hear the calls of the great God for so long a time, can you think it hard of Him that He does not grant an immediate answer to your prayers? Would you have help all of a sudden when you made Him wait for your hearts so very long? He waited on us to do us good when we ran from Him, when we spent our thoughts, our strength, our lives, and our time in vain. After all our rebellions, our undutifulness, and our disobedience, He moved upon our souls by His Spirit. He excited us to mind our interest and gave us space wherein to repent. Let us remember these things to humble us and to increase our patience, and to keep us from thinking it strange if God, even for a long time, delays His help.

2. Consider the sovereignty, the greatness, and the wisdom of God. We are His own, and He may do what He will with us. Because we are His creatures, He may cause us to serve whatever purpose He pleases; and His wisdom will guide even our miseries to make them useful to others, though they are sharp and severe to us. His ways are far above us. His greatness and His glory are so far above our thoughts that the most suitable temper of a creature towards so great a God is to be silent and wait, to see what a period infinite wisdom will at length put to those dispensations of His providence which are so dismal and terrible to us. If all the comforts we have in this world, all that we most value and esteem, are taken from us; if our afflictions are long and tedious, and accompanied with such stinging particulars as have scarcely been mingled with the crosses of others who have gone before us—still God may do what He will with us. We can have nothing to say to Him because we are the work of His own hands.

Our hearts, in sore distresses, are apt to say, "Why are we so much and so long afflicted? Why are we compassed with such terrible calamities when others are at ease who, to all appearances, have sinned as much as we?" But these first risings of murmuring and disquiet are to be resisted by the considerations of the majesty and the greatness of God. God may put His creatures to whatever uses He pleases, and such as may, though with pain, promote the good of others, and their own final good.

Stephen Charnock observes, in his *The Existence and Attributes of God,* that though Job was a pattern of patience, yet he had deep tinctures of impatience. He often complained of God's usage of him as being hard, and stood much upon his own integrity. But when God came, in the latter chapters of the book, to justify His carriage towards him, He charged him not as a criminal, but considered him only as His vassal. He might have found flaws enough in Job's behavior, and corruption enough in Job's nature, to have cleared the equity of His proceedings as a judge, but He used no other medium to convince Job than the greatness of His majesty and the unlimitedness of His sovereignty. And this so appalled that good man that he put his finger on his mouth and stood mute, with a self-abhorrence before God as a Sovereign rather than a Judge.

God's wisdom, which makes the night to precede the day, and storms to clear the air and make way for a fairer season, ought also to silence and pacify our souls. Isaiah 30:18: "And therefore will the Lord wait, that He may be gracious unto you; and therefore will He be exalted, that He may have mercy upon you. For the Lord is a God of judgment; blessed are all they that wait for Him." He knows the most fitting times and seasons wherein to heal our diseases, to remove our fears, and to do us good.

3. Consider how great the mercies are that we are to wait for. We wait for heaven and glory, and we have His promise that our faith and our patience shall not be in vain (Psalm 37:3–7). And, after all the dangers, snares, hindrances, and temptations of this world, to come to salvation at last is so great a mercy that it is surely worth waiting for. Though we labor six days, yet the rest of the

sabbath refreshes our spirits; and so, after the sufferings of this mortal life, that eternal sabbath that is to be kept above with God will give us great refreshment. Our time on earth is a season wherein, by various trials and afflictions, we are prepared for that happiness and glory. As the night frightens us, the morning will surely bring us joy. It is but a little while and our Lord will come and save us; let us not surrender ourselves to our spiritual enemies.

James 5:7–8: "Behold the husbandman waiteth for the precious fruit of the earth, and hath long patience for it, until he receive the early and the latter rain. Be ye also patient, establish your hearts, for the coming of the Lord draweth nigh." The husbandman does not give his grain up for lost though it is covered with snow and storm; he expects to see it rise with the returning spring. And neither should we despair of finding comfort though the prayers we have made bring us no present satisfaction.

David had the promise of a kingdom, but what strange difficulties did he meet with! And what a long time was it before he came to sit upon a peaceful throne! We must have conflicts before we get the victory; we must run the race and strive hard before we get the reward. But once it is bestowed upon us, it will abundantly recompense us for all our years and all our heaviness. We are to take up our cross daily; every day on earth will afford us cause of patience; we are to watch, for all our time is but as a moment compared to eternity. Let not our Lord, who will bless us with a long and unspeakable felicity, have cause to say to us, as He did to His sorrowful disciples, "Could ye not watch with Me one hour?" (Matthew 26:40). He looks on us, knows our weaknesses, and will give us help. He could immediately solace, refresh, and save us if He would; but, seeing that He is not pleased to do so, let us humbly be silent and acquiesce in the wisdom of His appointment and decree. For though He delays, He is not unmindful of our sorrows, and in the very minute that is most for His glory and our good, He will come and save us. Isaiah 64:4: "For since the beginning of the world, men have not heard, nor perceived by the ear, neither hath the eye seen, O God, beside Thee, what He hath prepared for him that waiteth for Him."

Entertain a secret hope that it will not always be this sad and dismal with you. Though you have made several prayers that have not yet received a gracious answer of peace, yet pray still, and do not be discouraged, but, like blind Bartimaeus, cry all the more earnestly. You know that the woman of Canaan persevered in her attendance on our Lord; though the words He spoke seemed to have in them a great deal of sharpness and severity, yet she was resolved not to leave Him nor be denied. And, at last, our Savior highly commended that faith of which He seemed to take no notice before. "It is good that a man should both hope and quietly wait for the salvation of God" (Lamentations 3:26). The reason whereof is alleged in verses 31–32: "For the Lord will not cast off forever; but though He cause grief, yet will He have compassion according to the multitude of His mercies."

Though everything that you look upon within your hearts terrifies and perplexes your thoughts, yet the vastness of the mercy that is in God, and which through His Son He is willing to communicate to you, may afford you support and relief; the very possibility of help, though never so remote, may calm and quiet your souls a little. For though you see nothing for the present but frowns and anger in the face of God, yet you cannot, you ought not to say that it will never shine again. Though His strokes are increased and are every day more painful than they were the day before, yet you must not then conclude that He who chastens for your profit will not lay aside the rod. Though you are sinking with your fears, and have no power left, yet lay hold on the strength of God. He will not strike your trembling hand, but will encourage your dependence and trust in Him. You have not everlastingly perished; you have not yet received your final doom; it is still possible that you may escape.

There is great comfort in a "maybe I shall be saved, though as by fire." And there is even more in an "I fully believe I shall be saved." Zephaniah 2:3: "It may be ye shall be hid in the day of the Lord's anger." Joel 2:14: "Who knoweth if He will return, and leave a blessing?"

Though you are afflicted and tossed with tempests, and though you have no comfort, there is yet a prospect of a quiet shore. Christ is not far off with His pleasant and reviving consolations. Hold out a little longer and your expectation shall not be in vain. Length of pain and continuance of sorrow tire and exhaust the natural spirits; and long attendance upon God, without any manifestation of His appearing to help us, dulls our motions, enervates our souls, takes the wheels off of our chariots, and greatly tempts us to despair that, because He does not help us now, He never will help us. Jeremiah 8:18, 20: "When I would comfort myself against sorrow, my heart is faint within me; the harvest is past, the summer is ended, and we are not saved."

But let us hope still, for when we are at the lowest, then is the proper season for God to work. We are indeed altogether desolate, but in Him there is complete and suitable salvation. It is an honor that we give to His promise when we believe it, and rely upon it when all things seem flatly to oppose our faith. Isaiah 8:17: "I will wait upon the Lord that hideth His face from the house of Jacob, and I will look for Him." (See also Psalm 27:13–14).

When we let our hope go, we pull up the sluice and deluge ourselves with miseries and calamities that are inexpressible. The God who raises the dead does so, many times, after long despair. He gives our departed hopes a resurrection and makes our broken bones rejoice, so very merciful and so very good is He.

Chapter 10

People under great trouble and anguish of soul are not to look for assurance or great joy all of a sudden, but, as far as they can, are to inquire into the reasons for God's displeasure towards them, and to look up to Him through their great Mediator, and not to further provoke Him; also how they may know when afflictions are sent in wrath and when in love

When you are under the sense of the anger of God, do not look for assurance and great triumphs of soul all of a sudden; if you have encouragements, it is a great matter, though, as Mr. [Paul] Bayne used to say, you do not know what spiritual festivities and jubilation mean. If you have daily bread to maintain your life, it is what you ought thankfully to acknowledge, though your tables are not covered with dainties, and though you do not fare deliciously every day. Only three of the disciples were admitted to the sight of our Lord's glorious transfiguration. He does not treat all of His followers with the same dishes, with the same joys and transports. We are sufficiently privileged if we are of His family. If we are adopted, there may be several who are greater favorites than we, and whom He is pleased to set at His right hand while we are on His left. He may choose whom He will to be His beloved disciples, to whom He will manifest more of His presence and love, and an extraordinary care.

Do not think that, because you have read of some who have had heaven meet them with angelic triumphs and consolations, therefore you must drink as full draughts of the same rivers of pleasure, or that they will follow you as much as them in this wilderness. Some of the eminent servants of Christ who have been very laborious and useful, who have been remarkable for their patience, their faith, and their self-denial, have been blessed with a nearer access to God, and have seen more of the Lord of hosts in His glory. But it is enough for such unprofitable servants, and such great sinners as we have been, that we look for the promised land. Though we do not have many clusters of the grapes of paradise to cheer us on our way, our Master uses us very well if He does not turn us out of doors. Though we do not fare as well as others do, it is a mercy that we have the crumbs that fall from His table.

This advice is needful because, if we look for extraordinary joy and delight, and do not find it after waiting so long, we will be ready to give up our work when we do not receive the pay, in the hope of which we flattered ourselves for a long time. Some, after long desertion and sore trials, and after a long absence of Christ, have cried out, "He has come, He has come, oh, now He has come, whom I longed to see. Now salvation has come to my house. Now I am fully satisfied. Now I am content to die. Oh, the riches, the depths, and the greatness of the grace of God! Now I see that my fears were too great and my thoughts of Him too low. I see that He who inhabits eternity, even the great Jehovah, will deal familiarly with the sons of men. I could not have thought that I, who was so faint, could ever be revived; that I, who was so full of despair, could ever be full of hope; that I, who was so near to hell, could be brought to the gates of heaven. But my own experience now tells me that it is so."

Song of Solomon 2:3–4: "I sat down under his shadow with great delight, and his fruit was sweet to my taste; he brought me to the banqueting house, and his banner over me was love." This is the language of those whom the King of heaven delights to honor. These are the golden vessels which he fills with the house of gladness. These are the Elijahs to whom He sends His chariots of fire to convey them home.

But this is not the lot of all His subjects; this is certainly not what we are to expect. If we go to heaven, even though it is by dispensations that have in them a great deal of cloud and darkness, yet it will be very well for us. If we believe, we shall be safe. Though there are some who, with Simeon, embrace their Savior in their arms, and see His salvation before they die, most of us must wait for this sight till after death. The greatest part of believers have a comfortable and reviving hope through grace that they shall come to heaven; but there are few who are so well assured of it as to have no remaining doubts and fears. But, notwithstanding what I have said, we must endeavor to work out our salvation and, by a diligence in good works and holy duties, to strive so that we may be among the blessed number of those excellent saints whom God is pleased to clothe with the garments of praise and joy.

The passionate feelings of praise and joy are not essential to holiness, though when they are bestowed they greatly quicken our obedience and enlarge our hearts. If we resolutely adhere to God, He will give us what will be sufficient for us. Our very fears shall increase our comfort afterwards. By the way in which we least expected it, joy and pleasure shall come as the ravens, those greedy creatures, brought meat unto the prophet.

Inquire into the causes of God's anger. He is never angry, as I said before, but when there is very great reason, when we force Him to be so. What is that accursed thing in our hearts or our lives for which God hides His face and frowns upon us? What particular disobedience to His commands is it for which He has taken up the rod? Job 10:2: "I will say unto God, 'Do not condemn me; show me wherefore Thou contendest with me.' " That is, "Lord, my troubles and my sorrows are very well known; every eye beholds my calamity; every ear is astonished with the report of my sore distress; and all who know me or have heard of me wonder why, above all others in the world, I am made so miserable a man that there has not been an example of this great and strange affliction since the beginning of the world. I myself, who feel these wonderful sorrows, am most of all perplexed. Show me for what and why it is that I should be so."

Job was an upright man, and, not being conscious of either secret allowed sin or open transgression, might be at a great loss to know the cause of his affliction. But most of us are as far from the grace he had in his troubles as we are from the riches he had in his prosperity. We may soon know that God is angry for our sin, and yet at the same time we must not cease to be solicitous to know what are the particular sins that have made Him tear us up by the roots and throw us down as with a whirlwind—what it is that has made Him be angry with us for so long, and for so long to delay His help—so that if any evil is undiscovered in our souls, we may lament it with a seasonable grief and get a pardon for it.

It is not the common course of God's providence to cover His servants with so thick a darkness as that which our troubled souls labor under in the day, or rather in the night, of His displeasure. And therefore we may, with humility, desire to know why He proceeds with us in a way that is so singular; for it is in some way delightful to the understanding to pierce into the reasons and causes of things. Psalm 74:1: "O God, why hast Thou cast us off forever? Why doth Thine anger smoke against the sheep of Thy pasture?" However angry He is, we must make our addresses to Him. And seeing that to be cast off, to be separated from Him, is so terrible a thing, He allows us to inquire into the reasons of His proceedings, and to debate the case. However, our debate must end in prayer and supplication, as here in verse 2.

It is very true that when a man has fallen into a pit, the business of the poor man is not to inquire how he fell there, but how he may be drawn out again and escape the danger that has overtaken him; yet in this case of the sense of God's displeasure, the knowledge of the causes of it may produce many good effects which, though they do not appear in our depths and troubles, yet will show themselves afterwards. They will cause us forever to dread the same thing which brought so many miseries upon us.

Suppose that a mother gives birth to children who die at an early stage of their life. After all the pain of bringing them forth, and after all the care for their future welfare, she sees them snatched away from her, one after the other. To know the reason for so terrible a stroke will greatly support her spirit. If it is to wean her from earthly comforts, and give her those that are eternal; if her children are taken away to give her more of God; if she must bury her dear offspring so that her declining graces may have a resurrection, or that her comfort in the living may be more sensible to her when there are so many who are dead—this will calm her soul, and make even a disconsolate mother rejoice.

Thus, when a man is exercised with long and sharp sickness and affliction, to know the causes of it may be useful to promote his humiliation at the present, and make him avoid the like for the time to come, if he recovers.

When you are under a sense of God's displeasure, fly to His mercy and grace in Christ. When your Creator is angry, nothing in the world can give you relief but Himself. Fly to God, considering His greatness, justice, holiness, and majesty; to Him, revealing Himself through the Mediator. The hills and mountains cannot be a shelter from His wrath; where can you go from His presence? Where will the sense of His anger, and your own guilty thoughts, not pursue you? Take yourselves to Him, and, when you think of Him, think of Him as a God in whom there is the greatest tenderness and pity, and to which all the compassion that is in human nature is but a weak resemblance.

It is all the same to Him, with regard to temporal deliverances, to save by many or to save by few; for what dangers can resist omnipotence? So it is as easy with Him to forgive a million sins as to forgive one sin. If we are never so unworthy and vile, yet mercy seeks no other qualification of its object but that it is in need and seeking to avoid ruin; and it is a good way to fly to His mere grace and mercy, for we have undone ourselves. Poring upon ourselves merely increases our load; we are apt to say in our distress, "If we were more mortified to the world, if our hearts were purified and cleansed, then we might approach Him with some boldness who is altogether holy." This is true, but yet we must first ask Him to make us those in whom He may delight. And as we sorrowfully cast our eyes upon our wounds and our miseries, let us look at the same time to that Physician who has provided a remedy for us in Christ, and who can heal all our backslidings and teach us to apply that divine remedy. If we are the worst and most sinful creatures on earth, yet a Savior is offered for our acceptance and our choice; and if we will receive Him, all our transgressions, however heinous, will be blotted out.

As we have a very deep sense of hell and destruction, so let us have the most enlarged thoughts of the pardoning grace of God. And to this we are encouraged by the disclosures He has made of Himself through His dear Son. His forgiveness is like Himself: it is, as Dr. [John] Owen says in his treatment of Psalm 130, an object for faith alone, which can rest in that which it cannot comprehend. Were forgiveness not in God, something beyond that which men can imagine, no flesh could be saved. Isaiah 55:8–9: "My thoughts are not your thoughts, neither are your ways My ways, saith the Lord; for as the heavens are higher than the earth, so are My ways higher than your ways, and My thoughts than your thoughts."

It is not the manner of men to pass by multiplied

transgressions as He does. The consideration of His infinite mercy removes all those obstructions which our unbelief, viewing the greatness and aggravation of our sins, throws in the way. And though our sins have been in every way inexcusable, and, upon every reflection that we make upon them, frighten and trouble us, yet the mercy of God will surely yield us some relief. For there is no other reason why He does good to this or that sinner but His own grace (Hosea 3–4). He freely chooses, justifies, adopts, and renews the souls of His elect; and it is not at all from their merit, or from anything that He foresaw in them, but from the good pleasure of His will (Ephesians 1). All that He does for them, all that He will do for them to eternity, will be to the praise and glory of His own grace.

This is the true way to humble us, when we see nothing in ourselves but what exposes us to misery; and true gospel obedience is the fruit and product of His love shed abroad in our hearts. This is the only Rock whereon we are to build our comfort when the storm comes. This free grace of God is that which the saints admire on earth, which revives their drooping spirits, and which they will wonder at forever. It is a shelter from the accusations and malicious insults of the devil. For though he sets our sins, with all their overwhelming circumstances, before us; though we cannot deny the charge, and believe that we are miserable in ourselves—yet we resolve to fly to the mercy and love of God in Christ.

We would disparage the excellencies of His nature, and the offers of His goodness, if we did not lay hold of them. And this is that which some call a natural Novatianism in the timorous consciences of convinced sinners, whereby they doubt and question pardon for their sins of apostasy and falling after repentance.

Beware of running into further sin, and so provoking God to further anger. When our hope has perished, there is nothing so evil which we shall not dare to do. If help does not speedily come, we are apt to say that it is a vain thing to pray, that it is vain to look up to a God who has thrown us off. Jeremiah 2:25: "Thou saidst, 'There is no hope; no, for I have loved strangers, and after them will I go.' "

"You are lost forever," the devil will say, "and therefore it makes no difference if you sin or not; you are lost still." This is one of his fiery darts; and if by our compliance we allow it to take hold of us, it will terrify us all the more. He will rejoice at our fall, and put our souls, by every new transgression, into much more violent and scorching flames.

What monstrous injections, what unbecoming thoughts of God he suggests! And, alas, how frequently do we entertain them! They come upon us thickly. In the time of God's displeasure, when the edge of His holy spiritual laws wounds our souls, what vast multitudes of corruptions do we then discover which we never saw before! How our old sins amaze us, and new ones arise and spring from them! And what can we do in the swelling of Jordan? What, in so great an inundation, but endeavor, in our poor, feeble manner, to look up to Christ for help.

Beg the Spirit, one man has said. There is no heart so unclean which this Spirit will not cleanse; no soul so feeble which He does not fortify; none so sorrowful which He does not comfort; none so desolate which He does not cause to rejoice; none so slavish which He does not set at liberty; none so sick which He does not heal; none so dead which He does not quicken. Surely He will regard us, for He knows that, of ourselves, we cannot bear up against the winds and waves.

And let us always remember that, among so many cruel enemies, it is unbelief that leads the van. It encourages and draws them on; and when we have obtained the victory over this, all the rest will be daunted and run away. By unbelief we open our hearts and let in all the thieves and robbers who deprive us of our peace. It is the defilement of our consciences, by manifold acts of sin, that makes us like the troubled sea which cannot rest. And for a conscience guilty of so many neglects to lay claim to God's mercy is to do as we see mountebanks sometimes do, who wound their own flesh to find out on their own bodies how strong the salve is. Yet often they come to feel the smart of their own presumption by long and desperate wounds. As Richard Sibbes says in his *The Soul's Conflict,* let us in the case even of sore afflictions be afraid to sin; for that devil who tempts us will immediately vex and torment us all the more for it.

Do not mistake those things for evidences of the certain wrath of God which, perhaps, are not really so. He may suspend the expressions of His love, though He loves us still. Joseph had the tenderness of a brother, while his brethren thought he was very angry with them. Nay, in our secret supports we are not destitute altogether of His care, though we may not know how it comes. Metals that lie deep in the ground partake of the influence of the sun, though it does not shine upon them directly with light. There are few afflictions but have rather the marks of a fatherly kindness, in the seasonable correction of our faults, than the marks of displeasure. No outward losses or inward troubles, that are but for a time, are the certain signs of wrath; no, though they are very long and very grievous. It was not so in the case of Job.

Some of us will ask, "How shall I know when afflictions are in wrath?" It is a question to be answered with great tenderness and caution.

Divines have answered in this way. Afflictions are said to be in wrath:

1. When they come with great violence and suddenly destroy, as in the case of Sodom and Gomorrah, and in the great deluge. Psalm 58:9: "Before your pots can feel the thorns, He shall take them away as with a whirlwind, both living, and in His wrath." Nahum 1:9: "He will make an utter end; affliction shall not rise up the second time." And yet this must have some limitations; for a good man may be seized with a violent disease and die suddenly, of whom we ought not to say that he died by the wrath of God.

2. When there is no discernible mercy in the cross, but only what is evil.

3. When one evil makes way for another, and none are sanctified.

4. When the affliction brings some special sin to remembrance, and when sin itself deprives us of a mercy; when intemperance brings sickness, ambition brings disgrace, or covetousness and an overeager desire for riches bring poverty.

But then, even great crosses are in mercy:

1. When God not only afflicts us, but teaches us at the same time.

2. When we can be thankful for that comfort which

we have lost, that is, if it is an outward loss; for I do not see how any person can be thankful for desertion while it remains upon him. That would be to thank God that He has departed, or that He has restrained the manifestations of His love, which no man is obliged to do.

3. When all our losses are made up in God, and in the graces of His Spirit.

Chapter 11

Present distress of conscience is no sign of reprobation. There may be too great trouble for sin. And when it is excessive, former experiences may be helpful to afflicted people. God will not judge persons who have been good according to what they are in the woeful disease of melancholy

Do not judge your eternal state by what you now feel. You may, by the terrors of the Lord, be in anguish and tribulation, in the very suburbs of hell, and yet never go there. God may be displeased, and yet, after a moment's sorrow, you may find Him to be your gracious and everlasting Friend. You may be now thrown down, but His hand and His promise can quickly raise you up again. You may conclude, through the power of your dismal thoughts, that you are reprobates, and yet God may bring you to salvation at the end. You may lie in terror for many years, but you cannot, you ought not to say that it will be so forever.

I myself have been so afflicted, in such great anguish and perplexity, under such dreadful apprehensions of the wrath of God, and of His power and greatness employed against me (as I thought), that I thought myself in hell (thinking of it as not so much a place but as a state). I thought that my soul would be gathered with sinners, and that I would be found at the left hand of Christ. I thought that I was cut down forever, banished from the courts and from the presence of the Lord, and should never see light, comfort, or refreshment any more. Yet, through the grace of God, you see that I am revived, and that I am not without hope, as I once was. From the very gates of death, from the very door of destruction, I have come to tell you that, though God is just, yet He is also gracious. There is mercy with Him that He may be feared. And as the night comes, so will the morning also; for though we have provoked Him, which was our folly, yet He will not contend forever, which is our comfort.

Psalm 31:21–24: "Blessed be the Lord, for He hath shown me His marvelous kindness in a strong city. For I said in my haste, 'I am cut off from before Thine eyes.' Nevertheless Thou heardest the voice of my supplications when I cried unto Thee. Oh, love the Lord, all ye saints. Be of good courage, and He shall strengthen your hearts, all ye that hope in the Lord." When we are in deep and sore affliction, such as smarts and makes us groan, it is hard indeed to believe that what makes us so sick will promote our health, or that what breaks us in pieces will join our bones again. But our sense and present feeling are not to guide our thoughts. We feel ourselves indeed to be miserable, but we ought to believe that our present misery may promote our happiness, though by ways that for the present we may not see. We are not to judge God by the darkness of His providences, but by the light of His Word; not by His afflicting strokes only, but by His promise, which obliges Him to correct us for our sin, but yet not altogether to destroy us.

Remember that it is an evil thing to be overly troubled, even for sin itself. This advice does not concern the greatest part of mankind. Most are secure, breaking the laws of God and not trembling; they pollute themselves with manifold abominations and are not ashamed; they sin with lofty looks and hardened hearts, and do evil with both hands earnestly. They take the name of God in vain, they profane His sabbaths, they slight His Word, they defy His threats, and they scorn His messengers; yet few or none strike their thighs and ask, "What have we done?" They are daring where they ought to fear, and rejoice where they ought to mourn. The greatest part of the world are in a deep slumber, in misery and danger, but they are insensible; they do not know that the end of these things will be very bitter and vexatious.

But I am now speaking to those whose consciences are awakened with a sense of the greatness, majesty, and justice of God, and the strictness and holiness of His law, and who have, at the same time, a deep sense of their own guilt and liability to condemnation. Their thoughts in such troubles are too much apt to sink and to be overwhelmed. Indeed, the view of all their sins set in order before them is too terrible for them to look upon. The burden and the weight of them is too heavy for any mortal man to bear.

But they should consider that God is not only severe, but very good; that He is not only angry, but reconcilable and willing to be at peace again. This will represent His love toward us, and it is that, and that alone, which will melt our hearts with a kindly grief, and keep our sorrow from overflowing the due bounds, as it is very prone to do. And it does so in several cases.

The first case is when our sorrow for sin hinders our

regular proceeding in the true judgment of things. We know that in dark and cloudy seasons we cannot distinctly perceive the various objects that we clearly discern in fair weather. So when our sorrows have raised a mist before our eyes, we obscure our reason and weaken our faculties, and do not see things as they really are, but as they appear in a dark and confused manner. When we are not able to apprehend things as they are in themselves, but as our afflictions represent them, that is a false medium whereby to form our judgments; they make us heighten our troubles, and, it may be, make them greater than they really are; moreover they make us altogether inattentive to those directions, methods, and advices that are suggested for our help.

Second, when our sorrow for sin drives us away from God, the sight of our wounds should make us hasten to the Great Physician for speedy relief. When I have thoroughly beheld my sin, the next thought should be, "Oh, what need I have for God to forgive me, for a Savior to plead my cause, and for the Holy Spirit to renew me! What need I have to throw myself at the feet of Him whom I have provoked! I need to say, in the submissive terms of the poor prodigal, 'Father, I have sinned against heaven and before Thee, and am no more worthy to be called Thy son.' But because I have once wandered, I am not still to wander in a strange country, far from my proper home."

Our grief for sin is too great when it causes us to totally despair, to give ourselves over as hopeless and lost forever. This we ought never to do. We weep too much when we cannot see the goodness and mercy of God as well as His justice and severity; when we think that it is good to Him that He should oppress and crush the works of His own hands; when we judge Him to be tyrannical and cruel, as if He intended nothing but our ruin; when we peremptorily say that He will not hear our prayers, nor show us any favor; when we have no suitable thoughts of His amiable nature, His covenant, and His promise. We weep too much for sin when, by the painfulness of the rod, we call into question all that He has ever done for us when, because He frowns, we say that He has thrown us off; when, because He delays His help, we say that He will be gracious and favorable no more; when we charge Him foolishly, and either deny His providence or blame His conduct, because He does not use as gentle a method as we would have Him take; or when, from our distress, we draw desperate conclusions regarding Him or ourselves.

Most of all, we weep too much for sin when we see others, whom we reckon to be as great sinners as ourselves, to be in health and peace while we groan and languish, and say that we have cleansed our hearts in vain (Psalm 73:11); that it is a vain thing to be religious, to fear such a God who allows His servants to be so very much afflicted, and with such sorts of sorrows that are more spiritual and, consequently, more bitter than the rest of the world is acquainted with.

Third, we are too much troubled for our sins when that trouble not only indisposes us for duty—for if it is attended with pain and trouble it will be apt to do so—but when it makes us altogether omit our duty that we owe to God; when our sorrows dampen our affections, which are the wings of our souls to carry us up to God; when they cause us to mind nothing else but what is sad and grievous; when our sorrow swells to so great a height that it covers with its imperious waves all the foundations and grounds of peace and comfort. It was not so, as some have observed, with our blessed Lord. When He was upon the cross, He was in extreme pain and in violent agonies. Yet these did not take away from Him His care for His mother. The good thief, in the midst of his pangs, labored to gain his fellow thief and save his own soul, and to glorify Christ. These were extraordinary instances; our sickness may be such that all that we can perform for God is a quiet submission to His will, and a desire for the prayers of others. Thus our sorrows for sin are excessive when they make us give up praying, hearing, or the like duties; when they unstring our harps, dull our praises, or make us unfit for our calling.

The fourth case is when our sorrow puts us upon indirect means for relief; when we put that trust in men that should be placed in God; when we expect that cure from them which He alone is able to give; when we seek relief in vain company, in recreations, or in the things of this world. But if our sense of God's displeasure is very great, we soon know that all these things are of no value.

Call to mind those experiences that you have heretofore had of the goodness of God; remember the years when you have known the right hand of the Most High. You are now fearing His wrath, but can you not remember the time when His love was your daily solace and delight? You are now complaining that He does not hear your cry, but how many prayers has He sent back with a gracious answer? How many times have you lain at His feet in humiliation and tears, and His hand has wiped your tears away? How many times, when you have been fainting, has His Word revived your poor, troubled souls? And though His Word is now bitter to your taste, and fills you with gall and wormwood, yet it is still able to revive you. Those places of Scripture that heretofore revived you are still able to refresh you; those breasts are still as full of consolation as they ever were; but you are for the present under a decay of spirits, and have lost your appetite, so that you cannot draw that consolation from there that you used to do.

Do not forget the many mercies of your infancy, your childhood, your youth, and your riper age. Do not forget how seasonable, how unexpected, how necessary your mercies have been, both for your bodies and your souls. And though I know it is your abuse of them that grieves and troubles you, yet remember that He who once forgave you can forgive you still, and that He who once did you so much good is still able to do you good. Paraphrasing Judges 13:23: "If the Lord had meant to destroy us, He would not have received a sacrifice at our hands, nor have done all this for us."

Shall we distrust, shall we forsake, shall we limit a God who has been heretofore so very merciful and so gracious? And though it is very true that it is no comfort to a poor man to think that he was once rich, or to a sick man to think that he was once in health (for the bitterness of his present evil takes away the relish of his former comforts, and when a man has lost God in his terrible apprehensions it seems more intolerable than if he had never enjoyed Him), yet having once had communion with Him by His grace and by His Spirit may give us some reason to hope that the root of the matter is in us, and that God will cause it to bud and spring forth again, though it now lies under water and is covered with many storms and tribulations. And, I may also add, it may be covered with many sins and corruptions with which we were not troubled before.

Remember that God will not judge you according to what you are in such a woeful distemper as that of melancholy, but that it will go with you as you were in the time of your health. This is highly necessary to be considered, for many good people, when they are under the disease of melancholy, which can no more be prevented than tuberculosis or a fever, are very apt to express themselves after this or a similar manner: "I thought I had once been serious, but now I see that it was all a deceit. I see that I heard and prayed and received the sacraments in vain; for if I had been a true believer, this would never have befallen me." This is a very false way of arguing, for if you had been never so sincere, that sincerity would not have kept away diseases, nor this one in particular. For in melancholy we think and speak according to our present apprehensions and fears, and these are greatly caused by the disorder of our imaginations, which is owing to the confusion and the hurry of our thoughts; and that confusion is the product of a great and unusual stagnation or fixing of the spirits, when the blood is corrupted and the body indisposed, and this is most frequently occasioned by the want of rest or sleep.

It is commonly said by others who do not know what melancholy is, "Why do you think and pore so much? Divert yourselves; think of something else." But it is no more possible for people, where this disease comes with violence, to divert their thoughts than it is possible for a man to be alert in an apoplexy or calm in a raging fever; no more than a man who has a broken arm or leg can walk and act as he used to do before. As

Mr. [Richard] Baxter says in his *Christian Directory,* rational and spiritual methods will not suffice to cure this; for you may as well expect that a good sermon or comfortable words will cure epilepsy, palsy, or a broken head simply because this disease works on the spirits and fantasy, on which words of advice also work. Therefore, such words, and Scripture and reason, may somewhat resist it, or may palliate or allay some of the effects at present; but as soon as time has worn off the force and effects of these reasons, the distemper immediately returns. And it is as natural for a melancholy person to fear, and to meditate on terror, as it is for a sick man to groan, or for one in health to breathe. It is certain that tenacious, obstinate distempers, such as this one of melancholy, will not be relieved by mere words or sentences; they cannot indeed cast out their troubled thoughts; they cannot turn away their minds; they can think of nothing but what they do think just a man with a toothache cannot forbear to think of his pain. To not so think is to be cured, which they would be glad to be. Though others urge us to rule our thoughts, it gives us no relief, but only adds to our misery to be frequently urged to do that which we cannot do.

But my advice to such is that, in the use of such things as they find to yield a natural refreshment to their spirits, they would look up to God, who can make the winds and storms cease, and make that unquiet agitation that is in the blood and humors be still again. And when He shall be pleased to give you the rest of night, and the clearness and activity of your natural spirits, then your troublesome and uneasy thoughts, by the help they will then receive by reading or advice, will wear away. I speak nothing but what I myself have experienced to be true; for this disease magnifies our sorrows.

What I am aiming at is this: when any are in deep melancholy, so far as they have any reason left, they should not increase their own terror by thinking that all their former prayers and endeavors have been to no purpose because they do not perceive at that time what effect they have had. God is certainly more gracious than to reckon the unavoidable attendants of a disease that none but Himself can cure to be a sin. Men are not to be judged by what strange actions or expressions they are guilty of in a violent sickness; and among all diseases that are so, I think this is one of the most violent.

Chapter 12

The various ends that God has in allowing His servants to be under long afflictions, spiritual distress, and anguish

Consider what ends God may have in letting the apprehensions of His wrath continue for a season. Here I know I am entering upon a thing whereof we cannot have a certain, comprehensive knowledge; for the judgments of God (and great, long, and severe trials) are too deep for us to easily fathom, or to tell particularly what God's design is in this or that matter. The arcana of His government are not obvious to everyone who desires to pry into them; and there is an abundance of very dark and mysterious providences in this world, the reasons for which we shall never know till the great day.

Who can tell the very cause why God allows one religious man to be in affliction for several years, while another, who is perhaps no better than he, scarcely knows what affliction means? One shall be crossed and disappointed in all that he goes about; he meets with losses in his estate and in his family, and his health is damaged, while another prospers, is well, and dies an easy death. In what a smooth path do some good people go to heaven, while others are torn with thorns and briars, and go mourning and weeping all the way! Who dares to presume to say why this is so, and not otherwise?

A great modesty should become us in our inquiries, when we endeavor to pierce into the designs of the great God, whose throne is established in righteousness, but surrounded with clouds and darkness. "It is the glory of God to conceal a thing" (Proverbs 25:2). His infinite majesty will not be accountable to us for what He does. There is a thick veil upon the reasons for His judgments and decrees, so that He may procure a greater veneration from His creatures. Psalm 77:19: "Thy way is in the sea, and Thy path in the great waters; and Thy footsteps are not known."

Therefore, when we say that God does this or that for such and such a reason, we must do it with great humility, and only so far as the Scripture is our guide. And from that we may learn that God suffers His people to be under the apprehensions of His wrath, and under long afflictions, for such ends as these:

1. It is certainly good for the universe, for God does nothing in vain. And when any part suffers, it is for the good of the whole. We may not be able to discern how it may be so, though, until His hand has finished His entire design.

2. He does this so that others may be convinced by their very senses what a dreadful God He is, and how terrible a thing it is to sin. "The lion hath roared, who will not fear?" (Amos 3:8). When men see those who were once as pleasant as themselves shedding tears, and crying out in the bitterness of their souls that they are undone and miserable, their sad looks and their doleful expressions bear witness to the being, and to the severity and justice, of God. Sometimes, in the extraordinary joys which His love produces in the hearts of His people, He shows heaven upon earth; and some-

times, in the fears, amazements, and terrors of awakened consciences, He shows hell upon earth—and both are designed for the good of others by His wise and holy providence.

The language of their groans speaks to all who behold their sorrow: "Oh, do not sin against so great and so terrible a God, lest the flames begin to scorch you that have almost consumed us. We no more thought of falling into His hands than you do; we no more thought that our sinning would cost us so dearly than you do. But you see what we have felt, and what you may expect if you do not repent and turn and make your peace with so holy a God as He is. His power will amaze you, His arm will crush you if ever you provoke Him to send on you such a stroke as ours is. Endeavor therefore to profit from such a sorrowful example."

3. God does it to keep us from carnal security all our lives. Psalm 9:20: "Put them in fear, O Lord, that the nations may know themselves to be but men." When our sin has fallen upon us like a giant who is newly refreshed with wine, surely the remembrance of that horror, pain, and smart will keep us so that we shall not dare to sleep in sin, nor be unwatchful and presumptuous any more forever. Surely this will quench all irregular desires, and cause us only to desire that God whose favor we need so very much. This has surely shown us how great our weakness and our folly are, and how low we sink when we think that He has left us. This will make us be humble and walk softly all our days, remembering that we are not, every hour, any more than what God makes us to be. If He ever left us for but one poor moment, where would we be?

We who have tasted so much of His displeasure have

cause to rejoice with trembling. Every remembrance of that doleful time must be to us as a new motive to obedience, and a powerful restraint of sin. Hebrews 12:10: He chastens us "for our profit, that we might be partakers of His holiness." Oh, what an abundance of folly must have been lodged in our hearts, that God is forced to use so sharp and severe a method to whip it out! How numbed were we that nothing else could awaken us! How diseased were we that nothing but a potion so bitter could promote our cure! How great was our pride that He was forced to beat it down by so violent a stroke! Deuteronomy 8:15–16: "Who led thee through that great and terrible wilderness, wherein were fiery serpents, and scorpions, and drought, where there was no water; that He might humble thee, and prove thee, to do thee good at thy latter end." And so it was that Paul had a "thorn in the flesh" (2 Corinthians 12:7).

4. God does this to convince us of His own all-sufficiency, and the nothingness of ourselves and of all other creatures. He lets us fall to show us how small our strength is, and that if we would have our goings established we must depend upon Him alone. In our prosperity, we are apt to think that this or that creature, this or that person, will yield us relief; but in spiritual troubles God shows us that all men, even the best of men, are vanity, and those from whom we expect the greatest help do us the least good. Nay, those watchmen of whose skill and kindness we have the greatest opinion are frequently allowed to smite us by their imprudent or harsh speeches and censures, so that we may not look to those cisterns which we find to be broken ones, but to that heaven whence all our consolation flows.

When we go to created things with the most raised

expectations, we meet with the most unlooked-for disappointments. And, indeed, while we look only to them, we are like people who go begging to the doors of the poor. Our fellow creatures have nothing but what they receive; unless God helps us, they cannot help either. Unless the wind blows, neither all the skill of the pilot nor all the industry of the mariner can make the ship sail forward to the port. We think that if our friend was sick, we would hasten to his help and immediately relieve him; but our best Friend stays a long while before He delivers us, not from any pleasure that He takes in our sorrows, but that He may render His power and His wisdom more illustrious. Thus it was with Christ in John 11:6–7. When He heard that Lazarus was sick, He stayed two days in the place where He was so that the glory of God might be more conspicuous in Lazarus's resurrection. And when the season that is most beautiful comes, we shall discern the reason for His delay. He lets us fall low so that He might display His power that is almighty, and His wisdom that is never at a loss, so that we might know, when all other methods have been tried in vain, that it is He alone who can make our broken bones rejoice; that when we are beset with difficulties which we think insufferable, we may still stand and see how glorious, how suitable, and how speedy is the salvation, the grace, and the help of God, and that He alone is the God of comfort (2 Corinthians 1:3). He wants us to see that all other things are inconsiderable, but that He is all-sufficient.

It is an excellent lesson that He teaches us by our heaviest crosses. None can calm the tumults and uneasiness of a troubled soul but He alone. Our spirits are so remote from human observations, our diseases are so inward and so great, that men cannot reach them; but nothing is too hard for Him who is the Father of spirits, and He calls us peculiarly to regard this as His mighty work. Isaiah 57:17–19: "For the iniquity of his covetousness I was wroth, and he went on frowardly in the way of his heart. I have seen his ways, and will heal him; I will lead him also, and restore comforts unto him, and to his mourners. I create the fruit of the lips; 'Peace, peace to him that is far off, and to him that is near,' saith the Lord, 'and I will heal him.' "

God creates peace. He not only brings peace, but brings it from nothing by His all-powerful efficacy so that nothing can resist. I say again, this I believe to be one of the principal lessons that God designs to teach us by our inward and spiritual troubles, that in Him alone our help lies, and that even the best of men are vanity. We must not look for much from them, for, if we do, we shall most surely be disappointed. They do not have the patience to hear our complaints or to understand the particulars of our case; or, if anyone does have such great patience, and so much tenderness as to hear our sad story, they will, it may be, sigh or shake their heads at it, but, alas, they can give us no relief.

5. Another end that God may have in the continuance of long and sore afflictions, and great inward troubles, is to reveal more clearly to us the corruption and defilement of our nature. In a calm, the waters of the sea appear to be clear enough; but when the storm comes, it throws up the mire and the dirt. In prosperity and health, we think we have very good hearts and considerable degrees of sanctification; but when sin is set home upon us, the spiritual law of God begins to show its purity. And, oh, what multitudes of iniquities then

appear! What unbelief, what impatience, what murmuring, what unbecoming thoughts of God, such hideous and strange thoughts as we have never had before!

In times of health, strength, and peace, there are a thousand secular affairs and contrivances that take up our time and divert our minds, turning us to the view of things outside us; but in the trouble of our consciences, our eyes are turned another way to behold with attention our own souls, and to see what lusts, what impurities, what venomous creatures, what vipers have been entertained there. And, oh, what a ghastly sight this is, to see such a numerous brood of transgressions, when we imagined that all had been very well with us! It is even a wonder that God, who saw so much evil in us, should let us alone so long.

These spiritual afflictions show us what a sorry, contemptible creature man is, what cause he has to be debased when he is most proud, and what cause he has to be covered with shame and blushing when he is most fearless and undaunted. When God does not blow upon our garden, instead of those spices and graces coming forth that may be for His glory and for our comfort, there is nothing but weeds and thistles, nothing but thorns and briars to tear and wound us. Our soul is then like a dead carcass—full of putrefaction, with no sprightly motions towards heaven, no spiritual desires, no warm desires; it is like the cold regions of the north, which the sun visits only with its fainter and weaker beams, and not like those eastern countries, where its greater heat produces spices and fragrant flowers.

6. Another end that God has in the continuance of spiritual troubles and afflictions, and the sense of His wrath long upon us, is that from our experience Christ

may be forever very precious to us. When we are at ease and think ourselves whole, we seldom think of Him. But our pain, our smart, our guilt and our fears, the sight of our present danger and of approaching wrath, all cause us to run to this Physician and beg His help when we are sinking. They will make us stretch out our hands and say, "Master, save us or else we perish!" Never did a poor man beg for alms with more earnestness than we shall beg His help; never did a diseased person, after a violent, racking pain, more long for rest and a cure than we shall long for Christ. Having fallen among lions, having been the slaves of fear, and having been held in captivity by the temptations of Satan, we shall most gladly shake off our chains and embrace liberty and salvation when our Lord comes to set us free. The sight of Him as our Savior will make us run to meet Him and say, "Welcome, Thou only Friend of our souls; welcome, Thou dear Physician and Healer of our souls. Hosanna to the Son of David; blessed is He who comes to us in the name of the Lord!"

Oh, how our very hearts will melt with love when we remember that, as we have been distressed for our sins against Him, so He was in greater agonies for us! We have had gall and wormwood, but He tasted a more bitter cup. The anger of God has dried up our spirits, but He was scorched with a more flaming wrath. He was under violent pain in the garden and on the cross; ineffable was the sorrow that He felt, being forsaken by His Father, deserted by His disciples, affronted and reproached by His enemies, and under a curse for us. The sun was under a doleful eclipse; this living Lord was pleased to die and, in His death, was under the frowns of an angry God. That face was then hidden from Him that had always smiled before. His soul felt that horror and darkness which it had never felt before. Though there was no separation between the divine and the human nature, yet Christ suffered pains equal to those which we deserved to suffer in hell forever. God so suspended the efficacies of His grace that it displayed in that hour none of its force and virtue on Him. He had no comfort from heaven, none from His angels, none from His friends, even in that sorrowful hour when He needed comfort most. Like a lion that is hurt in the forest, He roared and cried out, though there was no despair in Him. And when He was forsaken, yet there was trust and hope in the words, "My God, My God."

Have we been abandoned by God? He was much more so; and He was deserted for a while that we might not be so forever. Oh, how frequently should we remember such a Savior! How delightfully should we think and speak of Him, who thought nothing too much to suffer for us. We have, by feeling the wrath of God, drunk in some measure the cup whereof He drank. We do so justly for our sins, but He does so out of love and kindness, that He might make an atonement and a propitiation. And if what we have felt was so terrible, how much more dreadful was that which He endured! If the smaller drops that have put our souls into a flame have filled us with anguish, what torment did He undergo who was plunged into a sea of wrath! Surely such a Friend, such a Physician, as He has been to us, must be ever valued. We cannot pray but in His name; we cannot be justified but with His righteousness; we can hope for nothing but by His merits and His intercession; we cannot live, we cannot die without Him. Let this be the constant language of our souls:

"None but Christ, none but Christ!" (see Song of Solomon 3:1–4).

7. God also does this so that we may put a high value on the Scriptures, that we may search and look into them with more earnestness and frequency, to see if there are any promises in them that are reviving, and place in them that may afford hope and comfort to souls so miserable and so guilty. For when our consciences are awakened and pierced with the sense of wrath from God, if His Word would speak peace to us, we could have ease; but the terrible threats thereof are the things that wound us deeply and put us to a greater smart, and we then know and fully believe beyond all doubt that this is the Word by which we are to be tried in that great and solemn day.

8. Another end of God in continuing afflictions and a long, remaining sense of His wrath upon us is that we may be everlasting admirers of the freeness of His grace when we are delivered. Oh, with what wonder should we behold His condescension and His care for us, that when our wounds were very deep, He poured in wine and oil; when we were inwardly bleeding, and no creature or friend on earth could help us, He did not allow us to bleed to death. Whatever gifts we have, whatever advantage above some others in knowledge and in understanding, whatever opportunities we have of doing good, and whatever zeal we use in doing what that opportunity offers to us, we ought to say with Paul in 1 Corinthians 15:10, "By the grace of God I am what I am, and His grace which was bestowed upon me was not in vain; but I labored more abundantly than they all, yet not I, but the grace of God which was with me."

The hand of God is so strong, and His wisdom is so

admirable, that He turns to our profit and advantage not only the evils which are caused by cross events, or by the world, but those which we commit ourselves, and that seem to be contrary to our salvation, even those sins which we are guilty of. He changes these poisons into medicine, these scandals into edification, and from the thickest darkness He brings out light. For example, by David's adultery and murder He opened the eyes of His servant to consider the horror of his fault, and that which was likely to have thrust him into perdition instead, by divine providence, confirmed him in the way of salvation. By his fall he was made to know how feeble his nature was, and, on the other side, to know how admirable the grace of God was. This obliged him to quit all his opinion of himself, and not to seek his happiness anywhere else than in the mercy and grace of God. As for other faithful persons, this sorrowful example of his was beneficial to mortify their vanity and pride, and to teach them to put all their trust in God.

With what wonder should we daily cry out, "Will God indeed dwell familiarly with men?" Will He pity, will He pardon such impatient, such murmuring, such unbelieving sinners as we have been? Will He cause us to hear the joyful voice again, who have so long had the voice of ruin and destruction in our ears? Will He return and be my God again, when I have so often thought that He was my enemy? Will He give me the hope of heaven, when I have been so long at the very door of hell? Will He put out His hand and take me into His ark, when my poor uneasy soul has been wandering to and fro, seeking rest and finding none? His end in these afflictions and sore trials is that the delivered Christian may be always employed in wondering at His love, and that, when he has lost himself in wondering, transporting joy, he may say, "Oh, the height, and breadth, and depth!" (Romans 11:33).

What, will He be so gracious to me, who has had such hard thoughts of Him? Will He embrace me, such a prodigal as I am, in His arms? Oh, why should He let me live when others, who have been less sinful than I, are dead and have perished? Why should He be kind to me, when I was so undutiful to Him? What, will He give me leave to pray yet again to Him, when in my unbelief I so often said that it was vain to pray? Will He suffer me, who has spoken so unadvisedly with my lips, who has darkened counsel by words without knowledge (Job 38:2), to take His name in my mouth? Will He suffer a mortal man, and a vile sinner, to say, "My Lord and my God"?

Yes, He will! I see, I feel, that there is with Him plenteous redemption, and I must forever admire the riches and the freeness of His grace. Let others talk of merit, of the power of their own will, of the light of their own understandings, and of the force and strength of their reason; as for me, I know that I have none of these things whereof to boast. I was laid low in the very depths of misery and desolation, and there I would be laying still, for all that I was able to do. I was helpless, and He filled my despairing soul with hope. I was very guilty, and He forgave me. I was near to hell. I saw the flames and smoke of that infernal pit. I smelled the fire and brimstone, and He who alone could help me brought me back again. I was fainting, and He revived me. I was dying, and He made me live. How many has He passed by and allowed to pine away in their iniquities, and yet He has said unto me, "Live!" If He will accept my poor prayers, my weak endeavors, then my heart and my soul, my thoughts and my affections shall all be employed for Him and for His glory. When I have so long heard the rumor and the noise of war, He has sent me the tidings of peace and joy. Oh, whence is it but from His own grace that I, who was so far from Him, should be brought nigh; that I, who hated Him so much, should be so greatly beloved! Enter into thy rest, O my soul, for the Lord hath dealt bountifully with thee.

9. Another end why God suffers His servants so long to remain under the impressions of His wrath is that they may learn to be merciful and helpful to such as are in the same case, and to such as are sinning, and have not yet felt the displeasure of God for their sins.

First, as for such as are under trouble of conscience and the apprehension of God's wrath, as our heavenly Father has been merciful to us, so we must be merciful to them (2 Corinthians 1:3–4; Luke 22:32). And, having met with a Fountain that has quenched our thirst, we must lead them also to the Spring of living waters. Think of yourself as a Joseph, sold into the Egypt of a wounded conscience, where your feet were hurt in the stocks and the irons entered into your soul, so that you might provide food for the famine of others, and especially to be a purveyor of comfort to your brethren who shall follow you down into the same doleful condition. We must not grieve them by a sharp or unseasonable discourse; when they are in the furnace, we must not make it to hotter by imprudent bitterness. They are wounded in their souls, and those wounds require a gentle, skillful, and tender hand. Every one of us should say, "They are troubled on every side, and so was I. They are afraid that God has departed, and so was I. Those arrows of the Almighty that stick in them only a little while ago stuck in me. That cup that is now in their hand was but a little while ago in mine. As they sigh and complain, groan and fear, even so did I. Therefore, let me visit these sick, direct these wanderers who have lost their way, and see if these prisoners will become prisoners of hope by the sight of my liberty. I must lead them to my Physician and tell them the nature of my cure."

When others have fallen into the same pit that we have just gotten out of, let us strive to draw them up. Let us put on bowels of compassion; let us patiently hear what they say, and not rebuke them for complaining; let us not be weary of their discourse because it is doleful and troublesome; let us not smile at that which makes them weep, nor simply call that fancy which is the anguish and trouble of their souls. Let us remember all that speech and usage that made us worse when we were ill and avoid all such with them. Let us remember what it was that gave us some support, and let us minister the same to them.

When any of our friends are very sick, if we know anything that has been beneficial to us under the like case, we make all the speed we can to fetch it, and we cannot see them faint without finding at the same time a very sensible commotion in our own hearts. No outward affliction, though never so painful, is as terrible as these spiritual troubles are. Let us therefore be more affectionately concerned for such distressed persons than for any others when we see the anger of God beginning to kindle in their consciences. Let us use all the methods that are most likely to quench the beginning flame, for as God commanded the Israelites to be kind to strangers, because they themselves were such in the land of Egypt, so let us be very kind and pitiful to all who are in distress, since we have been so ourselves. Let us take all opportunities to visit, to exhort, and to direct them. Let us wrestle with the God of Jacob on their behalf; let them see that we sympathize most heartily with them, and that, though the grace of God has wiped away our tears, we can still weep with those who weep. Let us take all the ways we can to make them believe that we are afflicted with their affliction and are sincerely concerned for the sadness of their case. And by this means, they will ruminate on what we say, and will more regard what we tell them, since we have once been as they are now. Then they will also listen to others who may speak well indeed, but not from their own experience. If a man is diseased in his body, he would rather have a physician who had himself been lately cured of that disease, rather than someone who was more learned by information and study, but does not feel the disease half as much as the former one does. The knowledge of the one is but speculative, but the other's is more distinct and practical. He knows how to make suitable applications to his patient from the remembrance of how he felt in his own body (Hebrews 2:17–18; 2 Corinthians 1:6).

Second, God continues the sense of His wrath very long upon the souls of His people so that they may learn to pity wicked men and instruct them in the way of happiness (Psalm 51:11–13), that they might teach them by their words, their serious exhortations, their faithful reproofs, their holy conversation, and every action that they go about. There are many lessons that we ourselves are not taught except by the rod and the frowns of an angry God, by a very smarting and severe discipline. We do not see, till after a long teaching, the real evil of sin and the true worth of Christ; and we must communicate some measure of this knowledge to others—though the misery is that most will scarcely believe our report until they themselves have come to feel what we have felt.

He who, by the mercy of God, has escaped out of long trouble of conscience can say this to sinners: "I have dearly paid for all the delight that I once had in sin, for all my indifference and lukewarmness, for my cold and sluggish prayers, for my lost and poorly used time. Beware that you do not provoke Him, for He is a jealous God. If you do, you shall also find that those sins which you make a slight matter of will tear you to pieces hereafter; you will find them, when your consciences are awakened, to be a heavy and intolerable burden; they will press you down into hell itself. I could not have imagined that the displeasure of God was a thing so bitter and so very dreadful. As the Scripture says, it is a terrible thing to fall into the hands of the living God, for He is a consuming fire. If His anger is kindled but a little, you cannot then fix your minds upon any pleasant objects, nor have one easy thought; you cannot then go about your business, your trade, or your secular affairs, for your souls will be so much amazed that you will be full of horror and consternation. Those of us who have felt the terrors of the Lord most earnestly persuade you to forsake every sin; for if you indulge and love your iniquities, they will set you on fire round about."

Oh, that you knew what you do when you sin! You are opposing that authority that will avenge itself of all its obstinate opposers; you are heaping up fuel for your own destruction; you are whetting that sword that will enter into your bowels; you are preparing yourselves for bitterness and trouble. And, though God is patient for a while, He will not always be so. The shadows of the night are drawing close, and the doleful time will come when all your mirth will end in tears, and all your false confidence and foolish hopes will expire and give up the ghost. And which of you will live when God shall enter into judgment with you? What will you do? Where will you go for help when He who is your Maker, He who has weighed your actions and observed your wanderings, shall call you to give an account of all these things?

Our blessed Lord, when He came near Jerusalem, lifted up His voice and wept, saying, "If thou hadst known, even thou at least, in this thy day, the things which belong to thy peace!" (Luke 19:42). What cause have we, then, to mourn over our fellow creatures, whom we see to be in danger of misery, and, alas, they do not know it! Can we see them sleeping on the very edge of ruin and not be troubled for them? Oh, poor sinners, you are now sleeping, but the Judge is at the door. You are rolling the pleasant morsel under your tongue, but it will be a great vexation to you in the latter end. How can you rest? How can you be quiet when you have none of your sins pardoned, no comfortable relation to God, and no well-grounded hope of assurance? How can you, with any assurance, go about those things that concern your buying, your selling, and the present life, when your poor souls, that are of a thousand times more value, are neglected all the while?

We have felt great terrors, inexpressible sorrows, from an angry God; and we would fain persuade you not to run upon the thick knobs on His shield, not to dare His justice, not to despise His threats, as once it was our folly to do, when we did not know what we were doing. We have come out of a great tribulation and a fiery furnace, and we would fain persuade you to avoid the like danger. Let what we have felt be a caution to you.

It was the desire of Dives in his misery to go to his brothers and warn them, lest they come to the same place of torment; but it was not granted. Some of us here have come from the very gates of hell to warn you so that you may not go there; nay, to warn you so that you may never go as near as we did. We wish you so well that we would not have any of you feel as much sorrow and grief as we have felt. We were once asleep as you are; we did not imagine that terror and desolation were so near. Then it came upon us; and now, having been overtaken with a storm of wrath, we come to warn you that we see the clouds gathering, that there is a sound of much rain and of great misery, though your eyes are so fixed on things below that you do not see it. You must speedily arise and seek for a shelter, if you care about the salvation of your souls; you must not put off serious thoughts for your own safety, not for one day, not for one hour longer, lest it be too late.

We were traveling with as little thought of danger as some of you, and we fell among thieves. They plundered us of our peace and our comfort, and we were ready to die, when that God whose just displeasure brought us low was pleased to take pity on us and to send His Son, that kind Samaritan, to bind up our wounds and to cheer our hearts. And we cannot be so uncharitable as not to tell you, when we see you going the same way, that there are robbers on the road, and that, if you do not either return or change your course, you will smart for your security as much as we have done. We have been saved indeed at length from our fears, though as by fire. But we suffered, while they remained, a very great loss.

Someone might be saying to himself, "I shall see no evil, though I walk in the imaginations of my own heart. These things you talk of are the mere product of a melancholy temper that always thinks the worst, that is always frightening itself and others with black and formidable ideas. And, seeing that I am in no way inclined to that distemper, I need not fear any such perplexing thoughts."

But know that no briskness of temper, no sanguine, courageous hopes, no jollities nor diversions can fence you from the wrath of God. If you go on in sin, you must feel the bitterness of it, either in this world or in the next; and that may come all of a sudden, notwithstanding all the strength of your constitution, and all the pleasures of your unfearing youth. That cup that is full of sparkling wine has dregs and poison at the bottom. Your souls are always naked and open before God, and He can make terrible impressions of wrath there whenever He will, notwithstanding when, by your cheerfulness and mirth, you seem to be at the greatest distance from it.

Chapter 13

What the duty is of those persons whom God has delivered from melancholy and from the anguish of their consciences under a sense of His wrath. Also, what a wonderful act of providence it is that allows a very sinful world to be in such great peace! And what cause there is for all people to pray against such diseases, whereof the devil serves himself to their great torment and vexation. And at the conclusion of this first part, what is to be thought of those who are distracted with trouble for their sins, and of those who die in great darkness as to their spiritual state

I now proceed to show how those persons who have long been under a sense of God's displeasure, and who have now come to some good hope through grace, ought to behave after so terrible a visitation. But my *Discourses on Sickness and Recovery,* which I published some time ago, where I mentioned what it is that we are to do after recovery from sickness, have, in a great measure, prevented my further insisting upon this subject, as well as addressing those ends that I have now mentioned which God aims at in these dispensations. And if we make it our great care to comply with them, we answer His designs; and even those sore afflictions will be a very great mercy to us. What I judge further necessary to be said, I shall comprise in the following particulars:

1. In all the remaining part of our lives, we must value this world very little. Our unmortified affections were the briars and thorns that pierced us and multiplied our sorrows. Let us look upon this world and its most admired glories as a poor, contemptible thing, for so it is indeed. The world, by the cares and variety of thoughts to which it naturally carries us, easily disquiets and throws us down, but it cannot, with all its charms, raise us up again; all its honors cannot save us from the contempt of God; all its pleasures cannot sweeten our cup, nor all its smiles cheer us when He frowns.

The more we are elevated above earthly things, the more we shall be freed from storm and tempest. It may be true what some tell us, that the tops of those mountains that are above the middle region are so quiet that the lightest things there lie still and are not moved. This world has been formerly, and will be still, a place of vanity and vexation of spirit. We have found it to be so; we have always met with trouble. When we loved anything here with an excessive love, alas, it was able to do nothing for us in our sore affliction! When our consciences were in a flame, there was nothing in it that could quench our thirst. Let us esteem such an empty world as this at a low rate. Its comforts are doubtful, but its miseries are certain; its griefs are long-lived, but its pleasures are very short.

2. When the sense of the wrath of God is removed, we must, by the remembrance of it, be fortified against the temptations of Satan. When we are tempted to distrust, we must say, "I will not entertain any more hard thoughts of a God whom I have found to be faithful." When we are tempted to impatience under some new

returning cross, we must answer and say, "I will not fret nor murmur any more against my gracious and loving God, who will, I am sure, remember me still in my low state, as He did heretofore." When Satan would persuade us that we are not sons of God because we are afflicted, or because we have suffered for so long, we must quench this dart also by remembering our dear Redeemer, who was never more beloved than when He was most severely tried. There is nothing that will so preserve us as the remembrance of the kindness and the mercy of God. His peace, which passes understanding, will keep our hearts.

3. Let our escape from such long and sore afflictions quicken us to duty. By that I do not mean only the duty of prayer, but the performance of all those acts of religion whereby we may glorify God and do good to men; let your prayers be more fervent, our meditations on Him more sweet, and our thoughts of Him more constant and abiding. Let us take heed of all formality and unaffectedness of spirit in all our attendance upon God; let us beware of inward and spiritual decays; and let us stifle and resist the first abatements and declinings of our love for God, seeing that He has withdrawn His hand from us, and that His dread does not make us afraid (Job 9:34). Let us draw near to Him and seek His face, and do it now with more delight; for as the earth is shut and bound up by frost and cold, and does not put forth her fruits till the warmth and heat of the summer call them out, so the heart, under the cold affections of fear and guilt, under the dark apprehensions of wrath and judgment, is so contracted that it does not know how to draw near to God. But when His love is shed abroad in it, then it is enlarged to the per-

formance of its duty, and the sense of mercy (and the hope of it) give us great encouragement to pray, for prayer is the child of faith. Let the love of God towards us quicken us to watchfulness, and to a daily care of our own hearts, which are so treacherous and deceitful. It once was night, a doleful night with us; but seeing that the day has begun to dawn, let us set upon our work with a greater diligence.

4. Our deliverance from such sad and terrible apprehensions of God's wrath, and from long and sore trials, should teach us to walk humbly with Him. We have seen Him in the terribleness of His majesty; we have seen the Lord of Hosts in His glory, and such a sight cannot but make us know that we are unclean (Isaiah 6:5). What have we wherein to pride ourselves? The archers have sorely shot at us, and we could not make our bow abide in strength. God has bruised us, tried us, and laid us low to show what was in our hearts; and, alas, we saw nothing there but what was very bad, such a sight as may cause us to wonder at His patience and His healing grace, and to abhor and loathe ourselves forever.

The time of our darkness was a time of provocation; when we were in the wilderness we murmured; and what a mercy it is that our carcasses are not fallen and our souls ruined, but that the God whom we so provoked has given us the prospect and hope of Canaan after all this! Those who would have told us, when we were in health and peace, that we would have spoken so harshly of God when we were in our distress, that we would censure His dispensations and sin so very much when His rod and His stroke were upon us—we would have thought of them as very censorious and uncharitable people. But no man knows how bad his heart is until it is tried by long and sore afflictions. Our anguish, our sorrow, and our despairing fears caused us to do a thousand things which we would, at another season, have trembled at. And such fools are we that even when we are beaten in the mortar, our folly does not depart from us. Though God has forgiven us, yet we ought to remember our murmuring, our unbelief, and the like sins, with a great self-abhorrence all our days. Isaiah 38:15: "What shall I say? He hath spoken unto me, and Himself hath done it. I shall go softly all my years, in the bitterness of my soul."

We have caused many to be discouraged, many to faint, many to reflect unfavorably on religion because of our sadness; and the dishonor that may hereby have come to God should be a matter of great humiliation to us, though there is, in the spiritual affections of the religious, something that is very tremendous to the wicked. It is as a judgment to harden them, and for the falling of many, that by this means they are more fixed in their prejudices against all religion; and by seeing those who have long pretended to embrace religion to be very sorrowful, they are tempted to believe that there is nothing real in it, and so they go on and sin and die. We have great cause to be humbled, and not to glory in our strength, for we have found it to decay; not to glory in knowledge, for we have known such distempers that have cast a cloud upon our understanding. We have been buffeted by Satan to teach us that we have need of more help to preserve us than our own. Oh, what is man when left by God? Nothing but weakness and vanity. "He withdraws man from his purpose, that He may hide pride from man" (Job 33:17).

5. We must beware of a relapse. As we are careful to avoid all those things which might bring upon us the same bodily diseases from which we need to be delivered, so we ought to be as careful to prevent everything that may bring a new indisposition and terror on our souls when we have just come out of the furnace. Let us beware that we do not fall again into such hot and fiery trials as those which we have felt. Let us forever be very cautious to avoid everything that has the appearance or the show of sin. And let us forever be jealous of our own hearts and watchful over their most secret motions, seeing that they have often—alas, too often—betrayed us. Let us forever absolutely deny all the most pleasing temptations of the devil, remembering that he is the enemy of God, and remembering with what cruelty and pride that enemy of our salvation exulted over us when it pleased God to leave us for a season. Let us remember how he suggested dreadful and amazing apprehensions to us, and let us no more come near the den of lions nor play with the hole of asps. We have felt the arrows of the Almighty; let us not provoke Him again to bend His bow, and to set us up for a mark of His displeasure.

It is not long since His waves and His billows went over us. Oh, let us not plunge ourselves again into the deep waters, nor cause Him to frown, whose frowns we have found to be so very terrible. Psalm 85:8: "God the Lord will speak peace unto His people, and to His saints. But let them not turn again to folly." It was indeed our folly to provoke so gracious a God; it was our folly to be indifferent and careless in our holy duties. Let the rod that has made us smart forever drive away the folly that was once bound up in our hearts. Doleful experience, along with anguish and tribulation, has told us what a dreadful thing it is to sin. By the judgments that we have groaned under, let us learn righteousness. We have come off of the rack with broken bones and with many wounds, which our good Physician has been pleased to set and heal again. Let us not rebel against His laws, lest we be put to the rack again. The corruptions that are within us will not bring us to it unless we cherish and approve them when they entice us to what is evil. Though they war against us, if our mind does not permit it they will not interrupt our peace with God. Let us not be secure; though the devil has left us, it may be only for a season, and he may return again with greater fury. Let us, during the comfortable quiet that we now enjoy, be preparing ourselves to resist and oppose all his assaults for the time to come. Let us, though we triumph through the grace of God, remember that our enemies are not yet fully overthrown; they are not ashamed of one defeat, but will rally their dispersed forces and come again.

What did we think of sin when it had caused the Sun of righteousness to be covered with clouds so that we could not see Him, nor feel His vital, quickening beams for many days? What did we think of it when it had set us on fire round about and brought us to the very gates of hell; when it sunk and overwhelmed and terrified us every minute? Let us never, henceforth, begin to parley with an enemy that has used us after such a barbarous and cruel manner.

6. After we are delivered from the dreadful apprehensions of the wrath of God, it is our duty to be publicly thankful. Psalm 66:16: "Come and hear, all ye that fear God, and I will declare what He hath done for my soul." It is for the glory of our Healer to speak of the

miserable wounds that once pained us, and of that kind hand that saved us when we were brought very low. It is for the glory of our Pilot to tell of the rocks and the sands, the many dangers and threatening calamities, that He, by His wise guidance caused us to escape. And now to see us on the safe shore may cause others who are yet afflicted and tossed with tempests to look to Him for help; for He is able and ready to save them as well as us. Like soldiers when a tedious war is over, we must relate our combats, our fears, and our dangers with delight; we must make our experiences known to doubting, troubled Christians, and to those who have not yet been under such long and severe trials as we have had.

7. The fears that we have had of God and His wrath must teach us to not inordinately fear any of those evils that are of a lower nature. Others who have been in ease and quiet all their days, who have had no trouble of conscience, or none for a long time, may be afraid of temporal evils and inconveniences; but to us who for a long time have been afraid of God Himself, how slight a thing the wrath of man appears to be! When we have been under the displeasure of Him who can kill the soul, what little cause have we to fear those who can only kill the body! Others may be afraid of a small distress, of a little bad weather, but it does not become us to fear who have been in so many storms for many months together. When we have been afraid of hell, there is nothing upon earth that looks so formidable. And if God has delivered us from the greatest dangers, we ought to believe that He will save us from the lesser troubles of our life. Our experience of so many terrible things should fortify our minds against all future afflic-

tions that are not of the same kind. I shall close this part of the chapter with these two bits of advice:

(1) If the servants of God are prone to such sad apprehensions of His wrath, then you have great cause to admire the peace that is in the world. Many a one among His people is crying, "The Lord has forsaken me. His wrath lies hard upon me." And if all His people, if all whose sins deserve His wrath, should all be so sensible of it, and complaining and crying out in like manner, oh, what a doleful cry that would be! It would be like the cry that was in Sodom, when it rained fire and brimstone; like the cry that was in Egypt, when they found all their firstborn slain! Oh, what a change would appear in the world if God should let out the sense of His displeasure upon all who have deserved it! This world would be like hell itself; all commerce and business would immediately fail, for what heart would men have for trading, buying, or selling if they knew that the very next moment they might be in hell!

It is one of the mighty acts of providence to maintain so great a calmness in a very sinning world; for if God were not infinitely patient, if He should open the eyes of all men to see His unspeakable majesty, holiness, and glory, combined with their offenses, the judgment they deserve, and their nearness to destruction, and then allow them (as He justly might) to be tortured with their guilty thoughts, to be tempted and overcome, and to sink into despair, oh, what lions and tigers men would be! They would tear themselves, and one another, to pieces. All the stillness of this earth would be turned into rage; all its joys would be turned into gloomy sorrows; all its laughter would be turned into weeping, wailing, and gnashing of teeth, and all the inhabitants thereof would be in anguish and curse their God and King.

Most are, for the present, insensible; they do not see where they are going, nor do they feel the horrors that they are capable of. They are treasuring up wrath, and it is His goodness that it does not immediately fall upon their heads in burning drops. There is but a thin partition between this world, that has in it so many various pleasant objects, and that world of flaming torture, where all is dismal and uncomfortable. And if the curtain were drawn aside, and the wicked apprehended that they were going there, oh, what consternation, what amazement, what paleness would be seen on every forehead that is now most proud and lifted up!

(2) Pray to God that you may not fall into such diseases, whereof Satan is apt to make very great advantage. And also pray that Satan may not be allowed to bring such sickness upon you as will indispose you for the service of your Maker. It is of long and severe afflictions that the devil makes great use, and in their own nature they lead to impatience, murmuring, and hard thoughts of God; and therefore they may be earnestly, but always with submission, prayed against. And though, if you are naturally melancholy, all the prayers in the world will not change your temper, yet by them that black humor may be kept from tyrannizing you, as it has done many thousands.

Pray against all such diseases as are not common to men, and which, being unknown, cannot be relieved; by affecting your natural spirits, they may cause you continually to think tormented, anxious thoughts, so that you shall be a terror to yourselves, and be unable to follow your calling. Yet these, by not affecting you as visibly as other diseases do, expose you to the uncharitable censures of your friends, and to the reproach of others.

We may also pray against such afflictions as disturb our reason, so that we cannot think nor exercise our faculties as we used to do. As it is lawful to pray for the removal of afflictions, so it is also lawful to desire that the strokes of God may not be heavy upon us, and that He would remember our frame, that we are but dust (Psalm 103:14).

If we have been in diseases that have overwhelmed us, it is our duty to pray, and to use all imaginable care that we do not fall into the like again, and to pray for others, so that they may never fall into any such; for of all other distempers, there is none so insupportable and so terrible. When we beg new favors of God for ourselves, we must remember others, and wish that they may never feel what we have felt. When beggars crave alms, they frequently use as a motive that the person of whom they are begging may be preserved from that misery whereof they themselves have had woeful experience. If they are blind, they will say, "God bless your eyesight." If they are lame, they will say, "God bless your limbs." If they are undone because of being burned, they will say, "God bless you and yours from fire." So we may say to our Redeemer, "Lord, mayest Thou never be put to fresh agonies by the deep distresses and agonies of Thy poor, bleeding servants." And to you who are good, we may say, "The Lord preserve your peace; the Lord bless you, and make His face to shine upon you; the Lord give you the sweet hopes and foretaste of heaven." And we wish that you may never drink so much wormwood and gall as we have drunk; that you may never see, know, and feel such terrors, and so much of hell as we have felt.

It is our duty, as I have said, to pray against such diseases which have an influence, for the most part, upon the mind—though it would be a very atheistic thought to imagine that all inward horror of conscience comes from bodily distress, for God, to whom all things are naked and open, can make immediate impressions of His wrath upon the soul, that shall fill it with sudden amazement and trouble. Yet I verily believe that of all the Christians who are under dreadful fears of wrath, and who are in long terror, there is not one in twenty but whose inward trouble comes either from a melancholy temper or from a multiplication of sharp and severe outward afflictions; and from these the devil takes an opportunity to throw his fiery darts, and to put them all into a flame. Those who know how great temptations attend long-continued afflictions will heartily pray against them.

To all of this I shall only add two questions, and so conclude this first section of this book.

QUESTION 1. If the anger of God is but for a moment, what shall we think of those with whom He is angry to their dying day, and who die in apprehension of His displeasure?

ANSWER. It is very true that His servants may die in these circumstances; and it is a very uncomfortable passage to their poor souls. It is very sad to the servants of God, for of such I speak, to go to heaven speaking, in one sense, the language of hell. It is a mysterious, and a very deep, transaction of providence that is wise and good, though it is not understood; but many a believer, even at the last, in his dejected apprehensions, thinks himself to be an heir of the curse only to find himself to be an heir of glory. Many a time the sun sets in a cloud, and yet arises in a marvelous light. Or, as Mr. [John] Dod once said to a minister who asked him what he could say to one who was leaving the world without any comfort, "What will you say to the Son of God Himself, who, when He was dying, complained that He was forsaken?" It is, as I mentioned before, sad to the person himself, and sad to his relations, whom he takes his leave of in such doleful expressions. His sorrowful departure may, after all their mourning, meet with joy in the great day; and their mutual sorrows at their parting may increase their joy when they meet again.

Many a one dies with a dreadful sound in his ears, as if he were a reprobate and a castaway, whom God will bless, and who, immediately after his dissolution, shall hear a comfortable sentence. Many a one Satan pursues and hunts like a bird upon the mountain, who shall arrive safely at his eternal home, where neither the devil's malice nor spite shall ever enter. Many a one wanders about here like Noah's dove, finding no rest, whom God will take into His ark. And though he seems to have fallen into the very belly of hell, yet he shall rise again in a blessed immortality. Those eyes, which were closed with tears, shall in peace see the Lord. We must not judge persons whose troubles continue to the last moment of their lives; for if they have been holy they shall enter into rest, though by a way that is very dark and frightful. Moses, by the displeasure of God against him for his provocation, died, and came short of that Canaan which he very much desired to possess. But when he was in heaven, he was fully satisfied; and in his

God he met with all that he could ever desire.

QUESTION 2. But suppose a person is distracted with the terrors of the Lord, and dies in the woeful condition. The anger of God toward such a one seems to be very great; and how is that consistent with the promise that all things shall work together for good to those who love Him? A person thus distracted cannot exercise any grace, cannot think of God aright, cannot commit himself to Jesus Christ, nor can he put his soul into any fit posture by faith and patience for his Lord's coming.

ANSWER. This is related to the former question, and what I said then may give some answer to this one. Indeed, all terror long continued in a sense of God's displeasure is attended with distraction. What man can have his eyes opened to see God against him (as he thinks), and to see hell (as he thinks) preparing for him, and yet have calm and quiet thoughts? It must fill him with horror and confusion; it must eclipse his reason, and put all his apprehensions into an inexpressible ferment to see himself so likely to perish. He can mind nothing else; he can think of nothing else but his danger and his misery. This always returns; this always perplexes and overwhelms him.

I have met with only one person [Richard Alleine, in his *Godly Man's Portion*] who ever handled this question, and, because of his judgment, his learning, and the good reputation he has in the churches of Christ, I will give you the substance of his answer.

1. This may be for the good of others. Is there not many a lesson that such as are not so afflicted may learn from so sad a providence? May they not learn to admire more the goodness and mercy of God to them,

that they are not in the same case? And to that extent it is so good for the person himself, though he does not discern it, that he is used as an instrument to promote the glory of God.

2. It may do him the same good as death will: it may deliver him from the evils to come, from beholding such sorrows to come on the church, or on his friends, as would have been a daily torment to him, and on which, being deprived of the use of his reason, he cannot reflect with so great a grief as otherwise he would have done.

3. By this means the wise God may have prevented his falling into many such sins and temptations as might have been very harmful to others, and might have more greatly defiled his own soul. And who knows but that this may be the case of the distracted person?

Thus, reader, we have been traveling as through a wilderness of fiery serpents. You have, I may say, borne me company while I have been showing you how God leads His children through a desert and the house of bondage. And I hope it has not been without some profit to some poor, troubled souls, for whose sakes especially I have so long insisted on this subject. In the next part, I shall, with God's assistance, lead you to the brighter side of the cloud, where you will not meet with things that are very doleful, but are rather very pleasant.

Part II

Chapter 14

"In His favor is life." Psalm 30:5

The several sorts of life that we enjoy by God's favor, and in what conditions of our present pilgrimage it more especially revives us

In God's favor is our natural life. We are the work of His hands, and His kindness and bounty continually maintain what He at first created. His providence secures us from innumerable dangers. He gives us meat and drink, health and strength; but His displeasure quickly deprives us of all these. It is said of all creatures, "What Thou givest them, they gather. Thou openest Thy hand, they are filled with good. Thou hidest Thy face, they are troubled. Thou takest away their breath, they die and return to the dust" (Psalm 104:28–29). It is this great God to whom we owe our peace, our plenty, our liberties, and the comforts we enjoy. He saves our bodies from plague and long sickness, from pining and wasting sorrows. All the delight we have in our friends, our families, or our relations flows from His goodness and His mere mercy. It is He who saves our houses from fire, our estate from robbers, and our country from desolating wars. Psalm 30:7: "Lord, by Thy favor Thou hast made my mountain to stand strong."

Man is the most noble creature, and the most dignified in all this lower world; and God has appointed the lower creatures to minister to his use and his delight. As one has observed, the air is his aviary, the sea and rivers his fishponds, the valleys his granaries, and the mountains his magazine. The first of these affords man creatures for nourishment, while the other affords metals for perfection.

The animals were created for the support of the life of man, and the herbs, the dews, and the rain for the same purpose; there is not the most despicable thing in the whole creation but is endowed with a nature to contribute something for our welfare, either as food to nourish us when we are healthy, as medicine to cure us when we are distempered, as a garment to clothe us when we are naked and arm us against the cold of the season, as a refreshment when we are weary, or as a delight when we are sad. All serve for necessity or ornament, either to spread our tables, beautify our dwellings, furnish our closets, or store our wardrobes. "The whole earth is full of His riches" (Psalm 104:24).

Spiritual life is in God's favor. It is He who draws the first lineaments of the new creature, and it is His hand that brings it to perfection. He first infuses a vital principle into the soul that is dead in sin, and it is He who maintains it afterwards against all the powerful motions of sin, against all the strategies and temptations of the devil. From His own grace He elected His people to salvation, and in time He gives them His Word and Spirit to quicken them, together with all those other blessings of adoption, justification, and sanctification, which are the product and the fruit of His electing love. The first quickening, and those exercises of life afterwards which His chosen perform; the first motion, and the renewed strength which they receive, to enable them to walk in His ways—these are His own gifts. It is His pardon that bestows upon His servants a new life when they were dead in law, and could see nothing ensuing but a terrible execution. It is His favor that contrived the way of our escape from death through the blood of Christ, and that was pleased to accept the sufferings of that holy Person in our stead. That faith which unites us to His Son, the Fountain of Life, and conveys quickening influences to us, is of His own operation. John 5:24: "He that heareth My Word, and believeth on Him that sent Me, hath everlasting life, and shall not enter into condemnation, but is passed from death unto life." This faith is of His bestowing, which enables us to be moderate in our prosperity, and to bear the cross when we are afflicted.

All those acts that are the fruit of the new birth, as well as the new birth itself, are the work of His own hands; for He gives both to will and to do. He teaches us to fight against our spiritual enemies, and His power, being employed for us, causes us to get the victory. When we are bewildered, His Word is our guide to direct us; when we are fainting, we have many great and precious promises to revive our spirits; when we are in darkness and danger, He is both our Sun and our Shield. His wind blows upon our gardens, and causes the spices to flow forth. He excites and quickens our graces when they begin to languish. And when we are lukewarm and cold, He makes us lively and fervent in the performance of our holy duties; for what the soul is to the body (to move it to natural things, to breathe, to eat, to walk, and the like), the same is the Spirit of God in our souls. It moves us to spiritual actions, such as the fear of God, love for Him, trust in Him, and all the works of righteousness, charity, humility, patience, and sobriety that are the motions of the new creature.

So we may say that this Spirit is the soul of our souls. Take away this Spirit and the soul resembles a dead body: it has no zeal for God, no compunction, no tenderness. When we are disconsolate, one look from God makes us of good cheer. When our hearts are numb and our eyes are dry, He melts them into tears with His love. When we are unfruitful, He sends His dew upon our branches, which makes us flourish in His courts and look fresh and green. When we are under spiritual decay, He causes us to thrive; when we backslide, He heals our backslidings. He brings us, through the great Mediator, into a nearness to and acquaintance with Himself. For as far as we are distant from Him, so far are we removed from true and real life. When we wander, He recalls us. He sends us fresh influences and establishes our goings when our motions are like those of a wounded body, very faint and tottering.

Eternal life is in His favor. Hence it is said in Romans 6:23 that eternal life is the gift of God. Psalm 16:11: "Thou wilt show me the path of life. In Thy presence is fullness of joy; at Thy right hand are pleasures forevermore." It is there that we are said to "see" God for the sight of His face is that which makes heaven such a glorious and delightful place. His wrath is that which kindles hell; the withholding of His favor makes it such a dark and gloomy dungeon. And the clear manifestation of His favor makes for all the glories of the celestial paradise. Therefore, when Jacob had a vision of God's favor to him, he said, "This place is none other than the gate of heaven" (Genesis 28:17).

Do not frame yourselves to a gross and material happiness; joy is all to be found in the love and favor of God. To see Him fills all the souls above with ineffable delight; to be deprived of this blessed privilege fills all the souls in misery with mourning and lamentation. To His saints, God will be all in all. His communications in heaven will be entire and full. The parts of creation are of divers orders; every one receives its portion of divine favor, different from that of others. He communicates Himself otherwise to the heavens than to the earth, otherwise to an angel than to a man. The earth has an image of His firmness; the sun has an image of His beauty; the heaven has an image of His immensity, and so with others. But there is no creature that has assembled in itself all the beams of the communications of God.

It shall be otherwise in paradise. God shall be all things in the saints, and they shall be filled with His favor. God is not so all in all in the faithful here. The troubles of our conscience, the weakness of our faith, the languors of our devotion, the shadows of our knowledge, our sins, our miseries, our sickness, and our death are the fruits of the fall and the malice of the devil. But in that felicity there shall be nothing of us in us, nothing of the impression of the devil. All shall be of God: our shadows shall be swallowed up by His light, and our weakness by His power.

It is a state of glory, and glory is a mixture of all the blessings of God, in a sovereignly perfect degree. That country that is above is indeed the land of the living: they live, and shall never die. But this earth is a region and a place of death. For besides the death which is natural, most men are dead in sin; and, truly, even those who are alive have but a weak and fainting life. There it is that the saints shall be admirers of the grace and favor of God, for it is that which, after various difficulties, innumerable temptations, and overwhelming fears, did at last bring them to that happy place.

When the poor, trembling saint, who thought himself cast off and forsaken of God, shall find himself in His arms, in His presence, in His heaven, how great will his joy and praise be! How he will ascribe all his life there to the mere favor and grace of God, who set him at liberty when, by his many sins, he had deserved to be bound in eternal chains! That favor and grace shall cause him to sing hallelujahs while others weep and wail forever. How will he admire that grace which has placed him in heaven, when so many others are in hell! And he will admire all the more when he considers that this distinction of states was freely made, and that the crown which will adorn his head was freely given. How every look at God will fill his soul with a wondering joy, because He freely gave His Son! How every view of Christ will increase his wonder! How he will wonder when he considers that Christ freely undertook the kind work of redemption, that He freely shed His blood and paid the debt which the sinner himself could never pay, and that He freely gave His Spirit, offering that salvation upon easy terms ("without money and without price") which cost Him very dearly! All the saints above will continually adore the riches of His grace, who admitted them to glory when they deserved to be shut out as well as others. They were deformed until He put His comeliness upon them; they were liable to death until He justified them; they were polluted in their natures until He renewed them, and were dying till He made them live; they learned nothing but what He taught them, and did nothing but what He enabled them to do. So that all must be wonderful in their eyes, from the beginning of God's design for their salvation to the conclusion of it. And when it is all finished, they must with loud praises sing, "Grace, grace!" Ephesians 2:8: "For by grace are ye saved, through faith; and that not of yourselves, it is the gift of God."

First, *no common mercy yields any comfort without the favor and love of God.* His loving-kindness is better than life (Psalm 63:3). If a man has all that he can wish for, everything that is splendid and delightful, everything that may please his eye or gratify his appetite, yet does not have these with the love of God, he is a miserable man. For it will mingle wormwood and gall with all his entertainments to think that God is his enemy, that these common blessings may conclude in hell, and that by all he eats or drinks he may be but fattening himself up for the day of slaughter. While he is allowing himself all the carnal gratifications, just a little consideration will allow him to discern that a two-edged sword is hanging over his head, and to see the gulf below that is ready to swallow him and devour all his hopes and joys; it will show him that all his comforts depend upon the slender thread of life, and that there is but a small partition between him and everlasting burnings. How this fills him with amazement and consternation, with fear and horror! And while he is most jovial, he may see a dreadful handwriting on the wall that may make his knees smite one against the other, and overthrow all his mirth and pleasure.

Alas, what does it signify to a man if all the world

smiles upon him, if he is under the wrath and frowns of God? They cannot shelter him from the coming storm nor screen him from the consuming fire. What small satisfaction it is to a condemned malefactor that the partakers of his wickedness applaud and caress him when his execution draws near, and when the day of his death will put an end to all his hopes. What peace can a sinner have who has the Lord of hosts against him? How can he lie down with comfort when he knows not but that he may awake in flames? With what ease can he look upon anything that he enjoys, when he knows not but that the next moment he may be destroyed and lost forever?

His next move may be to the grave and to a place full of torment! What comfort can he find from loud laughter, from cheerful company, or from vain sports when, it may be, the next moment he may be in a place where there is weeping and wailing and gnashing of teeth? Without the favor of God, all that is in the world—all its promises, all its pleasures, all its friendships, and all its entertainments—are mere vanity and vexation of spirit. If a man fares deliciously every day, if he drinks of the most sparkling wine, if he procures all the spices of the East and the riches of the West, those will not keep his heart from sorrows, nor will they secure him from the wrath to come. These things are wonderful while he can hear, smell, and taste, but what shall a man do who is a stranger to God when he is turned into a spirit? What shall an immortal soul do when all these corporeal goods have passed away? Where will his provision be? What will be his entertainment when he is lodged in the eternal world; when he shall no more hear the music that once charmed and gratified his senses;

when he shall no more see those beautiful things that he once admired and doted on? How must his soul, which pursued nothing but a temporal and carnal happiness, in his state of separation be filled with uneasiness and regret, with anguish and despair, to see itself stripped of all its ancient comforts, and to have nothing remaining that is comfortable; to be full of flaming desires and have nothing wherewith to quench the raging flame!

All that is present, without the favor of God, is but like grass on the housetops. It flatters us with a false opinion of its high station, and it looks fair and green, but the mower has nothing to fill his hand, and so it quickly fades and withers away. But God is the Fountain of Life (Psalm 36:9), a Fountain that supplies us with vital streams, and does not cease to refresh till it mingles with the river of delight that makes glad the city of God (Psalm 46:4). The glories of this world are soon covered with night and darkness, but He is a sun that ever shines, and from whence issues nothing but cheering and reviving light. Hence, a little that a righteous man has is better than the revenue of many wicked. Proverbs 15:16: "Better is little with the fear of the Lord than great treasure and trouble therewith." God's "little" is given with a blessing, and their multitude of things is attended with a curse. His temporal mercies are the forerunners of eternal ones. The righteous man tastes a sweetness in what he has because he is sure that it flows from the love of God. He can eat his bread with joy, and drink his wine with a cheerful heart, because his works are accepted (Ecclesiastes 9:7).

Second, *the favor of God is life in all temporal wants and afflictions.* No affliction can be borne if a man does not see that His fatherly goodness orders and directs the sharpest and most bitter cup. How can a man hold out in trouble when he knows not but that it may be to him the beginning of sorrow? With what grief must he weep, who does not know that his tears will ever be wiped away? How deeply must he sigh who looks upon his stroke to be the stroke of an enemy, and the chastisement of a cruel being (Jeremiah 30:14–15).

But the favor of God reconciles the soul to His most severe and mysterious dispensations, and teaches it to be silent under His hand. The favor of God teaches the soul to believe that, though He is angry now, yet He will not be so forever. When a poor soul looks round about and sees vexation and trouble over all the world, this favor of God encourages him to look above, where he finds calm and rest. When the men in whom he most confided prove to be deceitful, and when, from those from whom he expected the greatest kindness, he meets with the greatest disappointments, then he can have recourse to that God who will never change. When a man is left alone and forsaken, the Divine Presence gives him honey in the wilderness and turns his dungeon into a paradise. What he lacks in material things is plentifully supplied in his blessed and glorious Creator. And though he is poor in the world, yet he is rich in faith (James 2:5). Though he has nothing on earth that he can call his own, yet what a sweet support it is to think that God is his. Though he is cast off by all the world, what need he care if God receives him? If the world condemns him, what need he care when the sovereign Judge of all acquits him, and bids him be of good cheer because his sins are forgiven? He need not fear all their daring threats, their insolence and pride, when he can look up with Stephen and see Jesus at the right hand of God to plead his cause. Though he loses his friends and his earthly comforts, yet he has an almighty Friend that he can never lose.

Every correction is pleasant to a soul thus privileged; for however unpleasant it is for the present, he knows it shall promote his final good (Romans 8:28). He knows that his heavenly Father tutors him by so sharp a discipline for His own glorious kingdom, and so he relies upon His promise to bring him there. He knows that, when he is most pained, he is under the conduct of a tender and skillful Physician who, though He searches his sore, will not fail to advance and complete his cure. And therefore he is encouraged to entrust himself to Him, whom he shall praise as the health of his countenance and his God. He knows that when he is thrown down by sickness, the everlasting arms will be underneath; he knows that he shall be strengthened in his soul when his body begins to decay.

But without the favor of God, every little cross proves to be a burden too heavy for us to bear. When a man thinks to himself, "These pains that I feel are the wounds of an enemy"; when a man sees nothing but what is dismal, dark, and troublesome, and has no prospect of a dawning or approaching light—how sad and how overwhelmed must he be! How small a thing will sink us when the Comforter, who should relieve us, has departed (Lamentations 1:16).

Third, *this favor of God is life to us in the troubles of our conscience.* And there are no troubles in the world like these (Psalm 88:3–4). In all other troubles, our friends, by their kind discourses and pitiful expressions, may mitigate our sorrows; but how can they speak peace when God has declared war against us? Job 34:29: "When He giveth quietness, who then can make trouble? And when He hideth His face, who then can behold Him?" When God in His just displeasure raises a storm, who can make the waters smooth again? Once the sun has set, can all the power of nature make it rise again? Other troubles make the body droop, but these make the soul itself languish and pine away.

What but the favor of God can revive us when our hearts, under a sense of sin and guilt, begin to die within us? When our sins are set in order before us, who can free us from the formidable sight? Who but He can teach our hands to fight and to get the victory? When we are awakened with the sense of wrath, with the fear of hell and of destruction, who can close our eyes again? When we are under these inward wounds, who can pour oil on them; who can bind them up or heal them but He alone? When our consciences accuse us for our former and our latter sins, who can then plead our cause? Who can be on our side when God Himself has overthrown us? When the spiritual and holy law slays us, who can give us life? When the Word pronounces a dreadful sentence against us, who is able to reverse it? Who in heaven or on earth can be our helper if we do not find help in God? Who can give us any comfort when, through the terrors of our souls, we are looking for the wrath to come? Who will give us rest when we lie down and rise up again with a sense of the fury and displeasure of the Lord (Deuteronomy 28:66–67)?

When a soul is continually venting its presaging fears, and is saying, "Now I am troubled, but I shall shortly be in much greater trouble; now I am with my friends, but I may be shortly with devils; now I am on earth, but I may shortly be in hell"—then the favor of God brings life to the dying soul. One beam of His favor causes the disconsolate mourner to lay aside his mourning garments and rejoice.

After long terrors, how sweet is the voice of God that brings the news of a pardon! How welcome are the tidings of pardon to a malefactor at the very place of execution! And when God has brought us out of the deep waters and the miry pit, our very bones begin to rejoice. A cheerfulness is spread over every part when we think that the One whom we had so highly offended will yet be reconciled again; it raises us to transport and wonder: "What, will He be gracious and merciful to such as we are?" Is it not pleasant after a long war to be at peace, after hard labor to rest, and after a long journey to arrive at home? So it will be to see the face of God, after a long darkness, shine upon us again.

The Countess of Falkland, a devout lady, once said, "I have found Him whom I sought, the love of my soul and the joy of my heart, my Lord and my God. Now my joys return. I now behold the face of God, and feel His comforts in the service and worship of Him; and therefore every hour seems like five hours until the hour of prayer comes, till by contemplations and meditations I bring my God to my soul. I could wish every one of the days to be a day of solemn worship to God, to be a Joshua's day; the longest time of worship is too short for me, and my usual hours of devotion and meditation are too narrow a confinement for them. And when I am refreshed with the comforts of God, my heart dilates itself further by looking on the joys of heaven; for if there is such joy during the seedtime, how infinite is the joy of harvest!"

Indeed, what can be greater, more delicious, and more comfortable than to find that the Sun of righteousness will shine upon us with His healing beams, assuring us of His grace here and His glory in the world to come? What can be greater than to see hell, and that curse of the law in which we thought ourselves involved, to be under our feet; to see the yoke of sin broken and the power of death abolished; to see the heavenly sanctuary open and Christ our salvation on the throne, reaching out His hand to us, and guiding us to that happiness which He has purchased with His blood? Oh, how cold and miserable are all the delights of the world compared to such a delightful sight as this! And how happy are those people whose God is the Lord! No pleasures, no creature comforts, no merry songs can give quiet to a troubled soul without the favor and love of God. Till He comes, all other methods only make the clouds blacker and increase our sorrows.

Fourth, *His favor is life in the vehement assaults and temptations of the devil.* When the strong man comes against us armed, when he shoots his fiery darts, what can hurt us if God compasses us about with His loving-kindness as with a shield (Psalm 5:12)? He can disarm the tempter, restrain his malice, and tread him under our feet. If God is not with us, if He does not give us sufficient grace, so subtle, so powerful, so crafty an enemy will be too hard for us. How surely are we foiled and get the worse when we pretend to grapple with him on our own strength. How many falls, and how many bruises by those falls, have we gotten by relying too much on our own skill! How often have we had the help of God when we have humbly asked for it! And how surely are we to get the victory if Christ prays for us so that our faith does not fail (Luke 22:32)! Where can we go for shelter but unto God our Maker? When this lion of the forest begins to roar, how will he terrify and vex us until He who permits him to trouble us for a while is pleased to chain him up again!

Fifth, *God's favor is life, even in death itself.* He cures all the disorders of the soul. He weans it from the body and makes the passage to another world sweet and easy. He can take away the frightful, ghastly aspect of death and bestow upon it a pleasant and amiable look. And hence it is that sick people are often heard to say, "Oh, if I but had the favor and the love of God, I could be freely willing to die, even in this moment! If I but had His love, I could bear all these pains and quietly submit, though I have restless nights and weary days; for then I would be sure of eternal rest."

It is our estrangedness from God that makes us live in bondage all our days, and when our time to die comes it makes us very loath to depart. This sense of God's displeasure makes a deathbed into a bed of sorrow, and makes death the king of terrors. And who can but tremble when he finds himself leaving this world, and does not know what his portion will be in the next one; when he finds himself going to the judgment seat, but does not know whether he shall be acquitted or condemned there! How many times do the very thoughts of death cut us in our sickness to the very soul, because our spirits are clouded and our evidence for salvation has departed even before we depart, so that we stand trembling on the borders of eternity and would fain stay on earth, though we cannot? What but the favor of God will help us?

Psalm 73:26 tells us that when our heart and our flesh fail, He will be the strength of our heart, and our Portion forever. What but this will attend us through the shady vale! How can we part with our friends if God is not our Friend? How can we leave this earthly tabernacle if we do not have a house not made with hands? How shall we look upon so vast a change as that of time into eternity if we are not to change this mortal life for a better one?

But one smile from the face of God in that great and concluding work will keep us so that we shall not be afraid to die. One foretaste of heaven will make us bid this sinful world adieu with undaunted hearts. We shall then, like Moses, undress ourselves and die; we shall go down to the grave with the same cheerfulness with which Jacob went into Egypt, because our Mediator and our elder Brother lives, and has made good provision for us. We shall not be amazed to lie down in the dust once we have the hope of a blessed and a glorious resurrection. The day of our death will be a comfortable day if our blessed Lord is then pleased to tell us that, on the same day, we shall be with Him in paradise.

Chapter 15

Of heaven and hell, and of that spiritual death which has seized the greatest part of the world. The reason why good people are many times very willing to die, and the inexcusableness and misery of those who are without God's favor. And whence it is that some grow in grace more than others, and are more earnest for a share in the love of God

What a blessed and glorious place is heaven, which is full of God's favor! "The city had no need of the sun, neither of the moon to shine in it; for the glory of God did lighten it, and the Lamb is the light thereof" (Revelation 21:23; see also Revelation 22:2–5). It is the land of the living, and it is no wonder that death shall never enter there. Here indeed God hides Himself. He is hidden under the veil of the created world, and under the abundance of mysterious providences; for though His throne is established in righteousness, yet clouds and darkness are round about it (Psalm 97:2). Beams of His glory everywhere break forth through every creature, every providence, every law, and every ordinance of His; yet much of His glory that shines in creation is hidden by a train of second causes, through which few look to the first cause. His work in the world is carried on in a mystery. His interest lives, but is depressed; they who are devoted to him are supported indeed by His invisible hand, but in the meantime are for the most part low and afflicted. But in that eternal state, as Mr. [John] Howe points out in his *Treatise on Delighting in God,* the veil shall be rent and He will show Himself in a brighter manner. His glory will shine out with direct and pleasant beams to all the beholding and admiring eyes. He will there give forth the full and satisfying communications of His love that will cheer, satisfy, and refresh a vast multitude of grateful and adoring spirits.

Here the souls of good men are depressed by the misrepresentations of Satan, and by the frequent jealousies and suspicions of their own guilty souls; but there they shall see Him as He is, and what will increase their joy is to see Him to be their own God forever. No storms shall there molest their peace; nothing shall interrupt their eternal calm; not a vain, tumultuous, repining, or uneasy thought shall assault their peaceful and quiet hearts forever. No more shall they cry out, "Is His mercy clean gone? Has He forgotten to be gracious?" For they shall be with Him in His own presence. Here His family is composed of several distressed, mourning children, and when some praise Him their praises are disturbed by the groans of others, or by their own sins. But there they shall all be clothed with praise, and none shall be sick or die.

If we but knew that there was a place in the world where people never die, the love that all have of life would put them upon many inquiries as to how they might get there. This country is heaven; from thence death, fear, and consternation are banished forever. It is to there that we should lift up our eyes; there we should direct our hearts. In heaven the favor of God shines with an unclouded brightness. They who are inhabitants of that holy place are employed in an honorable attendance on their mighty King; they need not, they desire not, any of those enjoyments which are here below, any more than favorites of a prince desire a lower station, a poorer cottage, or some obscure and forlorn retreat.

And, alas, what are all our pleasures and our most splendid entertainments to that bread, and to those spiritual and intellectual joys, which angels and glorified souls feed upon! The first hour, the first day of joy above, is better than an age of joys here below. If one day spent in His courts, in His love and praises here, is better than a thousand elsewhere, what will one day in heaven be! There we shall not live upon things meaner than ourselves; we shall there have no mean complacencies, nor dishonorable cares. In the favor and light of God we shall have a taste of all excellencies and delights, without the least mixture of evil. And what transports shall we have when we come to the full view of Him, the light of whom, even at this distance, was so sweet and comfortable to us, when, after all our doubtings, fears, and sad thoughts, we find that we have, through many dangers, gained our port!

If the favor of God is life, oh, what a doleful place is hell, where this favor never comes (Job 10:22)! How black is their darkness, and how long and tedious is their night, who shall never have the dawn of day! Oh, how terrible and how frightful is the second death! It is a death that torments the separated soul, a death that banishes it from the presence of the Lord, a death that excludes it from all comfortable sight of God! There the damned see Him as a judge, and feel His amazing terrors; but they would gladly (if they could) wrap themselves in darkness, and never see such a frowning and dreadful God. There is anguish, woe, and tribulation, and the continual cry of that place is, "God has gone away from us forever! His face and His light cheer His saints, but they scorch us and puts us all into a flame." This is the language of their misery. They feel that God will show them no pity; that He is deaf to their cries and has shut up His bowels, that once yearned over them, in eternal wrath; that He once would indeed have been reconciled and they would not, and now they shall never have an offer of His favor any more.

Oh, poor, forsaken souls! What shall they do who have no God to give them help, no Mediator to plead their cause, no Physician to bind up their wounds, and no kind hand to give them the least comfort! For them, there is nothing but wrath, and no love; nothing but vengeance and destruction, and no mercy with it! The servants of God never taste so much of hell as when His face is hidden; it brings upon them desolation, terror, and the very pangs of death, but now and then they have some support, some beams of light. In that doleful place, on the other hand, there is nothing else but sorrow and despair. Here, in all the temptations of His servants, Christ is concerned. He sympathizes with them, and in His due time sends them relief. But He will never concern Himself with the damned, nor cast one gracious eye upon them. They are fallen, and He will not raise them up; they have perished, and they must perish; they thirst indeed, but shall never have a drop of water to cool their tongues.

What will these poor creatures do when they are overwhelmed with the wrath of the One who is almighty! Oh, how loud will be their cries, and how dreadful will be their complaints, when, after millions of years have passed, they have still as many more yet to come! When they have been long tossed upon the lake of fire, they will never be nearer the shore, never hear one comfortable word from the mouth of God! Oh, how glad they would be to have one smile of His face, one day's refreshment!

But it will not be; the gulf is fixed and the sentence is irrevocable. Isaiah 27:11: "He that made them will not have mercy on them, and He that formed them will show them no favor." Oh, what can be thought more desolate than to be forsaken by God, in whom alone is life, and to be cast out into outer darkness! And how great will be the consternation of the great day, when He shall say to the wicked, "Depart from Me." To hear that voice and those words, "Depart from Me," will be their hell. They shall not be able to turn their thoughts from the contemplation of their own miseries, nor their eyes from the sight of those objects that will fill them with grief and horror, and will be themselves abominable; for what a despicable, deformed thing even now is an apostate angel that has been stripped of the life of God!

If life is in the favor of God, the greatest part of the world is dead; for most are alienated from Him by their evil works. Most are stupid and insensible, in a dead slumber, and are His enemies. "She that liveth in pleasure is dead while she liveth" (1 Timothy 5:6). And if this is a symptom, and a mark of death, how many dead we have among us! How many find enough time for their games, their sports, and their recreations, and find no time wherein to call upon the Lord and seek

His favor! How many eat and drink and are merry, even while their souls are in the greatest danger, and their Maker is their enemy! It is a sign—when they are so insensible of their greatest interest, and have so little taste and liking of divine joys—that they are spiritually dead. How much greater is the number of the dead than of the living! How many families there are that are without prayer, without any sense of God at all, and in which the whole family is dead!

And in those families where some are alive, how many are there who are not yet quickened! How many good parents are mourning over their dying children, whom they cannot bring to life! They see them stepping into the grave, and all their entreaties, all their tears, and all their prayers cannot bring them out of there!

In our congregations, how many there are who have indeed a name to live, but are dead (Revelation 3:1); who have never yet been in earnest for their salvation, who allow days and years unconcernedly to roll over their heads, and are never the nearer to heaven at the conclusion of the year than they were at the beginning of it. They have, indeed, it may be, risen early and sat up late; but all their cares have been for the body, as if they had no soul. They have grown crooked from looking downward, and are as earthly and sensual as if they had no heaven to mind.

And what a heartless thing it is for ministers to find that they spend their labor in speaking to the dead who, in a great measure, remain dead still! They do not, however, do it without the hope that at some time or another their Master will say to them what He did to Ezekiel (see Ezekiel 37:2–6).

Oh, what a plague is among us, and we do not feel it! Gray hairs are here and there upon us, and we do not discern them. How many captives does the prince of darkness have who are in no way grieved at their own captivity! How many are strangers to the favor of God, who never saw His reconciled face, never felt the quickening influences of His Spirit to this very day, and yet rejoice as if all was safe and well! They sit down to eat and drink, and rise up to play, and in the midst of those diversions death seizes their bodies; and when their bodies die, their souls die, and are past our help. Oh, my friends, if you have any life or compassion, put on the bowels of Christ and take up a lamentation for the dead.

Why, then, are good Christians so willing to depart from this world? It is because the favor of God is their life, and when they are dead they can live again. Because they cannot see God and live, they are content to die that they may enjoy the blessed sight. They remember very well that they are strangers and pilgrims on earth, that affliction is as proper to this world as heat in summer and storms and snow in winter. They know that, however difficult their fare is, however harshly their are treated, they are traveling to their dearest country. And every one of those holy pilgrims on the way to Zion is continually crying out in this manner: "As for you, O city of God, how great and transcendent is your beauty! I desire nothing but you. I think of nothing but you. I pant, I thirst, I long for your felicity. How I long for you, you sure reversion of never-fading pleasures! O paradise, you are the recompense of my travels, and the sole aim of all my hopes. How fain would I leave these habitations of clay to dwell in your eternal and delightful mansions! What would I not give to enjoy the liberty of your citizens! O Jerusalem, Jerusalem, when shall I leave this ruinous and shaken house? Oh, that I had the wings of a dove; for then I would fly away and be at rest. Oh, when shall I arrive there? How long? Will it be before I enter the courts of heaven?"

Oh, how have many on whom the face of God has comfortably shone longed to depart and be with Him! They bear all disappointments and vexations in the hope of this; and pain and sickness are welcome because they are as the wheels of their chariots, and drive them nearer to their home. Such as these are like a well-freighted ship that is ready to sail, and waits only until a favorable wind presents itself. They do not die by surprise, for these happy travelers to glory are always on the road that leads them to the blessed place above. Death is not frightful to them because they have often meditated on what it is to die, and what is required for so vast a change.

There are, indeed, a great many formidable things in death—the separation of the soul, the many foregoing pains, and an innumerable army of sorrows and griefs that march before the king of terrors—all which, by faith, these holy persons overcome; they know that Christ has taken from death all its poisonous and hurtful qualities. Their distance from God is the trouble of all good people; and when He shows Himself they rejoice, just as when He hides Himself they mourn. And hence, many a religious person, when he comes to die, has been heard to say, "I would not now, for all the world, be without an interest in Christ. I always found Him to be a good Master, and I still find Him to be so.

He has taken away the sting of death, and I am willing to go unto the house prepared for all living; for my Lord has been there before, and has perfumed and sanctified the grave. You look dreadful, O grave, to flesh and blood, but not to faith; and I bid you welcome as the way to glory. I commit my body to you, to keep it safe until the resurrection, when my soul, which I now commit into the hands of my Savior, shall come and fetch it back again."

With this sense of the favor of God the martyrs so cheerfully persevered, and looked upon their dying day as the day of their coronation. This favor made them scorn the threats and the frowns of tyrants, and all their rage and fury. By this they went to the fiery furnace as to a bed of roses, because they knew God would be with them there. In the hope of His acceptance old and young, grave matrons and tender virgins, have embraced the stakes and kissed the flames, and freely died. They have rejoiced and looked with an unmoved countenance on death, while those who were spectators to their patience could not look upon them without flowing eyes. To these they have said, "Death would be frightful if we looked no further; but it comforts us when we see the crowns, the hallelujahs, and the glories that wait for us on the other side. This will deliver us from an evil world, from our corrupt hearts, and from all those sins under which we have long groaned. This will bring us to Him, whom all our days we have longed to see. Our friends bewail us here, but angels are waiting for our souls, and will be glad to convey them to Christ, their Lord and ours."

In such a way those forty martyrs, whom Basil and so many of the Fathers celebrated, encouraged one another. When neither promises nor threats would prevail with them to forsake their God, they were condemned to be exposed on ice so as to be killed by the cold. When they saw the place, they cast away their garments and ran to it with delight, not as if they were going to their death, but as if they were going to gather the spoils of victory. "As with our garments," said they, "we shall put off our old man, our sin, and all the corruptions of our nature. What a great thing is it if the servant suffers that which His Lord endured before Him! We were the cause that He was disrobed and afflicted. The cold is troublesome, but paradise is sweet. This ice afflicts us, but the rest we will find there delights us. Let us endure this cold a little while longer, and the warmth of Abraham's bosom will refresh us forever. We shall exchange this bitter and tempestuous night for an eternal day. Let us turn our backs upon the world, and, seeing that we are to die once anyway, let us now die so that we may live. And, O Lord, let us be acceptable to Thee when we are offered up to Thee by this painful death."

Thus they endured the cold night, rejoicing in the hope of glory. What wonders of courage and of zeal have been produced by the sense of the favor and the love of God!

And then, this being true, how inexcusable are those who refuse this favor of God, in which alone is life! Who would choose to be a beggar when he might be the King's favorite? Who would choose to embrace a dunghill when he might be treated with plenty and all suitable accommodations? Who would choose to be sick or blind when he might receive his health or his sight? And yet this is the sad case of sinners! God would be their Friend, and they will not have Him to be so. He would save them, but they will not be saved. He would bless them, but they choose instead to be cursed. How many are there who prefer a lust before a Savior, earth before heaven, and the applause of their vain, sottish companions to the approbation of the all-seeing Judge!

O blind sinners! Why will you lay hands upon yourselves, and do all you can to deprive your souls of life? As Joseph Symonds says in his *Treatise of Sight and Faith,* what a sad thing it is to deny sustenance to your own life! The breath of God is in you. What shall be done to the man who starves the child of a prince? What have we of comparable worth to spiritual vigor, agility, courage, and peace of soul? And shall we who have a door of life offer contempt to divine goodness, and violence to our own life, by not using what God has put in our hands for our relief? Is there so much allure in destruction, and so much beauty in eternal flames, that you cannot forbear going there? Why will you allow your souls to starve while you are contriving to gratify the flesh? Why will you still serve the devil and your own sins? Are they such good masters, and will they pay you so well in the latter end? Are you content to have the pleasures of sin for a season, though you lose your share in paradise? Oh, what bitter reflections on so bad a choice will this cause hereafter!

When you shall lift up your eyes in misery, and see the kingdom of heaven afar off, you shall say, "I was once offered that kingdom and those joys, and I would not have them. I was once fair for salvation, but I slighted it. I might have had the favor of God, but I would not have it. Oh, my cursed sins! How you have deceived me! You promised me delight, but you have brought me bitterness and woe; you promised me safety, but you have made me perish. Oh, that some angel or saint might be sent to bring me some relief! The Word of God told me of that glory. His ministers earnestly entreated me to prepare for it; my friends were always bidding me to leave my wicked course; my conscience checked me for it, but I broke through all these exhortations and these checks, and so have come, laden with guilt, to eternal misery. I was at my games and sports when I should have been upon my knees. I had time indeed, strength, health, and many helps and advantages. Oh, that I had, all my days, watched and striven and denied myself; then I would not have come to this place of torment! Oh, that my sun would rise again! Oh, that I might have another trial, and more time! But, alas, the Judge is now my enemy. I have heard my sentence, and He will not change His purpose! I am condemned, and I am lost forever!"

O sinners, if you would never fall into such a hopeless state, then now, even now, seek the face of God. Have you not already spent enough time in sin, in walking in the imagination of your own hearts, and in the sight of your own eyes? Have you not loved your sottish pleasures long enough? Oh, come, leave the tents of wickedness; come and love your God, for He is ready to receive you. Come to Him, and all your sins shall be forgiven! Do not let mercy itself, which is speaking for your hearts, be denied. Who will be so good a friend as God? Who will abide with you when life itself is gone?

And now, surely, the heart of some sinner begins to relent, saying, "Though I never prayed in secret before, yet now I will begin to pray. Though I lost the abundance of my youth and my health, I will strive to lose no more. I have put off God and my conscience with vain excuses and delays; I will put them off no more. God, who gave me life, shall have my thoughts, my heart, and my endeavors. And I will ever admire the riches of His love, if He will pardon such a malefactor, condescend to such a worm, and entertain such a prodigal as I have been."

In what a woeful condition, then, are those poor sinners who are without this favor of God! To how great a danger are they exposed every day! And, which is a part of their misery, they do not know it. Spiritual death has closed their eyes, and they do not see where they are going. What a sad object is a poor sinner who is yet a stranger to this God, who is every hour liable to His eternal wrath, who seeks the friendship and favor of men, and who has no thoughts of his Creator, no dread of His displeasure, no taste or relish of His love!

Surely they must be fallen into a deep sleep whom all the terrors of the Lord, all the threats of His Word, and all the calls of His ministers will not awaken! With what peace can you eat and drink, or work and rest, while so great a God is your enemy? Will His wrath, that makes the devils in their hellish agonies roar and tremble, be tolerable to you? When His vengeance pursues you, where will you run for help? When He frowns, what will it avail you though all the world should smile upon you? When He casts you off, who will show you pity? When He condemns you, who will plead your cause?

Do you not know that your life is short, that your change is near, and that the Judge is at the door? Do you not know that this world will leave you, so that you may quickly go into another? And can you dwell with eternal burnings? Can you venture to go to the judgment seat before you have an interest in Christ? Are you fruitless and barren here, and yet you think to flourish in the celestial paradise? Do you remain dead here under all the means of grace, and yet hope to live forever? What pleasures are those which enchant you that you will not come and taste the joys of God? Who will be a better Friend to you than He? If you laugh at destruction, that will not make it further off.

Oh, do not let the devil be your master, nor the world your god. Do not let sin cheat and impose upon you with its false and counterfeit delights. Others are mourning in secret after the Lord, and do you not have as much cause to mourn as they? Others are striving with earnest prayers and supplications and holy endeavors to enter in at the narrow gate, and will it open to you by itself? Or have you not also souls to save as well as they? Others read, hear, and pray, doing all they can for salvation, being afraid to fall under the power of eternal death; and have you no cause to fear? Why is it that when they are running so fast in the way of heaven, you run faster in the way of hell? Why do you tend and regard your bodies with great care to preserve them from pain, and yet allow your souls to languish and pine away?

If you knew how miserable you are without the favor of God, it would create a vast horror in your thoughts. How deeply you would groan if you were sensible of the vast load of guilt that is upon you! How earnestly you would cry for help if you saw where you are sinking, and where you are likely to be forever! How you would start if you perceived that the devil flatters you so that he might destroy you! It is his work you do, his lusts you embrace, and his designs you comply with! There is no dungeon so doleful, no place so full of torment, no fire so hot as that where he leads you, and which will be more insupportable to you because you let him lead you captive at his own pleasure. If we receive any life from God, let us bewail our dead; let us pity those who have no pity for themselves; let our eyes and our hearts melt and be troubled for them, though they will not shed any tears for the sadness of their own case.

Hence we see the reason why some grow more in grace than others do, and are also more serviceable in the world. Fear and sadness dampen and contract our spirits, but joy and comfort dilate them and cause them to act with sprightliness and vigor. The displeasure of God weakens the faculties and powers of the soul by the terrible apprehensions with which it is then filled; but His favor fills it with delight. Faith is then strong and unmoved when it can behold God, His Son, and the promises, all as her own portion. Love is then genuine and durable when it has a warm sense of the love of God; and under the constraining power and force of this love, the heart is dissolved into a tender sorrow and a true repentance. It is the shining of the face of God that makes us active for His glory and unwearied in His service. And under His pleasant and reviving beams, the Christian travels with delight and haste to His dearly beloved home. But when this favor is eclipsed, this sun covered with a cloud, then the poor Christian is as one who travels in the darkness of the night, one who has lost his way; he is full of fear and perplexity. And so is the deserted soul, but the first beam of day makes him go on and finish his course. And then the promise of Isaiah 35:1–2 is accomplished: "The wilderness and the solitary place shall be glad, and the desert shall rejoice and blossom as the rose; it shall blossom abundantly, and rejoice even with joy and singing."

The favor of God is as dew upon the grass; it causes fruit where there was nothing but withering and decay before. According as God is pleased to favor us or be displeased, so there is either a great ease on our spirits or restlessness and indisposedness. His favor excites admiration and praise, love and joy; and with these cheerful affections a man may do a great deal for God, whereas, most usually, with our departing comforts our strength departs. What can we do for the salvation of others if we are under a great fear that we ourselves shall not be saved? How can we work in the vineyard if we fear that our Master will cast us out in anger? Psalm 51:11–12: "Cast me not away from Thy presence, and take not Thy Holy Spirit from me. Restore unto me the joy of Thy salvation, and uphold me with Thy free Spirit."

And so it is that the favor of God, first, delivers us from those lusts and corruptions which chain us down so that we cannot run in the way of God's commandments. Second, it keeps us from being entangled with the affairs of the world that subjugate and enthrall our minds. Third, it is in us a spirit of adoption, and frees us from those slavish fears of the justice, sovereignty, holiness, and power of God which overwhelm our hearts. Job 22:26–27: "Then shalt thou have thy delight in the Almighty, and shall lift up thy face unto God. Thou shalt make thy prayer unto Him, and He shall hear thee."

The favor of God gives us access to the throne of grace; it takes off our unwillingness to perform holy duties, and our restraint in them; it gives us a freedom and enlargement of soul, and it is then as the flower that opens itself to the shining sun, says Jeremiah Burroughs in his *Excellency of a Gracious Spirit.* Though a man suffers no alteration in his constitution or outward appearance, yet, if God withdraws, all greatly decays within him. When the Spirit came upon Saul in 1 Samuel 10:6, "He prophesied, and was turned into another man." He was inspired with greater courage, and had a more heroic and better qualified disposition; but when this spirit was taken away, an evil spirit succeeded in its place. Then Saul was no longer the same; there was nothing but fear and horror; despair and vexation raged in his breast. He was in all respects a very miserable man. He had the name of a king, but was divested of all royal qualities when he was left by the God of Israel and went to ask advice from the witch of Endor. See his own complaint in 1 Samuel 28:15: "I am sore distressed; for the Philistines make war against me, and God is departed from me, and answereth me no more, neither by prophets nor by dreams."

Does not every Christian find by his experience that he is not the same in his duties at one time as he is at another? Sometimes his heart melts under a sense of the love of God, and he feels such a vital influence of the Spirit that it seems as the foretaste of heaven. He seems to be ever swallowed up with joy; he seems to be within the courts of God, and to set his foot within the land of promise. Oh, who can express the sweetness that spreads over all the panting soul when it sees the face of God! It lives indeed, but hardly knows whether it is in the body or out of it, so many wonders of grace and mercy it views!

And yet this same person who is now in triumph at the gate of heaven may, at another time, be bewailing his own case and in deep sorrows, as if at the very door of hell. When the dew of God ceases to fall upon him, he no longer looks so fresh and fair, but sighs and groans for his Savior, though a little while ago he could say, "I am my Beloved's, and He is mine." The same person may look upon God as a Judge who before thought Him to be a Father.

The life which God gives His servants may be weakened, but it is never extinguished; there is oftentimes upon them a spiritual fainting, though not a total death. When the Spirit does not produce any cheerful motion, nor display any of His usual beams of light—so that they are tossed between fear and hope, between the sentiments of life and the apprehensions of death—what dryness, what hardness comes upon our hearts! How little life, enlargement, or comfort have we in duty when the Spirit of God has withdrawn from us! All our endeavors, all our strivings within ourselves do not warm our spirits as He used to do. How little delight we have in prayer, and how loath we are to pray then. We know how lame and defective our petitions and desires are, and we are at as great a loss as was Job when he said in Job 23:3, 8: "Oh, that I knew where I might find Him, that I might come even to His seat. I go forward, but He is not there; and backward, but I cannot perceive Him."

And hence you see the reason why the servants of God so earnestly beg this favor, and are so deeply troubled when it is removed. It is their life, their portion, their all. Everything is strangely changed; all its comeliness, beauty, and glory vanish when the life is gone. Life is the pleasant thing; it is sweet and comfortable.

But death, with its pale attendants, raises a horror and aversion to it everywhere. The saints of God dread the removal of His favor and the hiding of His face; when it is hidden, a faintness, and a cold amazement and fear seize upon every part; and they feel a strange bitterness, anguish, and tribulation, which make their joints tremble, and are to them as the very pangs of death. Psalm 22:14–15: "I am poured out like water, and all my bones are out of joint; my heart is like wax; it is melted in the midst of my bowels. My strength is dried up like a potsherd, and my tongue cleaveth to my jaws; and Thou hast brought me into the dust of death." (See also Psalm 38:2–10; Job 23:8–9; and Psalm 13:1–4.) Psalm 27:9: "Hide not Thy face from me; put not Thy servant away in anger. Thou hast been my help, leave me not, neither forsake me, O God." Psalm 69:17: "Hide not Thy face from Thy servant, for I am in trouble; hear me speedily." Psalm 4:6: "There be many that say, 'Who will show us any good?' Lord, lift Thou up the light of Thy countenance upon us."

Chapter 16

The favor of God is diligently to be sought, and what is to be done that we may obtain it

1. Seeing that in the favor of God is life, seek it earnestly. If I were to bid you to take care of your lives or your estates, you would quickly think it a needless request because your own safety and interest would prompt you on to it. But if we ministers bid you take care of your souls, there indeed you can hear one sermon after another, one exhortation after another, and still be as secure and careless as before. We hear many people wishing for other things, and very few of them are desiring this favor of God. We hear the poor say, "Oh, that I were rich!" and the sick say, "Oh, that I were well!" The prisoner is sighing for his liberty, the trader is busily concerned for his gain, and the merchant for good returns; but, oh, how few there are who are saying, "Oh, that I might find grace in the sight of God. Oh, that I might be His, and He mine!"

Many have their eyes fixed upon the world, admiring and doting on it, though they see daily how vain it is, and how its fashion passes away. But, oh, how few there are whose eyes are fixed upon heaven, and whose hearts are panting after the living God! If I could teach you a way to be the favorites of a king or some powerful or great men, you would think to derive great advantages from such a privilege, and quickly strive to get it. But here is one greater than they, even the King of

Kings, whose favor is offered to your acceptance and your choice; though His majesty might confound you, yet His goodness bids you welcome into His presence. "Seek and ye shall find; knock and it shall be opened unto you" (Matthew 7:7). I think that every soul here would rejoice to know that it is possible for him to have God to be his own God; that however abject, however sinful he may have been, yet he may be advanced and honored by the Lord of glory if he will but return. When He bids us seek His face, we should answer, "Thy face, Lord, will we seek" (Psalm 27:8). And we should seek it presently, while He may be found, lest sickness, death, or judgment should prevent us, and lest, grieved with our delays, He should cover Himself from us by an eternal separation, and we should seek Him and not find Him. Because we did not hear His calls, He will shut out all our cries and laugh when our calamity comes like an armed man (Proverbs 1:26).

If you have no need of Him to forgive your sins, to heal your souls, to protect you from danger, or to bring you salvation, then leave this work alone. If this is your case, then be unconcerned whether you seek His favor or disesteem it, whether He is your Friend or your enemy. But if you have need of God, as I am sure you have, then pour out your supplications to Him for His grace and say, "O Lord, I have been dead in sin, but I know that nothing is impossible for Thee. Thou openest the graves and makest even the dead live. Let my soul feel Thy almighty power and have a share in the first resurrection, so that over me the second death may not prevail. Oh, let me be one of Thy children, one of Thy blessed family, one whom Thou lovest, and whom Thou wilt love forever. Thou hast pardoned many who were once as guilty as I have been. Oh, magnify the riches of Thy grace in blotting out my iniquities. Thou hast quickened many who were once dead; let me also be quickened by the vital influences of Thy Spirit. Many prodigals Thou hast received; let me not be thrown off. Many Thou hast blessed; many blessings Thou hast still in store; therefore, bless me, even me also, I pray Thee, O my God."

2. Join endeavors to your prayers, and use all the means of grace with appropriate diligence. 2 Corinthians 5:9: "We labor that, whether present or absent, we may be accepted of Him" (see also Psalm 119:58). Oh, do not mock Him with a mere form of words! Rather, let your affections and your words be joined together. Be as the hart that, when it pants for the water brook, runs with all the speed it can there. Once your souls are warmed with a sense of God, use all the care you can to maintain the sacred and the comfortable flame, lest by neglect it be extinguished and go out again.

For a man to wish that he had the favor of God, and not to use all His prescribed means, is foolish and ineffectual. This would be as if a traveler should sit in a lazy posture without any motion in the road, and yet wish to be at his journey's end; as if a man should wish to be learned, and yet never read or study; as if a soldier should wish for victory, and yet never fight; or as if a farmer should wish for a gainful crop, and yet neither plow nor sow. A careless wish for God's favor will not serve the turn. You must pray constantly, and resort to those places of worship where He usually manifests His presence in His own ordinances, and read His Word with reverence, humility, and frequency. You must seek Him with your whole heart; you must expect and wait, though it is long, for a gracious answer to your prayers. For how many days will men give their attendance for some preferment or high place in a prince's court! And it should not grieve us to stay for the favor and the love of God; for once it is bestowed, it will requite all your pains and labors (1 Corinthians 15:58).

In the quest for this, you will meet with manifold trials and great opposition; your carnal nature and your old sins will present motives to your sense to draw you back. Satan will perplex you with a thousand doubts and troubles. You may be sure that this lion will roar when he is likely to lose his prey. But none of this must be allowed to discourage you. The favor of God is so great a mercy that you may be justly importunate and restless until you get it, notwithstanding all the dangers that you meet with. No great things are obtained without difficulty. You will see hereafter that it was worth the trouble to take pains in a matter of so great consequence.

You now find that after all the pleasure of sin is past, it leaves a sting and fills your minds with bitterness and trouble; but you'll find hereafter nothing but comfort, nothing but an overflowing pleasure in the love of God. And you'll find it to be so very pleasant that you will wish you had done more for Him than you have done. There's not a soul in heaven who repents of the pains he took to get there.

3. You must be deeply sensible of your own miserable and undone state without God's favor. Luke 5:31: "They that are whole need not a physician, but they that are sick." Matthew 18:11: "The Son of Man is come to save that which is lost." Job 33:27–28: "He looketh upon men, and if any say, 'I have sinned, and perverted that

which was right, and it profiteth me not,' He will deliver his soul from going down to the pit, and his life shall see the light." Once you are convinced that your sins have made God angry, and that His anger is very just and yet so severe that if it continues it will be intolerable; once you are sensible what a great God you have provoked, what a holy law you have broken, what a hell you have deserved—you will reckon it as a great mercy that you are not already there, from whence there is no return. If your conscience has been awakened with a deep impression of His wrath, all the riches, honors, and pleasures of this world will seem to you to be very poor and empty things. The sight of the sin that has deceived you, that has defiled you, that has exposed you to so great a danger will fill you with shame and sorrow, with fear and trouble. Of all your desires this will be your chief and your only desire: "Let me have the favor of God, whatever else I lack. Let me have His favor or I die forever." You will be restless and unsatisfied till you have this hope.

The reason why men are so industrious for all other things, and so little concerned by the favor of God, is that they are blinded by the devil and their own lusts, and are under a spiritual insensibility. But once you find sin to be bitter, this will be very sweet. If awareness of sin has thrown you into painful agonies and deep distress of soul, this will greatly comfort and revive you. You will see then great cause to humble and to loath yourself; you will not find any cause of pride or of the boast of the Pharisee. Rather, in the better posture and temper of the publican, you will say, "Lord, be merciful to me, a sinner."

Never did a traveler, after a tedious journey, more

desire his home, or a mariner, long tossed with tempests, desire to see the quiet shore, than you will desire the favor of God. When you have been scorched with inward thirst, you will pant for this Fountain of love wherein you may quench your thirst. When you have been in a long war with God, and come at length to see the danger of it, oh, how beautiful will be the feet of those who are ambassadors of peace! You will then say what is said in Luke 1:53: "He hath filled the hungry with good things, and the rich He hath sent empty away."

4. The favor of God is to be had only in and through Jesus Christ, and you must apply yourselves to Him for it. It is not all your zeal, your repentance, your self-denial, or your mortifications that will, of themselves, be sufficient to bring you to the favor of God. Though you labor in His service all the day, and mourn for your miscarriages all the night, what satisfaction will this give to His offended justice, and to the honor of His violated law? We were happy indeed in His love at our first creation, and happy we would be still if we had persevered. But our first apostasy from that innocent condition by the fall has made a large breach between God and us, and there is no one found in heaven or on earth who can make it up but His only Son. The loss of original righteousness has made us lose His favor, and has occasioned a vast distance between Him and us. This has brought forth all the miseries of the world: irregular seasons, overflowing inundations, and dreadful wars; all the sickness and pain of our bodies, and all the guilt, unquietness, and disorder of our souls.

In Adam we all died; both natural and spiritual death come upon all because all have sinned. But God, in His mercy, has not left us hopeless. As soon as Adam fell, God was pleased to provide for his rising again; and as soon as he had wounded himself, God prepared a balsam to heal and cure his wounds. When Adam was stung and poisoned with the venom of the serpent, God prepared an antidote. The poor, guilty creature could have expected nothing but a curse, and yet God gave him the promise of redemption, and of a blessing by the seed of the woman that would break the serpent's head. When God drove Adam out of paradise, He might also have put him out of heaven, and out of His presence forevermore. He might have said, "Go and dwell with that devil who tempted you to sin."

Upon the fall, God indeed withdrew His usual favor. This raised a cloud that obscured the beauty of His morning glory, and that intercepted the beams a little while before they shone upon mankind's head. But though we had destroyed ourselves, in God was our help. He sent His own Son to die for us, and to give satisfaction to His justice, which would otherwise have flamed against us. And though we are enemies, yet He is willing to reconcile us by the death of His Son (Romans 5:10). It is by Him that He will deal with us; to Him we must address ourselves, as being ordained of God to make our peace. To His righteousness we must look, as being very sensible that our own at best is miserably defective. If our persons and services are accepted, it must be through His Beloved. He is the Principal and the great Favorite of heaven. All the mercy that we need will be bestowed for His sake alone; all the miseries that we deserve He will keep from us.

It pleases God to behold what Christ has done. He will be pleased with us if we are in Him. It is the blood of Jesus, the merit of His death, and our application of these two by faith that will reinstate us in His favor. And it is the power and the virtue of His intercession that will preserve us in it. Christ is the way, the truth, and the life. It is He who will conduct and lead us to His Father and make Him, who was our enemy because of our sin, our Friend again. It is His office as a Mediator and a Savior to heal the wounded, to reduce the wanderers, to call home the banished, and to make the lame walk and the blind see (Isaiah 61:1).

Our blessed Lord is willing to plead our cause and help our wants; for those who come unto Him He will in no wise cast out. If you believe, His Father shall be your Father, and His God shall be your God. For God has resolved that all the communication of His grace shall be made through His dearly beloved Son; and if you sincerely beg His favor for Christ's sake, you shall not be denied. "He that hath the Son hath life." You shall indeed flourish when you are united to this great and glorious Head, and the death that you found by the first Adam shall be removed by the second Adam. "As in Adam all die, even so in Christ shall all be made alive" (1 Corinthians 15:22).

The office of our Redeemer in heaven is still to be a reconciler, and neither all the angels nor all the saints there can do for us what He does. When you are complaining of the yet remaining defilement of sin, and are saying with the great apostle, "Oh, wretched man that I am! Who shall deliver me from the body of this death," then remember that there is help laid upon One who is mighty, one who is compassionate and has a tender sense of all your griefs and miseries. And therefore, when you are amazed with the view of your own guilt, terrified with the accusations of your own consciences, and perplexed with the violent assaults and temptations of the devil; when you are afraid that you shall be the stubble to the devouring wrath of God—then lay hold of His strength (Isaiah 27:5), of Christ, who is the power and the wisdom of God (1 Corinthians 1:24). And it may be said of you, as it is said in Ephesians 2:12, 14, In time past "ye were without Christ, being aliens from the commonwealth of Israel, and strangers from the covenants of promise, having no hope, and without God in the world; but now in Christ Jesus, you who sometimes were far off are made nigh by the blood of Christ. For He is our peace."

That you may have an interest in the favor of God, which is life, your natures must be renewed. It is not enough that your consciences are delivered from guilt, and from an inclination to punishment, but they must also be delivered from the dominion and power of sin. If your lusts are unsubdued, they will, by their unquiet and disorderly motions, create a hell within, and then you cannot expect a heaven without. If you relish only temporary, carnal joys, you must not expect to taste the joy of God, nor think that if you wallow in the mire He will place you on His throne.

Though God's Son gives refreshment with His cheerful beams to all the world, to the bad as well as to the good, yet the beams of His special favor will not shine upon a dunghill, nor visit those hearts which are full of all manner of pollution. His pure and holy nature will not allow Him to behold iniquity without approbation. Do not think to see the reviving smiles of His face as long as you turn your backs upon Him; so long as you love what He abhors; so long as, without any remorse or grief, you scorn His government and violate His laws. Till you are born again by the Spirit of God, you are in a state of death, and are unfit for the communications of the divine favor. If you are in that condition, then you are no members of the Body of Christ; for all who are joined to that glorious Head have life and strength from Him to mortify their lusts. "What fellowship hath righteousness with unrighteousness? And what communion hath light with darkness? And what concord hath Christ with Belial?" (2 Corinthians 6:14–15). There is no communion between God and you till your natures, your inclinations, your principles, and your designs are all changed from what they once were. "The righteous Lord loveth righteousness" (Psalm 11:7).

Till you have His image, and a resemblance of Him wrought in you by the Holy Ghost, you are not His favorites; you are not those in whom He can take a particular delight. Without holiness, His presence will not seem amiable to you; without holiness, you cannot see His face. Isaiah 59:2: "Your iniquities have separated between you and your God, and your sins have hid His face from you." And therefore your sins are compared to a thick cloud: they obstruct and dim the light that otherwise would shine upon your heads. Therefore David prayed, "Create in me a clean heart," and then, "restore unto me the joy of Thy salvation" (Psalm 51: 10, 12).

While sin is lodged and entertained in the soul, it is like wind in the bowels of the earth: it will cause convulsions and troublesome agitations there. It was the sin of Adam that made so many frowns in the face of God, that caused the first eruption of His wrath, that makes it so frequently flame out with terror against the guilty sons of men. Till you are born again, you will have an aversion to God. And how can you expect that His favor should be given to you while you do not care to think of Him? Till your darkness is removed and you are acquainted with Him, you cannot be at peace.

That you may have the favor of God, you must, in conformity to the new nature and those holy dispositions that you receive by His grace, yield Him a sincere and a constant obedience all your lives. "His countenance doth behold the upright" (Psalm 11:7). He encourages the weakness of that soul that is tender and afraid of sin. He will not treat you with the kindness that He shows to His honorable subjects if you take part with His open enemies. "Ye are My friends, if ye do whatsoever I command you" (John 15:14). Obedience is the genuine effect of so excellent and so near an alliance, and it is the proof and evidence thereof. John 14:21, 23: "He that hath My commandments and doeth them, he it is that loveth Me; and he that loveth Me shall be loved of My Father, and I will love him. We will come unto him, and make our abode with him." This is a promise full of mercy! These words have in them all that is desirable; they are big with consolation! What can a soul wish for more than to have God, the Father and the Son, for his friends, for his guests! And not only to tarry for a night or a day, but forever! Not to comfort him with a transient visit, which in itself would be a great privilege, but to dwell with him! Oh, blessed is the house that has such inhabitants! Blessed is the soul who is thus honored and esteemed! By obeying His commands, you show yourselves to be vessels of honor; and, when you are so, He will at one time or another fill you brim-full of joy.

If you serve the devil, you can by no means have that satisfaction that flows from the hope of being a son of God and an heir of heaven. Though God makes His showers fall upon the sands as well as on the manured and cultivated ground, yet, till you are fruitful, you cannot expect to be refreshed with His gentle and comfortable dews. There are peculiar influences of His grace that fall upon His enclosed gardens, and not upon the deserts. "Let favor be shown to the wicked, yet will he not learn righteousness" (Isaiah 26:10). God's favor would shine like the sun on a rock if He showed it to the wicked. And that wicked person would be no more fruitful, no more tender-hearted than he was before. If you embrace your ancient sins, if you hold onto your correspondence with your former lusts, God will not pour the oil of gladness into such old, depraved hearts. If we go on in sin, we violate our own serenity, and raise within our breasts a multitude of storms. Whereas, says Psalm 119:165, "Great peace have they which love Thy law, and nothing shall offend them." And Galatians 6:16: "As many as walk according to this rule, peace be on them, and mercy." Isaiah 64:5: "Thou meetest Him that rejoiceth and worketh righteousness." By these means, you shall obtain the favor of God.

Chapter 17

We ought to take heed that we do not lose the favor of God once we have enjoyed it; and what we are to do so that we may not fall into a condition so miserable as this would be

Take heed that you do not lose the favor of God again. It is true indeed that those whom God once loves, He loves to the end. They are not allowed totally to be miserable; yet they may lose the sense of His favor, and all the comfort that once flowed from the pleasant thought that He was their God. Those who have sailed with a very prosperous gale may, upon their negligence, be tossed with very many storms, and may be terrified with a thousand dangers and calamities while they do not see the sun, moon, and stars for many days and nights together; and though they do not at length fall short of heaven, yet they may travel as though through a wilderness on their way there, and not meet with those clusters of the promised land, with those joys and comforts, that others meet with. The Spirit may suspend His influences and leave the conscience in a very lamentable state, and take away the peace that He once gave, so that the poor soul in that condition cannot but look upon itself with as sad an eye as if it were a reprobate; and there are great difficulties and dangers before the Spirit returns again to repair the breaches which our sin has made. The disorders of our souls afterwards remain a great while, and it will cost us vast labor to remove them. When some river that is very muddy has overflowed the neighboring fields, though it returns to its ordinary channel, yet it nevertheless leaves those places all covered with slime and dirt.

The least eclipse of the face of God is a very formidable thing. It will shake all the powers of your souls, and will put you into such terror as will seem to be like hell itself. If you are so foolish as upon slight temptations to forfeit His favor, you'll pay dearly for that folly. You may do in a moment that which may fill you with astonishment and sorrows all your days, and make you go at last mourning to the grave. You may, by a sudden fall, have your bones broken and, it may be, never recover ease and strength. Do not, therefore, wound or bruise yourselves. If you are not careful, that candle of the Lord that shines upon your tabernacle may be removed; and then you'll know by sad experience that it is an evil and bitter thing to sin against Him. Though you do not now question your title to salvation, yet you shall then be full of doubts and fears; though you are now looking to God as to a friend, you shall then be forced to look upon Him as an enemy, and to think that your afflictions are not the rebukes of a Father, but those of an angry Judge. He will indeed be the same God still, as full of goodness and love as ever, but to you He will be as a Fountain sealed up, and your poor, mourning souls, like the mountains of Gilboa, will seem cursed and barren. There will be no dew or rain upon them. Though you are never so flourishing now, yet then the sharpness of the winter will blast all your fruit, so that the fig tree shall not blossom, neither shall there be any fruit on the vine, and the labor of the olive shall fail.

Consider how great the sorrow of David was when God, for a season, departed from him! How many were his tears, how heavy his complaints, and how sad his thoughts! Though he was (as is usually judged) of a sanguine and merry temper, and had a peculiar skill in music, which is the usual allayer and charm of grief, yet, in the sense of God's displeasure, his joy was turned into lamentation, and his harp, along with those songs with which he had driven away the melancholy of Saul, could not stifle or chase away trouble from his own soul. The storm was too loud to listen to those softer airs; the wound was too deep to be cured by those gentle and easy methods. Beware, lest you lose the sense of the favor and the love of God, and lest you make your heavenly Father visit you with painful rods and severe afflictions.

Take heed that you do not weaken yourselves, for "the joy of the Lord is your strength" (Nehemiah 8:10). Is it not motive enough to say that His favor is your life and His displeasure is your death? Let us take as many pains for our spiritual life as we do for our natural life, and all will be very well. When we find the least decays of nature, we are very industrious to repair them; when we find the least faintness or indisposition in our spirits, we have recourse to cordials, or to something that is very comfortable and reviving, to refresh them. When we are sick, we complain of our illness; we make an abundance of inquiries, and use a great deal of care, to know what it is that will do us good. We place a great value on our dear life, and are afraid of everything that may deprive us of it. And when we are in good health, what will we not attempt for our own preservation! What arts we will use! What provision we will make for meat, drink, clothes, houses, gardens, and other accommodations, so that we may live at ease!

And, my friends, is not our soul of more worth than our body? Are not its decays and its death more painful and more intolerable than all the languishing and decays of our outward man? Let us therefore, as we have a great horror of natural death, have no less for that which is spiritual. Let us keep, with a greater care, the favor of God, for that is our spiritual and eternal life.

Ways To Keep the Favor of God

And that we may not lose God's favor:

1. Let us not grieve His Holy Spirit (Ephesians 4:30). Though we are not so happy as to have a familiar conversation with Christ, as those did who enjoyed His presence here on earth; though He is withdrawn from our eyes, and we do not see Him in His exalted, glorified state—yet He has sent His Spirit to dwell in our hearts, and we ought, with all manner of obedience and respect, to treat and entertain so divine a Guest; to do nothing that is unsuitable to so great a Presence; not to pollute ourselves, nor to defile His temple with any sort of sin, lest we grieve and vex Him. The divine nature indeed is incapable of our passions; it is above our joys and our sorrows.

It is said of those who are upon Mount Olympus that they see the clouds gather below their feet; they see the hail and the thunder disturb and land on the plain, while they rejoice in the pure light of the sun. In such a manner the divine essence sees all the troubles and agitations of the creatures, remaining always in its own peace and tranquility. This expression is borrowed from human affections, and when the Holy Spirit does that in us which our nature does when it is seized with sorrow, then He is said to be grieved. And if we make Him sad, we cannot expect that He will make us rejoice; if we affront and abuse Him, He will not be our comfort; if He retires, all our evidences will be covered with darkness, and we shall be plunged into the lowest depths. Let us, therefore, obey all His suggestions; whatever He bids us, let us do; let our minds always be yielding to His good and profitable motions; let us not slight the revelation He has given, nor be unmindful to grow in all the graces that are pleasing to Him. Let us remember the kindness that He does for us, how He chases away our darkness and, when we are fainting, how seasonably He applies the promises, and brings to our remembrance those truths that are most suitable and refreshing to us. Let us not grieve Him by neglecting to read or meditate upon the Word which He has inspired, or by foolish communications, by rash anger, malice, bitterness, wrath, or contention (Ephesians 4:31), but let Him be the absolute master of our souls.

When we are afflicted, let us not grieve Him by our murmuring, or by impatient complaints in our afflictions, just as we should not grieve Him by security and hardness of heart in our prosperity. And when He would carry us towards heaven on the wings of spiritual desire and love, let us not suffer ourselves to be seduced by the world, the devil, or the flesh; if we obey Him, He will maintain a sense of the divine favor in our souls. The life that He will then give us will not be like that of the sick, the feeble, or the dying, but like the life of the most strong and healthy.

2. Let us beware of spiritual pride. The contrite and

humble are those whom He regards. The proud He looks upon from afar off. Psalm 138:6: "Though the Lord be high, yet hath He respect unto the lowly. But the proud He knoweth afar off," that is, with disdain and scorn. It is nothing but our ignorance that makes us proud. We are ignorant of God, and of the multitude and greatness of our sins. Would it be possible for us to be proud if we frequently considered the great majesty of God and our own vileness? His almighty power and our weakness? His holiness and our pollution? His glory and our darkness? His eternity and our own fading being?

What comparison can be made between the great Ruler of the world and us who dwell in houses of clay? It was a mighty condescension in our blessed Lord, and one of the chief parts of His humiliation, to be clothed with our nature, that is in itself so mean and low. One man has said, "The whole world, from east to west, lies very sick; but to cure this very sick world there descended an omnipotent Physician, who humbled Himself, even to the assumption of a mortal body, as if He had gone into the bed of the diseased." It is ignorance in us that is the cause of our pride. We do not remember how often we offend in thought, word, and deed. We forget how we are by nature children of wrath. And we make ourselves more so by repeated acts of sin.

God resists the proud, but He has a regard for the contrite and humble soul. "He fills the hungry with good things, and the rich He hath sent empty away" (Luke 1:53). All on whom He bestows His favor, He first convinces of their own misery, showing them the curse, the hell, and the condemnation they have deserved. And when they are pardoned after such a sight, that pardon fills them with low and self-abasing thoughts. Luke 15:18–19: "Father, I have sinned against heaven, and before thee, and am no more worthy to be called thy son." One sight of the face of God will dash all our confidence and will lower all our pride. And the more this is revealed to the souls of the faithful, the more they see cause to loathe and abhor themselves in dust and ashes. Hence it is that the apostle who knew so much of God was so very humble. 1 Corinthians 15:10: "By the grace of God I am what I am. I labored more abundantly than they all; yet not I, but the grace of God that was with me." Paul called himself "the chief of sinners," and admired the grace of our Lord, that towards him "was exceeding abundant" (1 Timothy 1:14–15). Elsewhere he called the mercies of the gospel the exceeding riches of the grace of Christ (Ephesians 2:7).

If ever you would have the favor of God continued, strive against all pride. A man is proud (1) when he attributes that to himself, to his own industry, wisdom, or prudence, which He has received from God; (2) when he attributes to or expects by merit that which is a free gift; (3) when he thinks he has that which he does not have; or (4) when he despises others and seeks preeminence.

It is usual with us to take the measures of pride from the garb or attire, from the outward behavior, gestures, or the use of some less grave or decent fashions. And, indeed, there may be an excess in these things that may be very justly blamable. But, my friends, there is a pride worse than all this, spiritual pride, that has in it the very image of the apostate spirit, and is truly diabolical. When a man is proud of the graces or the gifts of God, it alienates him from the divine favor, for which we are more prepared when we are covered with shame and sorrow. And when we are poor in spirit, then we may hope that He will enrich us with His love. When we are emptied of all self-conceit, or a flattering opinion of our own actions, then we may hope that He will fill us with both grace and glory.

What a sorry, unbecoming thing it is for a man, even the best of men, to be proud! Alas, how soon the great God can cause all his glory to wither and fade away! What a vain thing it is for a man to pride himself on things that relate to the body, when it is liable to agues, fevers, consumptions, convulsions, and many tedious days and years of pining sickness, and must at last be the prey of death and molder in the grave!

And it is no less evil and foolish for a man to pride himself on anything that relates to his soul, such as in his knowledge, faith, or serviceableness; for upon his sin an hour of temptation may come upon him that will be an hour of darkness, that will cause the light of all these to vanish. And what is man when his conscience is awakened with a sense of guilt; when his sins are set in order before him; when the devil is permitted to sift and vex him, to ruffle him with amazing terrors and the constant view of hell? If God departs from us, that envious, raging spirit, who has great power and malice, easily triumphs over us and treads us under his feet.

Oh, how vain it is for us to be proud, who live a miserable life, and may die a very painful death! All the designs of God are to exalt Himself and abase the creature. The consciousness that the saints have of their own unworthiness will produce an eternal admiration of His love, and they will all cast down their crowns before the throne. 1 Corinthians 4:7: "Who maketh thee to differ from another? And what hast thou that thou didst not receive?" See also 1 Peter 5:5–6.

3. That you may not lose the favor of God, you must beware of formality, and all slightness of spirit, in the very performance of holy duties. It will also be very prejudicial to us when we can omit them and have no great trouble or regret for so great a sin, whereas, if we were duly concerned for the welfare of our souls, we would refresh them with frequent thoughts and meditations, as we do our bodies, with two or three meals a day. When we bring dead sacrifices to the altar of God, we need not wonder that we have so little spiritual and heavenly life; we need not wonder that we have no more sense of His favor, when we often pray for it as if we did not pray. The coldness and indifference of our petitions show that we do not much care whether they are granted or denied. And God will not thrust His mercies upon us whether we will have them or not; none shall enjoy His gracious, comfortable presence but those who strive and wrestle, such as have the zeal of Jacob, those who will not let Him go till He blesses them.

Heaven and salvation are things we would all have, but God knows we beg for them in a very poor fashion; and He may justly expel us from the sight of Himself because we draw near to Him with so little fervor and give Him cause to complain of us as He did of those in Isaiah 29:13, who drew near to Him with their lips, but whose hearts were far from Him. We are guilty of slightness and formality in duty in the following instances:

- When we perform them as a task, and not with delight and love.
- When we do not excite and stir ourselves to call

upon the Lord.

• When we are satisfied in the bare, outward performance, and do not have those inward exercises of contrition, faith, holy sorrow, and vigorous desires which are the life and the soul of prayer.

• When we allow our thoughts to wander, or when we run to such duties hurriedly from worldly business, not considering the greatness of our wants or that Majesty that fills the throne before which we pray, and how He will be sanctified by all those who draw nigh to Him (Leviticus 10:3).

• When we do not look for the answers to our prayers, and when, having done our duty, we are unsolicitous whether it produces any good effect or not.

• When we are more studious to approve ourselves to the eyes of men than to the eye of God.

I might add that if we would not lose the favor of God, we must duly improve all His other ordinances. We must hear as if it were for our lives, and take heed that His Word does not at any time slip out of our minds. We must receive the glad tidings of salvation with obedient and joyful hearts. And in all fit occasions, in the celebration of the Lord's Supper, with holy affections and a melting zeal, we must keep up the remembrance of the love of Christ till He comes again. With great constancy and seriousness we must read the Scriptures, which direct us in how to obtain this favor of God that is our life. But if any person places so little value on the favor of God that he will not earnestly pray for it, he must go without it, and will smart for his refusal of so excellent a blessing when it shall be too late to repent.

4. That you may not lose the favor of God that is your

life, you must avoid all sloth. What pains has God taken, what exhortations, what promises has He used to bring you near to Himself! What hardships and sufferings did Christ undergo to gain your love! And will you do nothing in answer to that favor of His that is so graciously bestowed and so dearly bought? Be circumspect, and walk closely with your God; beware of anything and everything that may stir up your Father's anger, for though He will not throw off so kind a relation, yet His wrath is very terrible.

I beseech you to be very fearful of all inward backslidings and of spiritual decays, lest the warmth of your first burning love for God wear away again. Take heed lest the death that is in His displeasure steals upon you by degrees, and lest, from a lesser degree of zeal, there comes a total indisposition upon your hearts. For once you begin to slide, the descent is easy; as soon as you are sleepy, rouse yourselves by those powerful motives that you may fetch from the Word of God, from His promises, and from His threats. Slothful servants will never have their Master's approbation. You have good encouragement, manifold assistances, and the prospect of a great reward. Are your joy, your peace, your present consolation, and your hope worth nothing? If they are worth something to you, then let no dangers, no difficulties whatsoever make you part with the favor of God, knowing that it may cost you dearly before you obtain it, once it is lost.

Take heed that you do not begin to lose your awe of God, and that you do not grow bold with sin; take heed that you do not comply with the devil, who, being forsaken of God, would have you be so also, and who, being shut out of heaven, would hinder your arrival there, or at least make you go there uncomfortably. If he cannot hinder your walking towards Jerusalem, he will endeavor to make you halt, and go there with pain.

But to prevent this, and all of his malicious designs, be fervent in the Spirit, serving the Lord. Upon God's first withdrawing from you, be restless till you find Him whom your soul loves. As you now flourish in the courts of God, take heed that you do not blast your own fruit; seeing that you are fixed on the Rock of Ages, take heed that you do not pull up your own anchor so that your vessel is driven on the sands and your hope shipwrecked.

Make no excuses for not working hard; use no delays; apply yourselves to the most active and zealous endeavors, so that you may prevent your own sorrow. "For the field of the sluggard will be all grown over with thorns, and nettles will cover the face thereof, and the stone wall thereof will be broken down" (Proverbs 24:31). These thorns are evil desires that will spring up of their own accord without sowing; they will increase of themselves, and then you will be exposed without defense to every invader, to all the birds of prey.

Consider that, as Joseph Symonds says in his *Case and Cure of a Deserted Soul* [reprinted by Soli Deo Gloria], the duties of godliness are not only a debt to God, but a reward to us, and that in our sloth there is not only unfaithfulness only, but ingratitude. Both the majesty and the mercy of God are despised. Remember what the Church said in Song of Solomon 3:1: "By night, on my bed, I sought him whom my soul loveth. I sought him, but I found him not." She did not find him, for she sought amiss. It is no wonder that she was not blessed with His presence when she sought it in such a lazy manner; and therefore, though she took pains afterwards, she did not meet with Him. He chastised her former negligence with a longer absence; though there was no place which she did not frequent, no person of whom she did not ask, yet she heard no tidings of Him. He who suffered the cross for her might justly expect that she should leave her bed and quit her ease for Him (Song of Solomon 5:2–9).

5. That you may not lose the favor of God, which is your life, take heed of an inordinate affection for this world and for sensual delights. If the care and business, the riches and projects of this world take up your hearts and the flower of your time, you will have but few thoughts of Him, and, consequently, but little love. The more you advance in the mortification of your appetites and your dearest lusts, the more cheerful influences you'll find of His grace. Beware that you do not love anything in this world too much—no child, no relation, no creature comfort—lest He tear away these idols from you, and the loss of an over-prized enjoyment vex your souls. He wants to have your whole heart, and you must not think that He will show you His favor if you only give Him half, and share the other half among the various objects that your mistaken affections dote upon. If you prize the favor of God as you ought, you will not desire any present good too vehemently, nor bewail its departure from you too sorrowfully. Your life will be in God, and not bound up in any of your friends, lest, when they die, your peace and comfort die with them.

If the world is set upon the throne, the disorder that is thereby offered to God will cause Him to frown, and to fetch the rebel and usurper thence, though it is to your smart and grief. Sensual appetites will clog and vitiate your appetite, so that you will not so well taste nor apprehend the sweetness that there is in God. If you have seen His face, the beauties and glories of it will make all the world appear to you as a mean and despicable thing. The woman who was clothed with the sun had the moon under her feet. You will see such an attractive excellence in Christ that you will esteem Him the chief of ten thousands, and the tempting, fair-speaking world will not be able to lead captive that heart which you have already given to a better lord. While others feed upon husks, you will be treated to the bread of your Father's house; while others pursue the drossy, short-lived pleasures of sense, you will have the delights of angels and of an eternal heaven to feed upon. And your splendid satisfaction will keep you from envying those whose ignorance makes them content with lower fare, and who, when they might fly as with wings of eagles, choose to grovel in the dust. As the moon is eclipsed when the earth shadows it, and hinders its admission of the light of the sun that makes it visible—and as in such an eclipse, the nearer that planet is to the earth, the more durable is its darkness—so we suffer an eclipse of God's favor when this earth interposes between Him and us, and when its false allurements and promises turn our eyes downward, which should always be lifted up to that glorious Sun by whose light we see.

This world is a more dangerous enemy than we usually take it to be; and therefore it is that the apostle says in 1 John 2:15, "If any man love the world, the love of the Father is not in him." Its joys are like those false fires that wander up and down in a thick and foggy night, and which lead the deceived traveler into some pit or gulf. But the joys of God are like the brightness of a summer's day; their clearness, their comfortableness and their continuance render them worthy of our highest admiration. The smiles of the world, many times, cover a designed mischief; but the smiles of God are to make us happy. The question is, then, shall we most prize the Fountain or the polluted streams? The rich Ocean or the smaller brooks? Why should we love the creatures when we have a God to love? Why should we dote upon a bubble that every little storm blows away, and not embrace that salvation which is offered, and which is both suitable to our faculties and not liable to perish?

With angels and glorified saints, let us make God our all, our portion, and our heart's desire; for our great Creator is much more amiable than His own handiwork. Let us leave the men who do not know God, and who fall down before their idols of clay and dirt. Rather, let us, with the highest reverence, with the most cordial submission, adore Him from whose favor we have life. Let us leave them to dig in the bowels of this earth for a sordid happiness, and let us arise and go hence. Let us go and seek after God; let us go and seek till we find Him; and when we have found Him, let nothing in this world—no pleasure, no pain, no promises, no threats, neither life nor death—make us part with our dear God again. Let us never cease to sigh and to long for Him; let us never be weary of His work, nor ever think that we can do too much for so good a Master. Let us feast ourselves with the cheerful expectation of His eternal love, and so take up the good resolution of the Church in Song of Solomon 4:6: "Until the day break, and the shadows flee away, I will get me to the mountain of myrrh, and to the hill of frankincense."

6. That you may more carefully seek and endeavor to obtain the favor of God, improve your experiences to this purpose. Have you not found what a pleasant thing it is to be near Him, to have access to His throne, and to see His face? And, on the contrary, have you not known what a dismal and uncomfortable state it is to be without Him?

There are two sorts of experiences that may be very serviceable to you in this great affair:

(1) Those experiences that you have of all other things in common with the rest of men. Have you not found that the promises and friendships of this world have been very changeable? Have you not many times embraced a cloud when you have promised yourselves a real and solid happiness? Has the world given you that pleasant, that cordial satisfaction that you proposed to yourselves when you first let your minds run unto it? Have you not a thousand times called it a very vain world? Have you not a thousand times found it to be so? Have you not pricked your hands and vexed your souls when you thought to have gathered the pleasant flower that you doted on? Have you not seen that the most beautiful rose is attended with a neighboring thorn? Has it smelled as sweet and lasted as long as you once thought it would? Has not all your wine had some wormwood and gall mixed with it? And where you hoped for the greatest pleasures, have you not met with a sad alloy of grief? Have you not been eager, importunate, and restless for this or that creature good? And, when you have obtained it, has it been so suitable, so delightful, so amiable in every way as at a distance it

seemed to be?

He must be a young man indeed who has not found this world to be a cheat; and he must be a fool who, once he has been cheated, will allow himself to be imposed upon again. A few years' experience will make us all say with the wise man of Ecclesiastes that all is vanity and vexation of spirit. And if we hope to extract more from it than so great an observer of nature as he did, we shall be miserably deceived. In our first and rash desires, we flatter ourselves with something here on earth that is great, plausible, and charming; but in our more sedate and second thoughts, we find that all that is under the sun is but a show and a mere appearance. And when we find it to be so—as a great many have done already, and all shall in a little time—it becomes us to apply ourselves to something that is more durable and satisfying, and that is only the favor and love of God.

(2) Improve not only your common experiences, but your spiritual ones to this end and purpose. I suppose there are a great many people who have been under distress of soul, and who, in such distress, have been brought very low. Now, what was it, I pray you, that gave you relief in so sad a case? Was it that you had many friends, great estates, a flourishing trade, and an abundance of outward accommodations? I'm sure you will answer, "No, no, none of these things gave us the least help. We tried several methods for a cure; we tried several diversions and pleasures, the conversations of our friends, and whatever innocent recreation we thought might give us ease. We heard sermons, we read good books, and we inquired of our ministers, but we found them all to be physicians of no value. They did

not open our eyes, nor heal our wounds, nor answer our doubts, nor refresh our tired and weary souls, until God Himself was pleased to do it. Nothing in all the world availed us; nor could all the means we used pull out the sting that the sense of our guilt and condemnation pierced us with. Abanah and Pharphar, all the rivers of Damascus, and all the streams of sensual delights were not able to mitigate or quench our thirst. All was desolation, terror, and amazement until the face of God was pleased to shine through the threatening cloud. We lived in darkness, and in the deepest sorrows, till He became our light and joy; we were sinking till He held us up; we were dying till He was pleased to revive us. All the delight and mirth that ever the world gave us was but as a flash of lightning compared to that clear and serene day that His grace created in our hearts. His love mitigated our pains and removed our sores, and one beam from Him was as the dawn of heaven. He has fed us, like John the Baptist, with honey in the desert. His loving-kindness indeed quenched our thirst."

I know that this is the sense of your souls, you who have tasted how good the Lord is. Now, having had so pleasant a relish of His mercy, I beseech you, do not let the memory of it wear away. Oh, remember with delight the transports, the sweetness, and the satisfaction that you have found in God; the settlement and the quiet that you have had when you have cast your anchor on the Rock of Ages; what views you have then had of the New Jerusalem, and what a pleasant prospect you saw when you were upon the mount! Oh, remember how often you have failed, and His kind hand has raised you up; how often you have been at the very gates of the grave, and He has been your life; how often His bowels have melted over you when you were rebellious; how often He has embraced you when you were prodigals; how often He has forgiven you, and bid you be of good comfort, when you condemned yourselves!

You have found all the creatures to be as a drop in a bucket, and how unable so small a drop was to gratify your earnest longings, your pantings and desires; after many a weary step, you found no rest till He manifested Himself, and gave you that composure and stillness which in vain you sought from lower things. Have you not found more solace in an hour's conversation with God, in prayers and meditations, than in many days' discourses with the best of men? This world, I dare say, you have found to be worse and worse the more you have tried it; but the clearer views you have had of God have shown you something in Him still more and more excellent. How often have you come to hear His Word with entangled, perplexed thoughts, and He has sent you away refreshed and satisfied? How often have you, with sad hearts and mournful looks, knelt down in your closet and risen again, after having had communion with Him, with great calmness and serenity? So much so that you have cried out, "Oh, that I had known Him sooner, and loved Him with my first affections! For He very well deserves all my faculties, and all the powers of my soul."

Remember the large experiences you have had of the goodness of God! With what kindness He drew you at first! With what gracious promises He cherished your languishing and feeble hopes! How seasonably He awakened you from the sleep of death with His threats, calls, and seasonable chastisements! How He has made your broken bones rejoice! How often He has enlarged your hearts in duty, so that you have felt so much of His power and presence, and in so comfortable and sweet a manner, as if you had not only heard of Him by the hearing of the ear, but also seen Him with the seeing of the eye! How often He has renewed His mercy, when you thought He would never be favorable any more! And how often, when your unbelief has made you say that He has departed, He has returned again! How often He has listened to your doleful cries, and given you many a proof of His love in gracious answers to your prayers! How many times your heart and flesh have failed, and He has given you support! How many times you have been sorely tempted, and He has overthrown the tempter! How many storms have put you into consternation, and He has appeared to your help and said, "It is I; be not afraid"!

He has put you, perhaps, into the fiery furnace; but He has been there with you, and used even the most severe trials to purge away your dross. He has corrected you with a very tender and skillful hand, and has ordered, with a most exact wisdom, all your troubles, both as to the nature of them and as to their duration. They have not been too heavy, nor have they stayed too long (Psalm 119:75). I speak as to wise men; judge what I say. These experiences, well remembered, will be a means to preserve you from losing the favor of God, which is your life. As it is useful for your health to remember what hurt you and what did you good heretofore, so these spiritual experiences will be very beneficial. For may you not say with David in Psalm 119:96, "I have seen an end of all perfection; but Thy commandment is exceeding broad"?

Chapter 18

Assurance, and the false grounds upon which many are apt to conclude that they are God's favorites when they are not

Endeavor to be assured that you enjoy God's favor, which is your life. Endeavor not only to believe that it is so, but to feel this animating your faculties and spreading itself through every part, so that you may have not only His countenance, but the light of it, and so that you may not walk in darkness, without the pleasant beholding of this glorious and reviving Sun. His favor towards you, though it is undiscerned, will make you blessed; but nothing but the sense of it will cause you to rejoice. Though you are safe, yet it is very desirable to know that you are so—not only to be going towards heaven, but to see the crown of glory shining before your eyes as you go along. Though God is your Father, it is very terrible if you cannot think of Him but as a Judge. Fears and doubts are disquieting and uneasy things; the restlessness and the torment that they give you should excite you to try all means whereby they may be removed. It is much better to have a vigorous and a stirring life than the sickly, feeble motions of it that are scarcely discerned—as in apoplexies and other diseases, where the soul has retired inward and the spirits have so weak a motion that they scarcely make the pulse beat. What peace can you have without an evidence of your interest in God? What comfort from His promises can you have if you do not know whether they belong to you or not? Will it enrich you to see large treasures if you have no share therein? What if there are abundant fountains of consolations, if you are likely to perish and die of thirst?

You must endeavor to have hope, as an anchor that is both sure and steadfast (Hebrews 6:19). And you have encouragements given you for a hope so sure. And, as one says, hope would be but a poor anchor if it should leave the soul to the courtesy of a wave, to the clemency of a rock, or to the disposing of a storm. Hope would be but a weak anchor if it should let the soul be lost with uncertainties, or leave it in danger of shipwreck. Do not be satisfied that you think that God's favor is your life until you can say with David, "He is the health of my countenance, and my God" (Psalm 43:5). These two, combined together, will produce a very solid and comfortable joy, when you can say with the rapture of Thomas, "My Lord and my God!" or with the Church, "I am my Beloved's, and He is mine" (Song of Solomon 6:3). Use all the ordinances, the Word, and the sacraments to this purpose, that you may find Him whom your soul loves (Song of Solomon 3:3–4).

Oh, what will be your pleasure when you see the great God of heaven to be your own God! To see that Savior, of whom the prophets, the apostles, the martyrs, all your ministers, and your Christian friends have spoken so much, to be indeed your own Savior! How will you be at ease when you see His excellencies to be yours, and that you are among the joyful and adoring throng who wait upon Him. To love Him, and to have His love shown to you; to have these mutual delights increase, but never decay; to possess one another forever with renewed and repeated ecstasies—this is a heaven begun that no thoughts can fully apprehend nor words declare. In order to have this, you must give all diligence to make your calling and election sure (2 Peter 1:10). You must often try your hearts and your actions by the Word of God; beg for His Spirit, obey His motions, excite your graces, watch against sin, and deny yourselves.

The trader endeavors all he can to get a plentiful trade, and would have a great deal of business and money flowing in upon him. The merchant strives to have all the plentiful returns imaginable. Oh, let us strive not only so that our souls may be safe, but that they may prosper too; not only that we may pray, but pray with boldness to God, as children to a Father. And when we are able to look upon Him as so related, and as our Friend, our service will be more fervent, and all our work will be done with greater life and heart. Our slavish fears and despondency will give way to love and hope, and then everything that concerns us will undergo a most comfortable change. We shall be able to hear the thunders, the curses, and the threats of the law without astonishment and terror because we shall dwell as in God's pavilion; we shall be able to think of hell and not be overwhelmed because we shall look upon it as a dungeon from which we are saved by the grace of God; we shall attend to the messages of the gospel, for it will bring us glad tidings. The blessed angels will be our guardians, the ministers of the church our directors and our helpers; the malice of the wicked and the rage of devils will fall below us, and will not reach our happiness.

But take heed of presuming the special favor of God

from the common mercies you enjoy.

1. You must not conclude that you have this favor from any of your outward privileges. God may long dwell among a people by the outward testimonies of His presence—by His Word and the means of grace—and yet leave them at last. No one was once more happy than the Jews under His protection, and yet none are more miserable than they by His departure. Jerusalem, where He had placed His name, and which was once the glory of all cities, is now no more remarkable for its glorious temple and its stately towers, for its riches, grandeur, and splendor, wherewith it shone before. The Holy Land, the country of Judea, which our Savior blessed with His presence, which He instructed with His heavenly sermons and honored with His miracles, is now no more the same Judea that it once was. It is now groaning under the cruel dominion of the Turks. The seven churches have lost their golden candlesticks, and the blessed Guest who once walked in the midst of them. The stars that shone there are now eclipsed and their glory is gone.

It is a great mercy indeed to have the gospel, but it will not be so to you unless it shines in your hearts. If it does not prevail to the conversion of your souls, it will aggravate your ruin, inasmuch as you will go from the clearest light to the thickest darkness, from the brightest day to the most dismal night.

You cannot conclude that you have this favor from any common gifts of knowledge, or of understanding, unless you are sanctified throughout. When our Lord ascended, He gave gifts to men. Kings scatter their liberal gifts indifferently among their subjects on the day of their coronation without making a distinction between the good and the bad; and persons who least deserve them partake of the pieces of gold and silver that are distributed. But their great honors, and the principal offices of the crown, they reserve for their peculiar favorites, and for those who belong to the household or who wait upon their persons. So it is that Christ distributes many favors to all who enjoy His gospel. But there are some who are peculiar to His own family, as distinguished from the rest of men, who receive the gifts of faith, regeneration, and adoption. Happy was the womb that bore Him, and happy were the breasts that suckled Him, and yet more happy are those who keep His Words (Luke 11:27–28). "Neither circumcision nor uncircumcision availeth anything, but a new creature" (Galatians 6:15).

2. You cannot conclude from your outward prosperity, your riches or abundance in the world, that you have this favor of God, which is life. Our Lord, who by His own example intended to show men better things than the goods of this world, first caused His angels to appear to the poor shepherds, not to the courts of princes or the schools of the philosophers. He could have had kings, if He had so pleased, to wait upon Him, and to lay their crowns and scepters at His feet; but He chose a train of poor followers, whom He enriched with heavenly treasures, and not with those of this earth, though the whole creation and all its glories were at His command. The poor received the gospel, and "not many noble are called" (1 Corinthians 1:27). "The poor of the world are rich in faith and heirs of the kingdom" (James 2:5). Yet, though riches are no sign of God's election, neither is poverty a mark of grace. Nevertheless it is with the lower sort of people, and

with those who are not often very wise in this world, God often builds His church.

Afflictions and crosses are no mark of His displeasure, nor is a continued prosperity the proof of His love. For many times God lets His sun shine upon the wicked to their dying day. Their strength is firm; the rod is not upon them; they fear no evil, and they know no sorrow. There are no tears in their eyes, no sadness in their hearts, no complaining in their families (see Job 21:7–13). Riches are indeed of themselves great blessings; with them a man may do an abundance of good works which the poorer sort of people cannot do by reason of the straits and difficulties that they wrestle with. They are great talents, and are serviceable to great purposes; they afford men great leisure for the affairs of their souls, and, not being perplexed with anxious cares how to get a livelihood, they may read and meditate and pray with more devotion. But then these soft and easy blessings, meeting with the corruptions that are in human nature, frequently prove to be a snare. They frequently minister to pride, vanity, luxury, and excess, to sensualities and worldly lusts; and for that reason our Savior says, "A rich man shall hardly enter into the kingdom of heaven" (Matthew 19:23).

Few meet with heaven here and with heaven hereafter. In Luke 16:19–31, the rich man had all manner of accommodations—a stately dwelling, a throng of admirers, soft garments and curious entertainments, composed of everything that could be fetched from the land, sea, or air; and in the midst of all this plenty he had the curse of an uncharitable spirit. Poor Lazarus was clothed with rags while the rich man was ruffled in silk. While the rich man had his excesses and his plenty, the poor man did not have even that which is necessary for life. He was a modest beggar; he asked but for the crumbs that fell from the table, the sweepings of the rich man's house, but he was denied. And to all this want there was added an increase of miseries by his painful sores. The poor man had no friends to visit him, no physician to bind up his wounds, no cordial to support his spirits. In this sorrowful posture lay poor Lazarus. His carcass was putrefying before he was even dead; the dogs were the only kind creatures—they licked his sores and assuaged the vehemence of the pain with their healing tongues. As one has expressed it, the dogs were human, but their master was a brute! And yet through all this, this poor man was very happy. When his pain caused him at length to die, angels were sent to convey his newly delivered soul away, to carry him who starved on earth to the feast of glory, where he will never be in distress or trouble any more.

The poor man had a very weary journey, but most sweet refreshment when he came to his journey's end. He was exposed to the injuries of the weather, and the sharpness of the cold, but in Abraham's bosom he was inexpressibly comforted. He had plenty enough in His Father's house, though he could not obtain so much as a crumb here with all his begging.

The rich man, a little later, had his polluted and unready soul torn away, and was condemned to greater destruction for having been so cruel to this poor man. This proud and scornful wretch, who, with his flaming eyes, saw Lazarus at rest while he was in torment, and who had become the beggar, fain would have had one drop to cool his burning tongue, but it was denied. He who showed no mercy found none (verses 23–24), and his hell was hotter to him for having lived so much at ease here on earth; it increased his flames to remember how many were hastening to the same place by his ill example, and who, when they came there, would increase his torment.

So we may say to a rich man what a good old minister said to a lord, after he had shown him his stately house, his gardens, his fish-ponds, and his other conveniences for a pleasant and easy life: "My lord, you need to make sure of heaven, for it will be bad going to hell from such a place as this." Many people think, because their endeavors succeed well, their trades flourish, and their wealth increases, that surely they are loved by God, and that these things are the marks of His peculiar favor. You may live in pleasures, and yet be dead while you live. Your bodies may lack nothing, and yet your unregarded souls suffer under miserable decays. You may be lifted up to heaven with outward enjoyments, and yet they may only expose you to a greater fall and a more amazing danger.

It may be that you are healthy while others are sick; but your health is not anything other than a greater talent which is given to you, and of which you must render a very strict account. Your ways, it may be, are smooth, but do they not lead you to ruin and the grave? There is nothing more formidable than spiritual judgments; and of all spiritual judgments, none is so great as for God to let you alone to choose your own way, to take your own course, and to follow the devices of your own hearts. And it is a mark of His anger kindled at a more than ordinary rate when He says in Hosea 4:14, "I will not punish their sons and daughters any more." Do not rest in this, therefore, but seek for sanctifying grace, and the pardon of your sins, with your whole heart.

3. Do not think that, because your consciences are not troubled, for that very reason you have God's favor. The ease that many sinners have is distempered, and will fade away; it is like the ease of an apoplexy, that numbs the senses and weakens life; it is like the slumbers of the sick that are caused by opiates and stupefying potions. As many times believers fear where there is no cause of fear, so do sinners hope where there is no cause of hope at all. Many a saint weeps who is going to Jerusalem, because he does not see the blessed place that is before him; and many a secure soul is asleep at the very door of hell because he does not perceive the danger that is underneath. If he did, it would terrify him to see that the flood is coming, and his house is only built upon the sand; to see that the sword is drawn, and his adversary is on the way, and he has not prepared to meet him.

Some have questioned which is the greatest sin, presumption or despair? It is no question that they are both very bad. They are both rocks, and if a man is shipwrecked, it is no great matter on which rock he splits when he is cast away. Still, though, God will make allowances even for the despairing expressions and thoughts of His servants in great and long desertions. He was gracious to David, though he said despairingly, "I shall one day fall by the hand of Saul," and to Zion, though she said, "The Lord hath forgotten me. My strength and my hope is perished from the Lord" (Lamentations 3:18). Yet it is a sin that we ought to resist and strive against.

And presumption is no less a sin against which we

must strive; it slays its thousands every day. There are too many who eat and drink, and are merry, and yet do not know whether God is their Friend or their Enemy. Psalm 55:19: "They feel no changes, and therefore they fear Him not." But if speedy, serious, and hearty repentance does not prevent it, they will shortly feel a change that will spoil and blast all their hopes. They'll feel a change that will at the same time conclude their life and send them to judgment, lodging their souls in misery—and where will their hopes be then?

My friends, the way of life is difficult; there are abundant mistakes about it; there are abundant windings, turns, labyrinths, and dangers, by means of which you may be hindered in your pilgrimage if you do not take great care. There are several ways like this way, that have a resemblance to it and yet vastly differ from it. There is the peace of God, and there is the peace of Satan. It is the design of that malicious spirit to let you be quiet in your sins so that you may not see their evil nor feel their bitterness; and then you save him the labor to make you miserable, for you make yourselves so. Do not allow him to blind your eyes nor lead you to destruction while you never make so much as one halt, nor startle at it.

You hear others complaining of their sins, and crying out that they are forsaken, undone, and miserable; and you thank God that you have no trouble, that your consciences are still and quiet. I beseech you to take heed that it is founded upon good reasons, that it does not prove to be a short slumber rather than a lasting peace. It may be that you have never doubted God's love for you, and it is very well if you have no cause to doubt. You may think that such as are in soul distresses are so because they have committed greater sins than other men, and that vengeance, therefore, like the viper on Paul's hand, fastened on them because they have been guilty of some very great and monstrous sins. But you must know that the judgments of God are too deep for you to fathom. He has wise ends in those severe dispensations, though those who are at ease may have committed as great sins as those who are in trouble.

Many times a great calm precedes an earthquake; many times the sky is very clear just before the clouds gather and the lightning and thunder come. Beware, lest you be unsafe while you are most confident. Beware, lest you go down to the grave, as thousands do, with a foolish and ungrounded hope. Remember the foolish virgins, and the warning of the apostle in 1 Thessalonians 5:3.

Chapter 19

By what means we may know whether we have God's favor or not: first, by the grace of His Spirit, though its action may be neither so strong nor so comfortable at one time as at another; second, by our hatred of sin and being satisfied with all providences

The next thing is to examine and to try whether you indeed have this favor of God, which is life. There are a great many people who think God is their Friend when He is really their Enemy; and a great many troubled, distressed Christians think that He is their Enemy when He is really their Friend. Let us, I beseech you, be very careful in a thing that so nearly concerns both our present and our future peace. Let us take heed that neither the devil nor our own hearts cheat us in a matter that is of so vast a consequence. And we have need of the greater care lest we should flatter ourselves with a foolish hope that we are God's favorites when we are truly not so; as our vain expectations would leave us at the last, so the ruin that it would bring forth would come with a double weight upon us, for to fall from great hopes is worse than never to have hoped at all. To be miserable after we have thought ourselves happy gives a more acute and bitter sting to that misery. There is many a one in hell, now groaning under the eternal wrath of God, who thought that He would see the smiles of His face, and not have been terrified with His frowns; who thought that he would have walked the streets of the new Jerusalem in liberty, light, and peace, whereas he is now in chains of darkness and in inexpressible anguish.

With what tenderness, with what caution, and with what holy fear should we manage such an affair as this! With what solemnity ought we to proceed when we are inquiring whether we are a favorite of God's or not; whether we belong to the living or yet remain among the dead; whether we are an heir of heaven or an utter stranger to the blessed place, and to the God who makes as blessed as it is?

And there is not one person reading this who does not have cause to make such an inquiry, and to say to himself, "I feel by the warmth and vigorous motions of my spirits that I have a natural life. I eat, drink, and sleep, and take great care, using a thousand projects to maintain this same dear and pleasant life. But while my body is indulged and thrives, is not my poor, slighted soul in a state of death? And while men show me favor and are friendly to me, have I the favor of that God who is to be my Judge, and who is either my best Friend or my worst Enemy?"

Now in this matter we may proceed by these rules:

RULE 1. Have you those graces of the Spirit wrought in you which are the certain pledges and tokens of God's favor? Are you rich in faith and yet poor in spirit? Are you hungering and thirsting after righteousness? And when you find your own best actions falling vastly short of the strict and pure demands of the divine law, do you prize and seek the righteousness that is in

Christ? Is that sin now bitter to your taste and grievous to your thoughts which was once highly esteemed and prized? Do you hate and bewail that with a relenting spirit that was one your dearly beloved and your joy? Are you mortified to this world, and do you walk humbly, wisely considering how weak you are, and how liable you are to be surprised and to fall, always considering that you are very sinful and very frail?

These graces of faith, mortification, humility, and the like are certain tokens of the love of God; and in a soul thus qualified He delights to fix His habitation (Isaiah 57:15). In such a soul there is a heaven begun; and it not only lives, but will attain new strength and proceed to further degrees of life. Though it now flourishes in the courts of the Lord, yet His light shining upon it will cause it to take the deeper root, and to look with a more amiable freshness. The self-conceited shall miss an abundance of refreshments that a soul so lowly will meet with, as those showers of rain that slide away from the tops of mountains descend into the valleys and make them more fruitful.

"Where the Spirit of the Lord is, there is liberty" (2 Corinthians 3:17). He does not give this Spirit to remain for a small space only, but to remain with His servants till their work is done. It is called "the earnest of our inheritance" in Ephesians 1:14. An earnest, you know, is part of the payment which is not to be returned again. And we are said to be sealed with this Spirit "unto the day of redemption" (Ephesians 4:30). God does that sealing in order to distinguish believers from other men. Seals are employed to make a difference from other things that are not so much to be regarded. We seal our own goods, or papers, or some particular thing that is most precious, so this expression of "sealing" calls us to meditate on the infinite tenderness of God's love toward men; for a man does not love anything so much as that which is his own. He looks upon other things in which he has no ownership with an indifferent and unconcerned eye; even the stately glories of a palace do not affect him with so great a joy as the little conveniences of his own unobserved cottage because it is his own.

Further, a seal often carries the arms of him whose seal it is, or the image of some great person. So the work of the Spirit is to engrave on our hearts faith, hope, and love. These are the signs of the new covenant and form in us the image of God, which consists in righteousness, peace, and holiness. God sets this mark only upon those who are indeed His favorites, those who, by the tenderness and softness of their hearts, are prepared to receive His impressions. But in this matter we are, in a great measure, passive, just as is the wax which receives the same marks that the seal stamps upon it. These are saving works of the Spirit to which I here refer, whereas a great many common gifts are bestowed upon those whom God abhors. Many a man may have light enough to show others the way to heaven, and yet never walk therein himself. And he who was a star in the firmament of the church on earth may sit in darkness. 1 Corinthians 13:1–2: "Though I speak with the tongues of men and angels, and have not charity, I am become as sounding brass or a tinkling cymbal. And though I have the gift of prophecy, and understand all mysteries and all knowledge, and though I have all faith so that I could remove mountains, and have not charity, I am nothing."

There are two things here that you must not expect: (1) do not expect to be equally strong in every grace; (2) do not expect to have the same comforts at all times.

You must not expect to be equally strong in every grace. We ought to strive to be complete, to have all the pieces of our Christian armor polished, fit for action, and well-fitted and put upon us. But those parts where there is most danger of a wound, those parts where the seat of life is, we are principally to secure and guard. So those graces we are first of all to look after and to cherish are those which produce and keep the rest in vigor, such as faith, repentance, and humility. It is most certain that all men, even among those who are God's favorites, are not of the same stature, nor the same strength, nor have they as much skill in every duty as they may have in one or two. It is so ordered by the holy providence of God that all in Christ shall have tribulations, but those, many times, are very different from one another, so that the different graces they are to exercise under their various trials may shine with a brighter glory.

Abraham was peculiarly eminent for his faith, Moses for his meekness, and Job for his patience. All believers, by the privileges with which they are invested, are stars; but even here one star differs from another star in glory. As there are several gifts of the same Spirit that are useful to the whole, so the graces that are wrought by Him do, according to His sovereign pleasure, produce various effects according to the subjects in which they are found, and are many times much advanced or obstructed by a good or ill temper of the body. Hence in those who have a choleric temper, the fieriness of their natural spirits, which upon every occasion is apt to be inflamed, very much hinders that meekness and calmness which is one of the graces of the Holy Spirit; and so others who are naturally tenacious, close, and narrow-souled many times smell too much even of these ill qualities when they are converted. But it ought not to be so, for if there is any particular sin to which we are more inclined by our constitution than to another, we ought the more industriously to set ourselves against that sin.

You must not expect to have the same comforts at all times. The Spirit blows where and when He will (John 3:8). Though the new creature is formed in you by the grace of God, yet you cannot perceive its motions with as distinct a sense at one time as at another. Though, by the intercession of Christ, His favorites are secured from a total and final apostasy, yet they may fall now and then, their life may seem to decline, a spiritual faintness may come upon them, and a very deep sorrow may cover and, as it were, bury their hopes and joys. Yet there is that vital principle that shall not see corruption, that seed of grace that will now and then flourish with acceptable fruit.

Your faith may, in violent temptations, be like the weak and undiscernible stirring of the soul. When the body is in a swoon, the soul seems for a while to be departed; but after the spirits are refreshed, it animates the whole body and exercises all the functions and offices of life as it used to do. When the ship was most violently tossed with a tempest, our Lord was there, though the poor, trembling disciples thought He did not care whether they were lost or saved. Thus Mary was drowned with tears after His resurrection, and, not finding Him where she expected, nor as soon, she gave way to sorrow: "They have taken away my Lord, and I know not where they have laid Him" (John 20:13), she said, when the very person she had then in view was the same dear Savior and Friend whom she longed to see. And when with great tenderness and familiarity He revealed Himself and called her "Mary," then she knew full well that it was her Master, and her poor, drooping heart was filled with joy and transport. The text tells us that "she fell at His feet, and kissed them."

God does not equally manifest His favor at all times even to the same person, who sometimes triumphs and is sometimes very desolate, just as the same vessel that is sometimes seemingly lifted up even to heaven itself by the rising and swelling waves is the next minute sinking to the bottom of the sea and is ready to be swallowed in the formidable depths. If we were duly prepared, the face of our God would indeed appear with as amiable an aspect at one time as at another; for if any frowns are there, our sins are the cause. But because we are sinful, it is necessary for us now and then to weep as well as to rejoice. The clouds and showers are as needful to the earth as are constant sunshine and fair weather.

Our graces yield no delight to us until the Spirit actuates and enlivens them. Until He blows on the garden (Song of Solomon 4:16), the spices do not flow forth, nor do the sweetest of the flowers smell with such a perfume and a fragrant scent as they then do. If we would have a warm sense of the love of Christ shed abroad in our hearts, it must be done by the efficacy and influence of the Holy Ghost. He brings the most suitable truths to remembrance, and He seasonably applies those promises that are most comfortable and reviving. He raises us in holy courage and hope, and He fills our sails with His favorable blasts. He banishes that fear and those perplexing doubts that enslave us, and sets before us the mercy and loving-kindness of God. And then He pours into our smarting and bleeding wounds the consolations of the gospel.

There are, indeed, some particular times when God is pleased to give to the soul the clear manifestations of His favor. Divines usually say that these occur in such particular circumstances as these:

• God is pleased to condescend to new converts who are suddenly cheered with mighty joys and filled with an admiration of His grace. He considers the weakness of these tender pilgrims, and His joy becomes their strength. He feeds them as with angels' food, for He knows they have a great way to go, and therefore He carries them in His arms and leads them gently along, and they do not meet with those sharp and heavy trials that more experienced Christians meet with. The sudden change that such persons perceive—when they go from gross darkness into a marvelous light, when their chains are struck off and their prison doors set open—makes them wonder and adore. Hence it is that they have vigorous affections, and are very active for the glory of their Savior. Hence it is that their zeal is so fervent, and that the flame of their love burns so clear and bright.

• God communicates particular manifestations of His favor to His servants at the Lord's Supper, for this is when they see their Redeemer crucified before their eyes; when they see the torments of His body and the agonies of His soul, how pained and how amazed He was, and that all this pain was for them and their salvation. And they see that as surely as they receive the bread and the wine, so surely do they receive this Jesus and all His benefits, including direction for the present and a title to everlasting glory. This carries them up to the top of the mountain; this makes them taste of the tree of life. This sight of a dying Savior, and of the heaven He purchased, makes them worship Him with praise and think of themselves as already being where He is. To this table of the Lord, the believing soul goes hungry and thirsty; from this same table the believing soul returns greatly pleased with so divine a banquet, though not without the most earnest desires for that entertainment that is reserved for it above.

• God is pleased to give His servants a clearer manifestation of His love when He intends to employ them in some remarkable or extraordinary service. He encouraged Joshua, who met with great difficulties, by saying, "Fear not, but be of good courage; I am with thee" (Joshua 1:9). When He sets before His servants the labors and dangers of the combat, He displays at the same time the greatness of the reward and the glory of the victory. Thus He animates His soldiers to fight His battles; thus He prepares His martyrs to witness to His truth. And then, with such a sense of His favor, no cup seems too bitter for them to drink; no danger seems too great for them to conquer. Hence Moses said, "If Thy presence go not with me, carry us not up hence" (Exodus 33:15). But with God's help, he was content to go to whatever place of difficulty he was called. He would rather (as Nathaniel Culverwell says in his *Whitestone, a Treatise of Assurance)* be in a desolate and howling wilderness than in a pleasant and fruitful land without the presence of his God. He knew there was no sweetness in Canaan without Him. There is more sting than honey in the land of promise unless He is there; and Canaan itself will prove to be a wilderness if He withdraws Himself. Thus God, Culverwell says, when He called Abraham to that great expression of obedience in sacrificing Isaac, first warmed his heart with His love and sealed up the covenant of grace to him. He spread before him ample and comprehensive promises: "I am thy shield and thine exceeding great reward." And this bore up Abraham and supported him, though the staff of his old age was taken away and, by his own hands, cast into the fire.

• In prayer, God is many times pleased to show His favor to a soul by giving it a secret assurance of His mercy, saying, "I am thy God and portion," and so sends it away filled with good things.

• In great straits, and in pinching wants, when there is the least of the creature, there is usually the most of the all-sufficient Creator. When all the cisterns of earthly comforts are broken, then this Fountain overflows and sends out His comfortable streams. He carries His people into a wilderness, and there He speaks comfortably to them (Hosea 2:14). He is most kind when the world will show them no kindness.

• God shows His favor to His people after they have gotten the victory over some lusts and corruptions that were both dishonorable to Him and uneasy to them. Such a conquest is attended with His approbation, and that gives them a mighty joy, like the joy that the poor Israelites had when they saw their enemies drowned in the Red Sea.

• God shows peculiar favor to His people on the day of their death. When all earthly delights are clouded and their sun has just about set, they lift up their feeble eyes towards heaven and He draws away the veil, and they see the Son of God standing at God's right hand as their Advocate and Mediator. And then it is that a poor, weary soul says, with Paul, "I desire to depart, and to be with Christ."

Mr. [John] Flavel said of Mr. [William] Lyford that, being requested a little before his death to let his friends know in what condition his soul was, and what his thoughts were about that eternity to which he seemed very near, he answered with a cheerfulness becoming a believer and a minister, "I will let you know how it is with me." And then he stretched out a hand that was withered and consumed with age and sickness, and said, "Here is the grave, the wrath of God, and devouring flames: the just punishment of sin on the one hand. And here am I, a poor, sinful soul on the other side. But this is my comfort: the covenant of grace which is established on so many sure promises is a salve for all. There is an act of oblivion passed in heaven: 'I will forgive their iniquities, and their sins I will remember no more.' This is the blessed privilege of all within the covenant, among whom I am one."

What a quiet and blessed soul this was! How full of joy in a time usually marked by amazement and terror! With what strength was he furnished to fight with his last enemy! God grant that you and I may have such strength and such comfort when it shall be our time to die.

RULE 2. That you may know whether you have the favor of God, in which is life, you must examine whether you esteem Him more than the world. There are two qualifications of this esteem: it must be serious and deliberate, and it must be prevalent.

(1) It must be serious, the product of many solemn, repeated thoughts, viewing God as being invested with many glorious perfections as He is represented in the Word, and as He shines in the face of Jesus Christ. This is a due consideration both of what He is in Himself and of what He will be to you. This esteem is not wrought by a hasty glance or a passing view, but by deep thoughtfulness, attended with calm and sedate reflections on our own guilt and His mercy; on our own emptiness and miseries and His all-sufficiency. It then comes from balancing all things that pretend to a share in our affections and submitting at length to the greater claim of God, saying after this or the like manner, "Lord, I yield myself up to Thee as Thine own. I was a little while dazzled with the bright pleasures of a vain world; but now I bid them all farewell so that I may come and taste Thy joys. I have served sin and Satan, but they have cheated and deceived me; they have given me vexation instead of rest, and husks instead of bread. Therefore now, O my Father in heaven, poor prodigal as I am, I return to Thee to live in Thy family, to do Thy work, and never to wander or to be extravagant any more. Oh, give me not all my portion in this world, but let me have an inheritance in that which is to come. Let others pursue their various projects, and obtain what they pursue; let them succeed in their affairs and bathe themselves in the softest pleasures. It is God whom I seek; it is He whom I will most value." It is a sign that a beam of heavenly light has shone upon your souls if this is your frame.

(2) Your esteem of God must be prevalent. The worst of men have some esteem of God as being a glorious, powerful, good, and happy Being; and they think

those to be the safest and most honorable ones who enjoy His favor. But then there are a thousand trifles that they esteem and labor after more, such as riches, ease, gain, or applause. But can you truly say, "I would not, if I might, have all the world without God Himself. I would rather have Him, though in poverty, disgrace, and trouble, than be compassed with throngs of flowing joys without His love"? If you have this favor of God, you will easily look through all the painted varnish of the world and see its real vanity. God and divine things will not only gain your hearts, but gain them in a sovereign and a powerful degree. And, till we thus prize and value Him, He is not our God, nor is His favor our portion. If you have this, you will say, with David in Psalm 4:6, " 'Lord, lift Thou up the light of Thy countenance upon me.' It is not outward prosperity or grandeur, the favor of men or the ease of the flesh, that I seek, but Thyself. Thou art my exaltation, my joy, my every good, all that I wish for and all that I desire."

RULE 3. If you have this favor of God, you will know it by the hatred that you have of sin. Wherever this favor comes, it will banish sin; it will weaken and expel it. And though it does not altogether destroy your sin, yet it will take away from it all its former amiableness and beauty. You will not sin with such boldness as you used to do; nay, you will be so far from doing so that you will not dare to commit the least iniquity. And if there is fixed in your souls a real and abiding hatred of sin, and if you use all good endeavors against it, it is a most certain mark that you have passed from death to life. You cannot forget what bitterness the remembrance of your former iniquities filled your souls with, what consternation then seized upon your poor spirits when you thought God was your Enemy and hell your portion! What would you have given then for the least beam of that Sun that now shines with His gentle beams upon your heads! How welcome was the voice of that Messenger who brought you glad tidings, and who assured you that there was mercy and hope even for you! Before you obtained this favor of God, you spent many a restless night, and many a weary day in a solicitous inquiry as to what would become of your immortal souls forever.

RULE 4. If you have this favor of God, in which is life, you will be satisfied with all His dispensations that bring you nearer to Himself. It is an observation not without truth that, wherever God gives grace, He will send afflictions to exercise that grace. And those who have the strongest grace must look for such conflicts, such temptations, and such assaults from the devil on their way to heaven as will put all their grace to the utmost and even the largest stretch. No one shall come to heaven without suffering; no one can tell how many millions of sufferings he may endure before the day of salvation dawns upon him. But he is a very happy person who is not overwhelmed with these innumerable calamities, and who, while he swims as in a sea of grief, can lift up his head and exercise his faith, saying, "Lord, let Thy will be done. If Thou wilt be with me in the fiery furnace and in the deep waters, I shall not fear, though those flames are hot and these waters roll fast one upon another."

Though it is our duty to withstand long, severe and heavy trials, it is a common thing in our prayers to say, "Lord, if Thou wilt save me at last, bring any sort of affliction on me, I will refuse nothing." But, alas, we generally do not know what we are saying. There are those arrows in God's quiver which, if shot against us, would cut us to the very soul and make us quickly change our language. There is such unspeakable weight in His hand that, when He lays so much upon us, we cannot bear it. There are those pains at His disposal, and which our sins deserve, that are in all things, except for their duration, like the very pains of hell.

He is the good man who does not desire affliction, for he will be sure to have it whether he does or not. The good man will submit to it when it comes upon him. He does not make himself a cross, but takes it up when he finds it lying in the way. He can say, "Lord, if I must be poor in order to have eternal riches, I am well satisfied. If I must be very low, contemptible, and despised before I come to Thee, that lowness and contempt shall be my real glory. If, during all the days of my pilgrimage, I must sow in tears, I will go on nevertheless, for I know that I shall reap in joy. If my corruptible body must languish away in pain, and my sinful soul have its troubles too, I will wait in hope and not repine or fret at Thy decree. If I must be friendless here, I will still prize Thee as my best and eternal Friend. Even when I am sorely oppressed I will stay close to Thee. I will lay hold on Thy perfections, on Thy covenant, and on Thy promises. I will not let Thee go till I am blessed."

This favor of God causes a person to rejoice in Him though the fig tree does not blossom. And when any dear comfort or any relation is taken away by death, it will make him say, "My God is better to me than ten of these comforts; nay, than many thousands of them put together. And though He snatches away from my embraces what I have valued most in this world, yet He shall have my best affections, my desire, my love, and my delight as much as ever." A soul thus prepared to be quiet under the most severe dispensations has life in the favor of God—that life that shall never expire but shall end in eternal life.

Chapter 20

Several other ways whereby a sense of God's favor may be preserved in our souls, and how we may certainly know that we are in that happy state

RULE 5. If you have this favor of God, you will desire the continuance of it above all things, and this will be both an evidence of your present sincerity and a means to convey to you a more pleasant sense of this favor. In all outward actions—such as prayer, hearing, giving to the poor, and the like—there may be a very great resemblance between a true Christian and a hypocrite; but spiritual desires, being the immediate offspring of the soul, are not liable to so many cheats. Your desires after God will be very strong and earnest, and will produce powerful and sensible effects, for they will be the fruit of a lively faith, and of an enlightened understanding that sees the value of this God. And this will render the motions of your souls more strong; for ignorance of Him is the mother of all feeble and languishing desires. Your breathings after Him will be like hunger and thirst, which are very uneasy to nature, and give us the most raging and eager appetites, and leave us unsatisfied until they meet with their proper gratifications. Psalm 42:1–2: "As the hart panteth after the water brooks, so panteth my soul after Thee, O God; when shall I come and appear before God?" Even as the hart, that poor creature, when it is pursued by hunters, and greatly heated by its flight, longs to be refreshed with the cool streams of water, so will you, when harassed with the temptations of the devil and his malicious and most cruel suggestions, fly with haste to the embraces and arms of God, longing and panting after Him. Nay, the warmth of your desires may be so great that you will, as it were, melt away in flaming zeal. Psalm 84:2: "My soul longeth, yea, even fainteth for the courts of the Lord; my heart and my flesh crieth out for the living God." And Psalm 119:20: "My soul breaketh for the longing that it hath unto Thy judgments." Proverbs 13: 12: "Hope deferred maketh the heart sick."

An eager desire for an absent, amiable good raises an agreeable sensation and something of disorder in the natural spirits. They are heated and stirred up with more vigor through the vehemence with which they move, though this very much abates their strength, and occasions that which we call fainting. Such is the sympathy that the soul has with its dearest body, that when the soul meets with a suitable object it is filled with warm affections and fills the body either with sadder or with more cheerful spirits, as it finds reasons of sadness or of joy.

These desires of holy men after God, however, do not always burn with an equal flame. In times of desertion, in some very perplexing difficulty, or in great bodily indisposition and sickness, they are dampened and cannot usually be so quick, so cheerful, and so sensible as at other times (though even then they may be very sincere and acceptable), for in so gloomy a time, one groan that comes from a humble heart may go up to God in as grateful a manner as many long prayers at another season. And in your desires after God's favor, you will have regard to these two things:

(1) You will remember what it was that once heightened your desires, and will endeavor by the same means to quicken them when they begin to languish. You will often consider what perfection in God it was, whether His goodness, His mercy, His truth, His unchangeable faithfulness, or the like; or what promise in Scripture, or what act of providence towards you it was that warmed your hearts. And then apply yourselves again to the same profitable methods. You will often recall those passages in sermons that you heard, or in the good books that you have read, that gave you the first amiable sense of God.

(2) You will carefully observe what it is that cools and dampens your desires—what passion, what worldly pleasure, what vain company, what foolish hopes, what tormenting cares, what enslaving fears—and avoid all these as much as in you lies. You will avoid those snares that entangled you, those temptations that have clipped your wings and made you, when you were soaring aloft, fall to this earth again. You will avoid whatever secret sin it was that weakened your holy breathing after God, or what omission of duty it was that estranged Him from you; and you will immediately begin to mortify that sin and to set upon that duty. Even when we have done all that we can, there will be a vast difference between what we are and what we ought to be, between our longing and the most glorious Object after which we are to long.

Do we find no longer any pleasure in our old lusts? Do we find our hearts dead to this deceitful world, to those objects we once called amiable and to which we sacrificed our time, our endeavors, our morning and our evening thoughts? Do the things that heretofore we most admired now seem less eligible? Does all that which we called beautiful seem deformed when compared with God Himself? Let every one of us sincerely say to our most beloved sins, and to the enjoyments of this world, "I once over-admired you, but I will never do so again forever. I bid you farewell; never pretend to have a share in my affections, for I have now found a better good. I have long pursued you to no purpose; but now, in finding God, I have found a sure way, a smooth way, and a near way to rest. You have cheated me with vain delusions too often, but you shall cheat me no more; for it is to God that I offer up my heart, though with grief I admit that I loved Him no sooner, when He is so infinitely good and amiable."

RULE 6. If you have this favor of God to be life to you at present, then you have felt by experience what a miserable thing it is to be without Him. As there is a wonderful variety in the works of God in nature, so there is no less in those of grace. His favor is not communicated in all respects in the same way. Though all are redeemed by the blood of the same Redeemer, yet some shall groan under the painful sense of their chains and captivity much longer than others. In some, the new birth is produced by His gentle hand in a little time; others do not have it till after many dreadful pangs and agonies. Some get to heaven with much less conflict than others who travel to the same place.

This variety is admirable and very wise, though we do not discern the reasons for it. Yet all who are blessed with the favor of God cannot, without astonishment, survey the hideous darkness and the woeful danger in which they lay before this glorious Sun was pleased to shine.

Such a person will say, "Oh, what would have become of me forever if He had allowed me to follow my own choice, and to take my own course and have my own desires when I was running to the very gates of hell? I now indeed see my sad state as it was then; but, oh, what would have become of me had He allowed me to continue in my fatal slumbers on the edge of ruin? If I had dreamed on, and had not awakened before the dreadful blow of death, where would my lot have been then? How many thousands of miseries was I under, neither perceiving my bondage nor feeling my misery? Death was creeping on me, hell was gaping to receive me, the law cursed me, and the devil led me captive, and I knew it not. And it was in this woeful posture that He found me. I was polluted, cast out, helpless, and in my blood. And it was then that He said to me, 'Live,' and made the time of my danger and my provocation into a time of love."

So great a change, and so happy a revolution, deserves indeed a frequent and thankful remembrance. It gives a mighty pleasure to the soul to find itself safe when it is even in the jaws of the roaring lion ready to be torn in pieces; it was then that the arm of the Almighty rescued the endangered and trembling prey. It is not with a greater pleasure that a sick man, who has long been confined with inexpressible pain, and at the very door of the grave, thinks of his present health and life. A mariner who has escaped shipwreck and the dangers of the sea, upon a plank or broken piece of the ship, and who with great difficulty and hardship has gotten to land, does not look with a greater calmness upon the waves, and upon that sea which had almost swallowed him up, than such a sinner looks upon his former miseries and his present privilege, his former enmity to God and his present reconcilation with Him.

It may be that you have experienced that nothing in all the world is so very terrible as God's withdrawing from you. Have you not found it to be a punishment much greater than bodily pain, sickness, or any temporal calamity? Have you not found that the loss of your dearest friend, your kindest and most comfortable relation, was much more tolerable than this? To lose the sense of His favor after you have once enjoyed it—has not this loss been to you even as hell itself, or like the departure of Adam out of paradise after he had beheld the beauties and tasted the pleasure of that amiable place? What fear, what anxiety, and what consternation seized upon him when he was to be kept from it, never to see the tree of life, never more to walk in that most delightful garden, nor to see angels visiting his sweet habitation as they once used to do!

And have you not been possessed with as great a fear when you have thought that God had been turned into your enemy because of your iniquities? "I could bear any other affliction," says the deserted soul, "but to be forsaken by God is so terrible that I cannot bear it. How can I see frowns in His face and live? I have had many disappointments, vexations, and crosses, and in all these I could lift up my head and have hope. But now I am destroyed on every side and my hope is gone. Heretofore, when the world had treated me ill, I could go to the throne of grace, and my heavenly Father would give my weary soul pleasant entertainment and speak comfortably to me. But now He does not visit and refresh me as He used to do. His blessed face, which I once saw with peace, is now hidden and covered with a cloud. I have my former worldly comforts, my friends, and my estate; but, alas, my God is gone, and what do these avail? I once read His Word with joy; now it fills me with gall and wormwood. I once sat under His shadow with great delight, and His fruit was pleasant to my taste; but now I am thirsty and have nothing wherewith to quench my thirst. I am now scorched with heat and have no shelter, no cool and shady retirement where I may fly for ease."

Job 23:8–9: "Behold, I go forward, but He is not there; and backward, but I cannot perceive Him; on the left hand, where He doth work, but I cannot behold Him. He hideth Himself on the right hand that I cannot see Him." You will most earnestly pray against so sad a state as this is if you have ever experienced the favor of God to be your life. "O Lord, hide not Thyself from my poor soul; whatever else I lose, let me not lose Thee and Thy love. Do not take me for Thine enemy, nor let Thy terrors fall upon me. Do not cast me off, O my Father, though I have been very disobedient."

And if God departs, your mourning for His absence will be like the mourning of a mother for the death of an only son, or like the sadness of so many poor children who bewail a lost father: they are left destitute, and can do nothing without his advice and help. You will follow your God with tears and supplications, and will say with Christ in great agony, but with great faith, "My God, my God, why hast Thou forsaken me? Why dost Thou forget the work of Thine own hands? Have mercy on me, O Lord, for I am weak. Why dost Thou leave me in this doleful wilderness where no water is, to be a prey to Satan and my own fears? I have indeed wandered about, seeking rest and finding none. Put out Thy loving hand and guide me to Thyself. I have indeed deserved this usage, for Thou wast with me and I did not value Thy presence. Thou didst call, but I did not obey Thy voice. Thou didst stand at my door, but I shut Thee out. Woe, woe unto me that I have sinned. Woe, woe unto me that I did not make better use of Thy grace, Thy presence, and Thy love as I should have done. But though I have been a prodigal, Thou art a Father still; and though I have not done as becomes a child, yet I will return to Thee, because Thou wilt not cast off the comfortable name of a Father."

Thus, I say, do those who have had experience of God's favor mourn for His absence. Their spirits are like the tender flowers that hang their heads when the sun is set; and they walk more disconsolately than any subject can be supposed to do who, after having once shared in the peculiar graces of his prince, sees the prince at length, because of his crimes, look upon him with a severe or a less favorable eye.

RULE 7. If you enjoy the favor of God, you will place a great value on His Word, on the Spirit, and on the blood of Christ. You will place a great value on His Word, as it reveals to you this God and persuades you by many comfortable promises and entreaties to accept Him. And not only this, but it conveys to you saving light and knowledge with its great and powerful efficacy. You will love the Word because of the many supports and consolations which you have received from it. You will love it as the rule of duty, and all its precepts will be dear to you, conveying to you life and strength. You will love it so as to read it often, meditate upon it, and lay it up in your hearts. You will love it as the instrument of your regeneration, and rejoice in it not only for a season, but forever.

You will value and obey the Spirit who brings home revealed truth to your hearts. When you were destitute of this life, it was the Spirit who convinced you of your miserable state, and who restored vigor and motion to those faculties of yours that were stupefied and numb, chasing away their ancient darkness and guiding them to their proper objects; and the Spirit then caused those objects to be revealed so as to produce glorious effects in your once-barren souls.

You will also prize the ordinances of God in which you may have communion with Him, ordinances such as prayer, hearing, meditation, and the like. And it will leave a sensible grief upon your minds when you miss these ordinances by your own fault.

RULE 8. You will be very humble and heavenly-minded. His favor fills all His servants with the lowest and most self-abasing thoughts. You will never speak of Him but in terms of respect, never pray to Him but with great reverence and veneration. The nearer access you have to Him, the more you will discern of His infinite holiness and purity, and how vile you are when compared to Him. You will wonder at His condescensions and cast down your crowns before His throne, imitating the humble language of David to Mephibosheth. In 2 Samuel 9:7–8, when David told him that he would eat bread at David's table continually, "He bowed himself and said, 'What is thy servant, that thou shouldst look upon such a dead dog as I am?' "

This will cause you to admire the distinguishing grace of God that is vouchsafed to you more than to many others in this world. Great numbers are buried in ignorance or open idolatry, and the rest are in profaneness or hypocrisy. Many, it may be, are passed by in the same families where you live; while you are alive, perhaps, your next-door neighbor is dead.

And then, if you have obtained this favor, you will be heavenly-minded. Your treasure and your hearts will be above; you will taste and relish spiritual and divine things, and will never be more pleased than when you are least earthly and carnal. And this holy temper will be your comfort and security against the temptations of Satan and the evils of this lower world, just as the birds that soar aloft are out of the danger of guns and the snare of the fowler, who catches the ones that fly too near to the ground.

RULE 9. You may know that you have the favor of God if you are industrious and zealous in the performance of all holy duties; if you perform them not only from the force of awakening convictions, but from love and delight; if you refuse no service that may glorify God, though it seems to thwart your worldly interest and be painful to the flesh. It is impossible not to find a calm and cheerful progress in your obedience when you know that God accepts what you do, just as it is a mighty encouragement to the labor of a servant when he sees that his master is well-pleased with his work. Darkness, you know, with its many inconveniences, greatly puts a stop to diligence, which yet is quickened and excited by the return of light. So if God's countenance shines upon you, it will make you not only walk uprightly, but even run the in way of His commandments with enlarged hearts (Psalm 119). And you will associate with all who are serious, holy persons; for the living do not take pleasure in being among the dead.

RULE 10. If this favor of God is your life, it will make

you patiently long for heaven. This favor will be sweeter to your taste than honey or the honeycomb. It will yield a more delightful relish to your renewed appetite than all the joys of this world. The little drops that now and then refresh your hearts will cause you to pant for those rivers of pleasures that are at God's right hand forevermore. Are you weary of sinning, weary of your imperfect faith, hope, and love? Does the prospect that you have of God at this distance render Him so amiable to your souls that you would fain be with Him where He is? Are you so sensible of the evil of your sin that you would fain be in that place where you shall sin no more forever, where your panting soul shall have all its longings turned into an eternal complacence and delight? You will often lift your longing eyes up to heaven and send there many a fervent wish, saying, with David, "Oh, when shall I come and appear before God?" (Psalm 42:2). "When will I see His glorious face, and feel beyond all doubt that I am loved by Him, and that I love Him better than I now do? When will I be where the joys of hope shall be turned into fruition, and where that which I now have only as a promise I shall have in the sweetest and most comfortable possession? When shall I be near His throne and see that glorious Majesty whom I have adored? When shall I see that face, all serene, and have no black or mournful cloud to interpose between my God and me forever? Oh, that I might join in the hallelujahs of the blessed! Oh, that I were in the land of eternal light and joy, and in that agreeable society of holy souls who have already passed the gulf, and who rest from all their labors; for I am weary with beholding vanity."

These, and such like, will be the motions of a holy

soul; for its warfare with sin, the world, and the devil is so painful that it cannot but desire to be released. Its ignorance is so great that it cannot but long to be overspread with pure and eternal light. Isaiah 51:14: "The captive exile hasteneth that he may be loosed, and that he should not die in the pit, nor that his bread should fail." But then this longing must be attended with patience; for we may sin even in desiring heaven when we desire it with too much precipitancy and haste. And, in this, good men are, many times, very much to blame; many times, when a person meets with some heavy sickness or some troublesome affliction, he is apt to say, "Oh, that God would now take me to heaven!" There is a great deal of self-love in this, and our nature, when it finds itself oppressed, would fain be at ease; but we must not forget that we must bear the cross and suffer before it will be our time to reign.

We must hold on in our race, though the weather is foul and stormy. Many thousands of pains may be our lot before God calls us from here, and the first thing we are to desire is that we may have faith and submission wherewith to bear those pains, and to persevere till He is pleased to call us. Some, indeed, He is pleased to dismiss from this earth to His heaven all of a sudden; but, if you consider, you will find that the greatest part of His servants have long troubles, manifold agonies, tedious conflicts, and heavy pains before they come to that glory. And in this respect, they find the gate that leads to life to be very strait and narrow. The land of promise is indeed a pleasant land; it flows with milk and honey. But there are many giants to conquer on our way there.

Your desires for heaven cannot be truly pure unless

you are content to glorify God by suffering as well as by doing His will. And even with patience there may be an earnest and affectionate desire to be with God. And thus some of the saints have breathed out their prayers: "Oh, time! Run fast, and remove days and hours out of the way so that I may enjoy forever the Beloved of my soul! Farewell, all my friends and relations, for I am now going to be possessed of an inheritance that is incorruptible and undefiled, that does not fade away. Farewell, eating, drinking, sleeping, and all my pleasures and recreations; for I am now going to the supper of the Lamb, and shall not need these weak supports of frail nature any more."

And others have cried out, "Oh, my God! Let me not still be in darkness, and provoke Thee and hazard my salvation; let me not please the devil and add sin to sin! Oh, why is my desire still unsatisfied? When shall I have nothing more to wish for? When will it be that I shall be delivered? Oh, come, Lord, lest I be weary of my work and duty; lest my graces be like poor, tired soldiers who fall into confusion and so lose the day. Happy is the man who loves Thee above all; happy is the man whose trust and hope is in Thee. But most happy is he who is with Thee, where I also long to be."

Thus I have finished the applications. And I hope there are several of my readers whose consciences, after such a trial, salute them with happy tidings and say, "You are those who have God's favor." And, oh, what happy people are all such! Happy shall they be in life; happy is their death, and happy are they forevermore. Some will say, "Happy are the men who are rich and great; who have thriving trades, numerous attendants, and swelling titles; who have plenty of silver and gold;

who need take no care how to live, and are free of all the pinching anxieties of a poor and low estate. But in truth, "Happy is the people whose God is the Lord" (Psalm 144:15). It may be said to every such person in the language of the angel Gabriel to the blessed Virgin, "Hail thou that art highly favored! The Lord is with thee. Fear not, Mary, for thou hast found favor with God" (Luke 1:28, 30). And what indeed can they fear whose Friend He is, who is so good and so powerful!

Chapter 21

The several privileges that belong to those who have God's favor

1. When you have this favor, all your sins are pardoned. Your God will not remember your iniquities any more. All the vanities of your childhood and youth, all your omissions and commissions shall not rise against you to condemn you. Though you have often quenched the Holy Spirit and stifled His convictions, yet this and many thousands of other sins that made you dead in the law shall be blotted out; all your sins of ignorance, and all those that have been done against light, love, and knowledge, shall be covered by this grace of God.

2. All your prayers shall be heard. Being pardoned, and having your guilt removed, you will have access with boldness unto God. Either He will give you the very things you desire, or those that are better and of another kind. Your persons are acceptable, and so will all your duties be; you are therefore successful because Christ is your Intercessor. As He has once purchased life for you with His blood, He will apply it to you for your further pacification (Hebrews 9:11, 14). Nay, you will not only prevail for mercies for yourselves, but, being favorites in the court of heaven, you will be in a capacity to obtain many blessings for others too. Matthew 18:19: "If two of you shall agree on earth as touching anything that they shall ask, it shall be done for them of My Father which is in heaven." God sometimes waits

to hear a number of voices before carrying out some public mercy because He delights in the harmony of many praying souls. He also loves to oblige and gratify many in the answer and return of the same prayer. And therefore it is our duty to beg the prayers of those we think of as good people because of their interest in God. Many seek the ruler's favor (Proverbs 29:26); their wants and their ambition push them forward, and make them very complacent and respectful to such in whose power it is to do them considerable kindnesses. They make a peculiar address to such as are principal favorites, and it is reckoned as a main step to promotion to have a friend in court. Similarly, it is to our great advantage to be remembered in the prayers of those who share in God's favor.

3. When you are the favorites of God, He will accept your sincere services, though they are mingled with many failings. The meanest oblations that you lay upon His altar shall be received gratefully, while the more pompous and costly sacrifices of others shall be disesteemed. Your inward groans shall move His tender heart sooner than their howlings and their loudest cries (Proverbs 15:8). He will cherish your most feeble breathings after Him, and will add more strength to the bruised reed and more flame to the smoking flax. He will register your good actions and will not upbraid you with your evil ones. There was some good thing in Abijah toward the Lord God of Israel in the house of Jeroboam (1 Kings 14:13), and He took particular notice of it. And at the last day our Lord mentions the charities and bounties of His people which they themselves had forgotten long ago. He will not reject your faith, though there are many doubts mingled with it;

nor will He cast off your desires, though they have a great deal of deadness, and lack many further degrees of life and fervor. He will remember His covenant though you forget your duty. Malachi 3:17: "I will spare them as a man spareth his own son that serveth him."

4. God will either preserve you from outward dangers or give you the strength to bear them. He will be afflicted in your afflictions, and will tenderly regard you as the apple of His eye. What can you fear while you have so great a Defender? What may you not hope for when you have so good a Benefactor? As He said to Abraham in Genesis 15:1, "Fear not, I am thy shield, and thy exceeding great reward." He is a reward to quicken your service, and a shield to keep you from hurt in the day of battle. Or, as we read in Daniel 10:19, "O man, greatly beloved! Fear not, peace be unto thee; be strong, yea, be strong." What safety must he have who has the Almighty for his helper! What honor must he have whom an angel called "greatly beloved"!

5. He will keep you in His favor so that you shall not finally be cast away. Though you are saved as by fire, and by great difficulty, yet you shall surely be saved. He may suspend His influences, but He will not change His covenant. He may be angry, but He will not be so forever. You may fall and bruise yourselves, but His gentle hands will heal your wounds (Romans 8:31–39). He who loved you when you were prodigals will not shut you out when you return home again. He who pitied you in your blood will not reject you when His image is upon you, though it is sullied with manifold defects. Your life is hidden with Him in Christ, and though it is weakened by various temptations and troubles, yet it shall spring forth again. Christ is the vine whereof you

are the branches. Though your life is exposed to many storms, yet in Him it is very safe; and you shall not expire by a total death, because Christ Himself will never die. The faithfulness of God and the life of Christ are both unchangeable supports to you. You need not fear the rage of your enemies while your Savior is your Guide, for He will bring forth judgment unto victory.

6. Sixth, and last, God will be your God. His wisdom and His power will direct and save you. If I could tell the tradesman who is setting up that I could help him to a plentiful trade; if I could assure the merchant of the successful arrival of his ships; if I could tell the poor how to be rich, and the rich how to get all that they wish for, I would be a very acceptable messenger. But to you who have the favor of God, here are better tidings! The Lord of heaven and earth is yours; and then, if you can count the stars, the sands of the sea, or the drops of rain, you may be able to number the benefits that will accrue to you by such a privilege. Whatsoever is truly useful to your spiritual welfare, whatever in all the large dominions of God will do you good, you shall be sure to receive. God the Father will be your reconciled Father, God the Son your Mediator, God the Holy Ghost your Sanctifier. You shall in no distress lack an all-sufficient and almighty Friend; you shall have all your holy prayers heard and granted; life and death shall be yours; the mercy of God will relieve you when you are in misery. 2 Corinthians 6:18: " 'I will be a Father to you, and ye shall be My sons and daughters,' saith the Lord Almighty." And He will say, as He did in Jeremiah 32:41, "I will rejoice over them to do them good . . . with My whole heart and My whole soul."

To be a child of a king sounds great, and carries

with it a high degree of honor, but to be the children of the King of kings is infinitely more honorable; to have so great a Father is an unspeakable and mighty privilege. All the dignities that ambitious courtiers seek with all their cringing arts are but little trifles when compared with this. All the renown that soldiers purchase with their sweat and blood is but disgrace when compared with the glory of being a son or daughter of the Most High God. If the Queen of Sheba—when she beheld Solomon who, in the splendor of his court and the wisdom of his actions, exceeded all the reports that she had heard—cried out with wonder, "Happy are thy men, and happy are these thy servants which stand continually before thee, and that hear thy wisdom" (1 Kings 10:8), how much more may we say, "Happy are the servants of the living God, who serve Him day and night, who wait at His temple, and who sing His praises, who see with what wisdom He manages all the great affairs of His vast and large kingdom." The same eye that is in the wheels watches for them, and all is carried on with a peculiar respect to His glory and their salvation.

The Father of our Lord Jesus Christ is their Father, the angels are their guards, the Spirit is their Teacher, and afflictions are their medicines. 1 Corinthians 3:21–22: "All things are yours; whether Paul, or Apollos, or Cephas." The stars that are in the right hand of Christ shine to give them light. The world is theirs, so much of it as is necessary to promote their real welfare. Life is theirs, wherein to prepare for happiness. And death is theirs, to convey them to it. They are Christ's, His brethren and His subjects; and Christ is God's, who is delighted with His Son, and with them in Him.

This is the privilege of a favorite of God. He is now, it may be, poor and low, affronted and disgraced; but the day draws near when the same person who is disesteemed by the sons of pride shall be owned by his great Lord. He shall be clothed with garments of praise and led out in triumph; and applauding angels will say, to the grief of the wicked, "Thus shall it be done to the man whom the King of Heaven delights to honor."

Thus you have set before you that which is life indeed, a life that shall never close with death. Keep your mind full of these pleasant ideas; endeavor to get a greatness of soul that does not cease aspiring after these glorious privileges, and look with contempt upon all other grandeur and magnificence. Having seen how honorable it is to be favored by the Lord of Hosts, let us all resolve that we will never admire this vain world any more, for now we have discerned a better world.

Part III

Chapter 22

The many miseries of this mortal life that are the usual occasions of sorrow to the sons of men, with respect to both their bodies and their souls

"Weeping may endure for a night, but joy cometh in the morning." Psalm 30:5

The life of man is full of sorrow, which yet is not so to be understood as that it is in every part full of darkness and calamity. We have, indeed, stormy days, but then we have fair weather too. We have not only the sharpness of the winter that pierces us with cold, frosts, and snow, but we have the mild and favorable summer afterwards that causes all the whole frame of nature to rejoice, and brings to us many grateful, pleasant things, giving us occasion to praise the wisdom of our Maker, who has made a world so beautiful wherein we are to dwell. He has provided for us all innumerable comforts, not only such as are absolutely necessary to maintain our life, but such as may give us delight and recreate our sense. We can not turn our eyes in any direction without beholding the wonders of His goodness—His sun, His moon, and His stars—whose influences are for our benefit as well as for His glory. And this gives us cause daily to say with David, Lord, "what is man that Thou art mindful of him, or the son of man that Thou visitest him?" (Psalm 8:4). He does willingly grieve the children of men. He does not make us always weep, but affords us frequent occasions of rejoicing, whereas all our time might be as one rainy day, from the rising of our sun to its going down. But His providence does permit us, however, to be laden with many miseries before we come to another world. And let us take a view of them, for it will be useful in subduing our pride, to keep us from vainglory, and to make us to remember that we are not at home, that here is not our rest, and that we ought earnestly to desire a better state.

1. Let us consider man in his first arrival in the world, or in his infant state. And there we discern this same creature, who in his later years makes so great a noise and bustle in the world, to be a poor, helpless thing, who is in no way able to cherish the newly begun life, nor to keep the candle that is lit from expiring in the same minute wherein it began to shine. Man comes crying into the world, an action very suitable to him as he enters a world whose pleasures are floating and transient, but whose griefs are very sure. Other creatures are endued with instincts and inclinations for their own preservation, and know, in some measure, as soon as they begin to live, how to maintain their own life; but man, of all others, is most destitute and helpless in this respect. He is so tender and frail that the least cold or dangers easily affect him.

God has put great love into parents, so that they, as well as they can, support and comfort and help their children; and with His blessing, and their own great care and labor, they attempt to rear these little plants.

But then there are abundant diseases that begin to set upon the newborn creatures, convulsions and other pains which greatly torment and vex them. They are not able to express, and so we do not know, what is bothering them so. But we are sure when they begin quickly to weep and be sorrowful that something is wrong; and their pains and sorrows make their parents also be afflicted and weep with them, when they see their children's miseries, indeed, but cannot help them. This soft and tender age is easily troubled and disquieted; every little thing troubles and molests them, so that the first hour of the night, in which we travel when we begin to live, is an hour of sorrow.

2. The second stage of life is when we have gotten over the weakness of our infant state and begin to have more strength, and reason dawns a little and yields us a little light to guide ourselves. That light is mingled with darkness; our small skill has an abundance of imprudence; and we run into a thousand dangers that we do not see. Those dangers make us weep and be sorrowful; our careless youth is full of miseries, and the blooming rose has many thorns around it.

When our reason begins to display itself with our increasing years, then the various tasks that are set for us to do, the various things we are obliged to learn in order to have a good and well-applied education, bring forth grief and pain. Our unwillingness to labor, and the correction we meet with if we do not do it, both afflict us. Our ignorance is our misery, and the difficulties that are planted about the tree of knowledge frighten and vex us. Many of our early days are spent in digging for this hidden treasure, which we cannot find but with a vast toil and sweating for it—and which, when we have found it, does not satisfy. It's true, indeed, that our early youth has many pleasures, many recreations and diversion to sweeten it, and we are then void of the many cares of life that afterward pierce our hearts. But even then we are so confident and so foolish, so apt to trust our own understandings, and so backward to receive the advice of others who are more experienced that we often wound ourselves. We often sow those seeds of sorrow that yield us an uncomfortable harvest many years later. And when, in our free time, we have some time to reflect upon what we have done, that reflection makes us weep to think that we have done so little for God or for our own souls; we weep that we have lost so great a part of our life in trifles and vanities. For we can then say, by sad experience, that childhood and youth are vanity (Ecclesiastes 11:10). The joys that we then were pleased with are past and gone; but the wounds that we then received many times smart and bleed afresh.

3. A third state is when we have gotten the yoke of our masters and instructors off of our necks, and begin to manage and guide ourselves and our actions; then we have many sorrows still in the common affairs of life, and with respect to knowledge and understanding, bringing along with them a huge train of cares, of grave anxieties and solicitude. If men have no employment or business, they grieve for the want of them; and if they are employed, they are hurried, disturbed, grieved, and vexed. They meet with many people who are false and treacherous, and with many businesses that are intricate and perplexing. And thus their plodding heads are stung with cares, and their breasts with sorrow, all groaning under the curse, and proving that

punishment to be true, that with the sweat of a man's brow he must eat his bread (Genesis 3). Ecclesiastes 2:23: "All his days are sorrows, and his travail grief. Yea, his heart taketh not rest in the night. This is also vanity." All his drudgery and toil are to small purpose; it is indeed vanity when a man deprives himself of sleep, the sweet repose of nature, and, next to the grace of God, the greatest blessing in the world. The poor are almost everywhere shedding tears of impatience and discontent for the straitness of their circumstances; they are mourning because they are likely to want what would bear their charges to the grave. Meanwhile the rich are troubled as to how to secure the riches they enjoy, and fear to lose them as many have done before, for they cannot live long without seeing many whom a few days and some unforeseen accidents have brought from the greatest heights to the lowest poverty—people whom the rising sun found rejoicing, and whom it left, for their sudden miseries, plunged in tears.

How many foreheads do you see covered with a cloud of grief because of their losses and disappointments! Look into the country fields, and there you see men toiling at the plow and scythe; look into the waters, and there you see men tugging at oars and cables; look into the city, and there you see a throng of cares, and hear sorrowful complaints of bad times and the decay of trade; look into studies, and there you see paleness and infirmities and fixed eyes; look into the courts, and there are defeated hopes, envys, discouragement, and tedious concerns. All things are full of labor, and labor is full of sorrow; and these two are inseparably joined with the miserable life of man.

4. In the next place, consider the miseries of the

body of man that make him weep and mourn. Persons of weak constitutions are liable to tedious and languishing pains that afflict them for many months together, and those who are of a stronger temper are liable to such pains as are so sharp and violent that they dispatch them, it may be, in a week or two. Man is seldom without pain, and always near sickness that will make him groan and sigh whether he will or not. And some sickness is all sorrow, such as melancholy, which is all sad, and does not have one bright or clear side, all disconsolate and grievous, stagnating the blood, changing the brisk and cheerful motions of the spirits, and fixing the mind unavoidably upon amazing and dreadful objects. That is verified by the example of Job: "His flesh upon him shall have pain, and his soul within him shall mourn" (Job 14:22).

The various seasons of the year have their inconveniences which annoy poor, mortal men. Not only is the winter full of storms, cold, and darkness, but the beauteous spring has storms and sharp frosts. The fruitful, teeming summer is melted with heat and choked with dust, and the autumn is full of sickness. And how can the eyes but shed innumerable tears when they consider the doleful pains to which they themselves, and all other parts of the body, are exposed! How can a man but groan to find himself present in such a body from which he cannot for many painful years be dislodged, and in which he has no delight or ease! What grief is it to him to have no help or relief when his spirits are broken and his heart is overwhelmed, to have many cutting afflictions upon him and the fear of more to come! Ecclesiastes 8:6–7: "To every purpose there is time and judgment, and therefore the misery of man is great upon him. For he knoweth not that which shall be; for who can tell him when it shall be?" To be daily dying in anguish and vexation, and not be able to die; to be surrounded with troops of diseases, of agues, fevers, consumptions, colic, gout, and stones, and not to be able to keep any of these off, nor to run away from them when they come!

5. Add to all these natural sorrows such as are distributed by God in judgment. Such are the tyrants whom God allows to flourish long and to triumph in the world, who tread upon the necks of others to advance themselves, and who glut themselves with the blood of the innocent, daring to do what is most unjust to gratify their lawless ambition and their lustful desire for empire. From them and their arbitrary designs flow innumerable injuries, wrongs, robberies, and mischief (Ecclesiastes 4:1).

There are other judgments, such as plagues and famine, spreading contagions, or bloody wars. There are plagues, that, at the same time, seize and kill; that conquer wherever they come, and send thousands of miserable mortals to the grave all of a sudden; that tear children from their mother's breasts; that separate one part of a family from another, and make them afraid of each other's company. These plagues send them together to the house prepared for all living; they turn flourishing cities into solitudes, and put a stop to all commerce and trade.

Then there is famine, which kills by as sure methods, but by slower ones. Famine makes people know they are dying before they die; it causes them to walk to and fro with pale, meager, and drooping looks, and turns a fruitful land into a barren one, where poor, starving children come begging to their mothers for bread; and those mothers, who have none to give, are forced to watch their children die before their eyes, as in Lamentations 4:4.

Then there is war, where many children are deprived of their fathers and wives of their husbands, where many who lived plentifully are bereaved of all their dear and pleasant things. War fills every place with blood and violence, with noise and clamor, with oppression and woe. War lays countries waste and desolate, and sacrifices multitudes of harmless people to its cruel rage and fury. These are the terrible voice of God, which will cause us to weep and to be afraid.

6. Consider men as associated together in their several relations, and so their sorrows and their causes of weeping are increased. The courts of princes have their occasions of grief and trouble; they grieve too, though their grief is more pompous, and clad in a more solemn dress. Those who have a numerous and great kindred and alliance are more often in mourning than others; for death more often visits their greater number of friends and acquaintances. Few families are without sorrow. That house which now rejoices is quickly turned into a house of mourning; and where this day there is nothing but the sound of the timbrel, the harp, and the viol, it may be that the next day there is the voice of crying and lamentation.

How many parents, who have long prayed for children and have at length obtained them, see them snatched away with an early stroke, and the flower wither in the blossom that they began to dote upon, their eyes closed by death as soon as they had but peeped into the world! And how many do we find in tears because they do but bring forth children to the grave, and will not be comforted because they are dead, and find a greater sorrow in parting with them than in bringing them forth! How many parents are there whose children live several years, to whose education they contribute all they can, and who hope to have them be the staff and comfort of their old age; and when they begin to flourish, a storm comes and blasts the fair and goodly fruit. And while they look for abiding joys from their dutiful obedience and holy conversation, they are forced to follow the promising and hopeful youths to their grave, and mourn as did David, even for a bad son: "O Absalom! my son! my son! Would to God I had died for thee! O Absalom! my son! my son!"

Nay, again, how many parents are there weeping for the disobedience of their children, who are likely to be the heirs of wrath, and to fall into destruction! It costs them many a tear and a sigh to think that their children are children of the devil and brands of hell! How it sinks their souls to see that all their prayers and exhortations, and all their cost and charge, are likely to be in vain! What sorrow can be greater than to think that what they have done for them will aggravate their condemnation, and that they must find their children, their now-dear and beloved children, at the left hand of Christ on that great day! The thoughts of this send them mourning to the grave.

How many congregations are mourning for the death of their faithful ministers, whom they shall never hear, nor with whom they shall never pray again! It grieves them to see those stars set that gave them light, and those ambassadors called home who entreated them to be reconciled. How many soldiers are bewailing the death of their general, who, in the midst of all his victories and their applauses, was all of a sudden snatched away!

7. Death is another occasion of weeping to the sons of men, as are also many of its violent and quick approaches. Ecclesiastes 9:12: "For man knoweth not his time; as the fishes that are taken in an evil net, and as the birds that are caught in the snare, so are the sons of men snared in an evil time, when it falleth suddenly upon them." Hezekiah turned his face to the wall and wept when he had his summons to depart. And if so good a man was so greatly concerned, how much more may most others expect to be concerned? It is a very melancholy thought to one in the flesh to think that he and his dear body must shortly depart, and that the body in which he has eaten and drunk and slept at ease, which has been treated so kindly and clothed so neatly, shall be turned into the grave, and there, in a very hideous manner, be consumed. As children cry when they come into the world, so do they generally weep when they go out again.

"Must I," often says a dying man, "leave you, my dear friends, my pleasant acquaintances, and never see you any more? I must never eat, drink, nor talk with you any more! I must not walk in my pleasant gardens, nor survey my habitation, nor visit my friends, nor they me, any more forever! I am going into the cold and lonely grave, and must, by myself, without your company, travel that unknown and solitary path."

The change of state, the greatness of the next world, and the different way of living when we are out of the body, and the many dreadful pains that accompany our last, concluding agonies make men see this period of life with weeping eyes; and when they are dying, it dissolves their friends into tears to see their wan and pale looks, to hear their last and dreadful groans. And immediately after death, it melts them to see the person with whom a few days before they comfortably discoursed and lived now changed into a mere lump of earth; for the soul that made it active and vigorous has fled away. It troubles them to part; it troubles them to think what their friend is, and what they themselves are soon likely to be. And when they come home the house is no longer as pleasant as it once was; they miss the one who made it so, the one whom they will never know again forever.

Thus mourners not only go about the streets, but are almost everywhere to be found in every country, and in every family. Job 14:1: "Man that is born of a woman is of few days, and full of trouble."

8. As for his soul, man is exposed to an abundance of sorrows. He labors under a miserable darkness in his understanding, and his natural ignorance creates an abundance of trouble and vexation in his soul. He has foolish hopes and extravagant desires, and a vain curiosity to know many things which he shall never know. And then the light of his understanding is apt to be eclipsed and confounded with the irresistible diseases of the body, so that it is impossible for him to think in sickness after the same manner as he used to do in health. His will also ministers to his sorrow; for he wills and desires an abundance of things that are contrary to his real interest. And if he has the things that he is apt to desire they give him new torment and disquiet, and he suffers innumerable miseries from his

precipitous and eager inclinations.

Knowledge is the greatest ornament of a rational soul, and yet that too has its troubles. Ecclesiastes 1:18: "For in much wisdom there is much grief, and he that increaseth knowledge increaseth sorrow." It is not to be attained without great pains and difficulties, without laborious and diligent search and vast perplexities—whether we consider the blindness of our understandings, the intricacy of things themselves, the many dark recesses of nature, or the implication of causes and effects, besides those accidental difficulties which are occasioned by the subtlety and entanglement of error. The variety of intricate opinions and the many convolutions of controversies and disputes, are apt to whirl a man about with a vertigo of contradictory probabilities; and instead of settling, they rather amuse and distract the mind, so that much study is wearisome to the flesh, as Bishop Wilkins said.

Besides, knowledge makes further trouble to the soul in that the more a man knows, the more he sees there is yet to be known. The higher a man climbs, the more he sees of the journey that is yet to go. And he who is versed in the knowledge of the world sees an abundance of mistakes and disorders which he cannot remedy, and which to behold is very sad. By knowing a great deal, he is liable to an abundance of contradiction and opposition from the more peevish, self-willed, and ignorant part of mankind, who are vexed because he will not think and say as they do. They are then very prone to censure and condemn the things they do not understand, for it is most easy to do so, whereas to pierce into the reason of things requires a mighty labor and a succession of deliberate and serious thoughts, to which the nature of man is averse. To judge lazily and hastily requires no trouble; and were it not that it is a man's duty to know, and that his soul, if it has anything of greatness and amplitude in its faculties, cannot be satisfied without it, it would be a much safer and quieter course to be ignorant. Study and painful inquiries after knowledge sometimes exhaust and break our spirits; they can prejudice our health and bring upon us those diseases to which the careless and unthinking seldom are inclined. Ecclesiastes 1:14–15: "I have seen all the works that are done under the sun, and, behold, all is vanity and vexation of spirit; that which is crooked cannot be made straight, and that which is wanting cannot be numbered."

Chapter 23

Showing that the fall of Adam was the cause of all our miseries; in how excellent a condition the blessed angels are; and the folly of such as expect to meet with nothing in the world but what is easy and pleasant

INFERENCE 1. Seeing that the life of man is a state of weeping, what sin must there be in the fall of Adam, which has so provoked God as to send so many miseries upon His own creatures! Had Adam not fallen, we would have always rejoiced and never mourned; we would have always sung the praises of God with delight, and would never have hung our harps upon the willows. We would have always lived upon the food of angels, pure and celestial joys, and would not have had that bread of sorrows which we now have to feed upon. We may justly cry out, "O Adam! What was it that you did when you tasted the forbidden fruit? Why did you ruin yourself and us, your helpless posterity, in one day? By one act you turned the pleasant world into a place of woe, and changed yourself and us from freemen into prisoners of this earth." It was a sad day indeed that opened a sluice to that vast inundation of miseries that have overwhelmed the lower world since that time. From thence came storms and tempests, wars and desolations, and all the burdens under which we groan and from which we cannot escape.

It is to this spring that we may trace all our troubles.

Oh, how happily, how pleasantly we might have lived had we not apostatized! And now we can only say, "Woe unto us, for we have sinned!" And when any plagues molest us, they are the fruit of our own choice, the product of our own iniquity! But thanks be to God that, through the blood of Jesus Christ, we have a way to escape at length from all those plagues and sins.

INFERENCE 2. Seeing that this life is full of weeping, how much happier are the blessed angels than we! At the view of the harmony and order of the world's creation, those sons of the morning sang together; it pleased them to see their Creator's glory appearing so, and they still continue to sing and praise Him. Not a troubled thought has possessed their minds; those holy spirits are always joyful, serene, and undisturbed; they are not linked to such bodies as we have and, consequently, are not liable to so many thousands of miseries.

A soul in flesh is forced to sympathize with its neighbor and companion, the body, and is altered or changed as to its joys and griefs according to the various objects that are suitable or disagreeable to the body. And yet our embodied condition gives us some privileges of which the angels, being spirits, are not capable; for by this means we can glorify God by suffering for Him, and by our patience in our various trials convert many to the faith of Christ, which the spiritual nature of angels gives them no opportunity to do.

As long as we are united to the body, so long must we expect to be afflicted; and when this union is happily dissolved, then the time of our freedom and our pleasure comes. In the resurrection we shall be as the angels of God; we shall not be busied with those perplexing and intricate affairs that now molest us. We shall be like them in vigor, activity, and joy. We shall have bodies indeed even then, but such as will be spiritualized, such as will not be capable of mourning and lamentation, nor by their heaviness, pains, and indispositions be any more a hindrance to the nimbler operations of our souls. And it should comfort us to think that one day we shall have such excellent companions, so knowing and so kind and loving as angels are, and that then we shall rejoice as well as they, and will, with our common praise, give our great Creator an eternal hymn of thanks.

INFERENCE 3. They have a wrong notion of the life of man who expect to find nothing in it but what is pleasant. These, because their mountain now stands strong, say with David, "I shall never be moved" (Psalm 30:6–7). However clearly their sun now shines, yet, sooner or later, storms and darkness will overtake them. The day is coming that will cast a veil upon all their smiling glory and turn their laughter into mourning and lamentation. For "man is born unto trouble, as the sparks fly upward" (Job 5:7). This world is like a hospital, full of various miseries and calamities; and therefore those who promise themselves nothing but diversion, mirth, and soft and easy pleasures labor under manifold mistakes, which arise from these two causes:

(1) Want of experience and consideration. Hence it is that young people, and such as have lived but a little while, are mightily taken with the sweetness and delight of life, whereas those who have tried it some years longer find several crosses and disappointments and vexations in it. And though the morning of

their day was clear, yet they see many thick clouds gather as the shadows of the evening are drawing on. It is nothing but gross ignorance that occasions the loud and mad triumphs of so great a part of the world; for if they surveyed even a little the condition of their suffering neighbors and the weakness of their own bodies, the uncertainty of their hopes and the vanity of their desires, they would sit down and bewail their miseries, and they would find their biggest joys to be confined with grief.

(2). They resolve not to disturb their present ease and pleasure with any mournful meditations. They'll shut their ears against all sad and doleful stories, and will hasten from the sight of all such dismal objects as would make them grave and solid. They will not ruffle their thoughts with anticipations of evil and future trouble; they are now at ease, and they hope they shall be so for very long. And this false expectation has no other cause than their unwillingness and aversion to think of a coming change; because they feel no pain, sickness, or inconvenience, they will not spoil their music with groans and sighs. They will eat, drink and be merry, and hang sorrow and cast care away. But as all the mirth of sailors cannot hinder the winds and the storms, so this insensibility and jollity does not keep the evil day further off, but rather swells the clouds and lays in matter for a more durable and intolerable sorrow. They may, in their jovial humors and with their full bowls, drown their understandings, but they cannot by this means overwhelm their miseries, which, after the fumes of the grateful wine have passed, will have a resurrection.

They may say indeed, as does Isaiah 56:12, "Come, we

will fill ourselves, and tomorrow shall be as this day, and much more abundant." But perhaps they will never see that morrow. Or, if they do, it may bring along with it some great or unavoidable calamity. We know that David said, in his prosperity, "I shall never be moved," and yet as soon as God hid His face, he was troubled (Psalm 30:6–7). It is unreasonable to conclude from our present delight that we shall never grieve. We may as well argue that, because we are now healthy, we shall never be sick, or that, because we are now alive, we shall never die. Such false conclusions and such vain hopes only increase our later troubles and make them heavier. It is said of Babylon the Great in Revelation 18:7–8: "How much she hath glorified herself, and lived deliciously, so much torment and sorrow give her; for she saith in her heart, 'I sit a queen, and am no widow, and shall see no sorrow'; therefore shall her plagues come in one day, death, and mourning, and famine."

Our miseries are sure, but our joys are uncertain; our pleasures endure but a moment, but our sorrows last a long time; our pleasures no sooner begin to live than they begin to die; and when we would prolong their time, their continuance occasions either torment or loathing. Senault, in his *Use of the Passions,* says that grief is more familiar to man than is pleasure, for one vain contentment is met with a thousand real sorrows. These come uncalled, and present themselves of their own proper motion. They are linked to one another. But pleasures are sought for with pain, and we are forced to pay more for them than they are worth. Sorrows are sometimes entirely pure, and touch us to the quick as they make us incapable of consolation; but pleasures are never without some mixture of sorrow.

They are always dipped in bitterness, and we are much more sensible of pain than of pleasure; for a slight disease troubles all our most solid contentments. A fever is able to make conquerors forget their victories, and to blot out of their minds all the pomp of their triumphs.

In some cases, though, we may make our sorrows greater in our imagination than they are in reality; for we are more ingenious and more particular in the computation of our grief than of our mercies. Many a thorn that annoys us is of our own planting; for one cross that God sends, our uneasiness and impatience make a thousand more. We apprehend some things to be evil which are not truly so; and sometimes we augment our real evils beyond their natural proportion, and so add new weight to that burden which made us groan before. Yet for all that, and abstracting from our irregularities since the fall, man is a very mournful creature. And our being so should excite us to take heed that we do not wound ourselves afresh when we are already wounded, nor lay in matter of new griefs when our unavoidable ones may be great enough.

There are two ways by which we aggravate our own miseries: (1) By putting a higher value upon things than they really deserve, and by loving them more than we ought; then the separation that is made between them and us gives a more weighty sorrow. (2) By seeking outside of ourselves for many things to make us happy, whereas we should labor that our souls be duly ordered, and our desires kept within their just and lawful bounds.

INFERENCE 4. We have cause to admire the wisdom of divine providence that, seeing that the case of man is so very miserable, He has ordered it to be very short.

Though our days are evil, yet they are but few. And though the days are for hard labor, there is a succession of comfortable nights wherein we may go to rest. We find it a long, tedious while to be in sorrows for fifty or sixty years, but how loud would our groans be if we were condemned to this toil and these weepings for many thousands of years! The greater our misery is, the less time it is likely to last. The sorrows of a man's spirit are like ponderous weights which, by the greatness of their burden, make a swifter motion, and descend into the grave to rest and ease our wearied limbs, and to knock our fetters off that eat us to the very bones.

Thus I have shown what sorrows are common to the sons and daughters of men. I am now to show what peculiar occasions of weeping Christians have above other men.

Chapter 24

The peculiar occasions of weeping that good Christians have more than other men

1. The Christian weeps for his own sins. He is convinced of his own folly and bewails it; he has, by the illumination of the Spirit, a more tender heart than others have, a more distinct view of the odiousness and malignity of the poisonous nature and dangerous qualities of sin; and that which was pleasant in the commission, he finds by dear experience to be bitter as gall and wormwood afterwards. This weeping is not the effect of mere softness or weakness of temper, or from a want of courage. There is nothing more reasonable, more just or honorable than to bewail the offenses that we are guilty of against the law of God. And to what purpose has He given us innocent passions but that they should be moved when suitable objects present themselves? The Christian says with David in Psalm 51:3, "I acknowledge my transgressions, and my sin is ever before me." And such a sign of an object so disagreeable pierces and wounds his very soul and makes it dissolve in a genuine and kindly grief and trouble, saying, "Oh, what have I done against my God, my Savior, and the Holy Spirit? Oh, how basely have I forgotten a gracious and loving God, a God who has remembered me all my days for good! He has loved me, and I have hated Him. He has called me, and I have disobeyed His voice. He has provided for me, and I have rebelled. He has been a

Father, but I have been undutiful, prodigal, and disobedient. And now His slighted, His forgotten love and kindness wound me to the very soul. Oh, what did I think of when I did not think of Him? What was it that my vain, foolish heart loved when I did not love Him who is altogether amiable? What was it that I cared for, or in what did I spend my time, that I did not care for my soul or for pleasing my God, who spared me and bore with me with an admirable patience? 'I have sinned; what shall I do unto Thee, O Thou preserver of men?' (Job 7:20). I will put my mouth in the dust. I will loath and abhor myself for my iniquities, if so be there may be hope. I have wandered, but my wanderings have cost me dearly. I have been in a strange land, and with tears I will return home, saying, 'Bless me, even me also, O my Father!' "

And then the love of Jesus constrains the poor Christian to be sorrowful, saying, "Did He leave heaven for me, and for me who many times would not leave a sin for Him; for me, who was a lost sheep, a dying malefactor, and an enemy by my evil works? Did He come to rescue me when I was in the very jaws of a roaring lion, and at the door of hell, and shall I not be grieved to think that I have requited Him so ill for all His love? It was my sins that made Him astonished, troubled, and exceedingly troubled even unto death; and yet, alas, I have done what I could to increase His agonies by my new sins. It was my sin that filled the bitter cup, that betrayed, that whipped, that exposed to such injurious usage the Son of God. It was my sin that wounded His breast, that raked in His sides, that nailed Him to the tree and made Him die. And can I look upon what I have done and not be troubled? Can my eyes behold

Him hanging on the cross and not have it affect my heart? Never was there any sorrow like His sorrow; never was there any love like His love. And never was there disobedience more inexcusable than mine has been; never was sin more sinful than mine has been! I have often made light of that which pressed Him down to the grave. I have rejoiced at that which made Him mourn and weep. But I will do so again no more forever."

And then it troubles the good Christian to think how often he has refused the motions of the blessed Spirit, and how, when the Spirit has moved upon his heart with a design to do him good, he has sent Him away grieved and vexed. All this is occasion of grief, though it does not always express itself in tears; for there is a rational sorrow as well as a sensitive one, and though the latter may be more passionate, yet the former is more lasting and durable. For those who are converted in their younger days, the warmth and heat of their glowing and beginning zeal more easily melts into tears, and then the rivers flow more than they do afterwards; but yet, when the flood ceases, the fruitfulness appears and, when their tears are dried up, their hatred of sin remains. For these outward expressions of sorrow are very much influenced by the temper and constitution of the body (2 Corinthians 7:10–11).

As it is in the first birth, so it is in the second: as soon as they are born they cry. No sooner are they brought from darkness into marvelous light but they wonder at their folly, and at the grace of God that saved them from it; and that wonder produces love and grief. First their hearts are softened with His love, and then they mourn for their provocations—though this with which good Christians bewail their sins is not a lazy grief, but is attended with serious endeavors of new obedience, as the husbandman, after the profitable showers of rain, sets himself with a renewed industry to cultivate the ground. And it is but reasonable that our eyes, which are too often the instruments of sin to us, should help us by tears to bewail that sin. Isaiah 38:15: "I shall go softly all my years in the bitterness of my soul."

2. Those who are good Christians weep also for the sins of others. The love they have for the name of God causes them to grieve for the reflections and dishonors that are thrown upon it by wicked men. They cannot without sorrow behold or hear of the sins of men in general: the sins of kingdoms, provinces, and towns; the sins of families; the sins of their fellow citizens, their brethren, and their neighbors. The tears that they shed are tears of compassion for the very sad and miserable condition of the world. While others make a mockery of sin, and through the blindness of their folly know not what they do, good men lament these persons' lack of concern and insensibility while they see them sporting on the hole of asps. They cannot see men treat their heavenly Father with insolence and scorn without their own hearts, in a just zeal for His glory, rising against them, not with indecent passions for their ruin, but in a hearty longing for their reformation. Psalm 119:136: "Rivers of water run down mine eyes, because they keep not Thy law." Thus said the prophet to his hearers in Jeremiah 13:17: "My soul shall weep in secret places for your pride; mine eyes shall weep sore, and run down with tears."

Our love for our neighbor and our zeal for God's

glory oblige us to this sorrow; it must grieve us to think what men are doing when they sin, how great a God they provoke to punish them, and how great a misery they are bringing on their own souls. It must grieve us to think how unsafe a way they go, and what a dismal end that way will have (Philippians 3:19). In Jeremiah 9:1 the prophet wished, "Oh, that my head were waters, and mine eyes a fountain of tears, that I might weep day and night for the slain of the daughter of my people." And yet, as [Pierre] Du Bosc has observed, when he pronounced these sad words the misery of the Jews had not arrived. Jerusalem as yet subsisted in its magnificence and splendor; its temple had not lost that admirable beauty which made it the wonder of the world. Its palaces had lost nothing of their pomp; its walls and fortresses were entire, and the daughter of Zion was princess among the provinces. But he spoke thus foreseeing that their abounding sins and their hardness and obstinacy would certainly bring upon them the judgments of God.

We must consider what we were ourselves when in the house of bondage and serving divers lusts, how enslaved and miserable we were. In this way the remembrance we have of our former danger may quicken us to do others all the good we can, so that they may not fall into hell while we are looking on, and to do all that is in our power to hinder their going there. To this compassionate sorrow we may be excited by the kind example of our Lord in Luke 19:41. He wept for those who rejoiced. He pitied those who had no pity for their own souls; because their hearts were hardened, His was very soft and tender. It is a matter of mourning and lamentation to consider how few there are who profess religion in its strictness, and, among those few, how many are scandalous or backsliders or hypocrites. It has often been observed that, among the bitter ingredients of our Lord's passion, this one was not the least, to foresee that there would be so many who, by their final impenitence and persevering in wickedness, would receive no benefit by it (see John Norris's *Discourse on the Beatitudes*). And if we may judge by proportion, the angels in heaven, who rejoice at the conversion of one sinner, also mourn and lament for the irreclaimable wickedness of so many millions in the world.

To a zealous magistrate, it is an occasion of sorrow to see in his dominions the great King and Ruler of the world so little valued, and his grief will stir him up to use all the wholesome methods he can, by good laws and a necessary severity, to keep the divine laws and authority from being scorned and trampled on by profane and blasphemous sinners. To a good parent, it is an occasion of grief to see the undutifulness and miscarriages of his children; it is very cutting to think that he has brought forth such as shall be his torment, and servants of the devil. To a minister, it is an occasion of grief when he meets with a careless audience or an unfruitful people, whom he is likely to see perish under the means of safety; for he is likely to be their accuser in the great day, and they are likely to be separated forever when the judgment comes. With a heavy heart and many tears he thinks of their forlorn state (Romans 9:1–2). Acts 20:18–19: "Ye know after what manner I have been with you at all seasons, serving the Lord with all humility of mind, and with many tears and temptations." Acts 20:31: "For the space of three years I ceased not to warn every one night and day with tears."

3. Good Christians weep for the manifold tribulations and persecutions they meet with. God is sometimes pleased to let loose the passions and the fury of wicked men for their chastisement, whose tender mercies are even cruelty. Song of Solomon 2:2: "As the lily among the thorns, so is my love among the daughters." She is beautiful and glorious, but surrounded with difficulties and tribulations. Psalm 84:6: "Passing through the valley of Baca, they make it a well; the rain also filleth the pools." They are satisfied indeed to endure trouble in the hope of heaven, but yet their sorrows and torments make them go there weeping. They have sense as well as religion, and their sensible nature, whether they will or not, will be affected. They cannot be sick but they must groan and sigh as well as others; they cannot feel tortures, racks, tedious imprisonments, or flames without shrinking a little at them.

Even the apostles, those great and courageous believers, were troubled and perplexed, though they were not overthrown (2 Corinthians 4:8). In times of persecution there is a general license of doing mischief, a bold oppressing of the poor, and a scornful despising of the afflicted and the desolate. This was the complaint in Psalm 123:4: "Our soul is exceedingly filled with the scorning of those that are at ease, and with the contempt of the proud." And the scorn of evil men is so base a thing that the most patient cannot but be somewhat concerned at it. Psalm 42:3–4: "My tears have been my meat day and night, while they continually say unto me, 'Where is thy God?' When I remember these things, I pour out my soul in me."

It is true that the servants of Christ esteem it an abundant matter of joy when they fall into divers tribulations. Their minds are quiet and well-satisfied; they love their Master, and will never leave Him; they will follow Him to the cross and die with Him there. But inasmuch as they are composed of flesh and blood, and have a nature that is tender and soft and averse to suffering as well as that of others, and which has several things that engage it to the world (such as various friends and relations to part with), they cannot, with respect to these, leave this earth without some grief and sorrow. The hearers of Paul wept that they should see his face no more; and it was likely to break his heart that he was to leave friends who were so affectionate, so loving, and so kind. And we must not think that they did not part at last without flowing eyes on either side (Acts 21:13).

4. Christians, however easy in their own circumstances, still have occasion of sorrow from that sympathy they have with their brethren who are in distress. The Spirit of our compassionate Lord dwells in their hearts, and as He is afflicted with all the afflictions of His people, so are they. They are all members of the same body, and one part of the body cannot rejoice while another part thereof is in pain. Thus they weep with those who weep (Romans 12:15). To hear of the desolation of others is extremely grievous to them; nor can they laugh and be merry while others sigh and groan. See Jeremiah 4:31, 8:21–22, and 14:17–20.

They cannot cheer themselves with music when the harps of others are hanging on the willows (Lamentations 1:12, 16; 2:11–12). This book of Lamentations is so very lamentable that it very well deserves to be read and considered by us so that the miseries of our neighbors may affect us as they ought to do. Job 30:25: "Did not I weep for him that was in trouble? Was not my soul grieved for the poor?" It must be a very hellish temper that has no relenting for the sufferings of others.

Such a diabolical temper reigns in France at this day whereby, by the encouragement of a cruel king and as cruel a clergy, the poor Protestants have undergone barbarous and more than heathen severities. If they had anything human left, they could not have used those poor, harmless, and innocent people as they have done. But they have long since degenerated into wolves, and to this day they retain their brutal and savage nature, tearing to pieces the sheep of Christ without any provocation. And though some have had such a brazen impudence as to say they have all along used nothing with them but sweet and gentle methods, yet there are enough witnesses, too many, in fact, in all parts of Europe who tell us melancholy stories of their hellish cruelties. Had there been the lowest degree of Christianity left in that execrable country, they could not, they dare not have proceeded to such barbarities as they have done, where neither the gray hairs of the most aged and venerable, nor the tears of widows, nor the sighs of prisoners could ever yet prevail for the least mitigation. They have exceeded the worst of former ages in the cruelty of their torments. Any other eyes but theirs would weep to see what they inflict on their fellow creatures; any other hearts would soften at the groans and cries of so many miserable people. But nothing can make an impression upon them; their dungeons, galleys, racks, and gibbets are the only things they can think of wherewith to vex such as are better than themselves, such as have been guilty of no crime unless it were an excess of loyalty to a king who is an enemy to mankind, as well as their enemy. By his allowance the vilest of men are permitted to do all those villainous and wicked things which raise a just horror in all who have any zeal for the glory of God, to see such feeding their cruel eyes with woeful spectacles of the distressed and sorrowful whom they have caused to be such. The most pathetic melting expressions have not been able to draw the least pity from the breasts of these inhuman monsters.

Will men never be ashamed of their antichristian barbarity? Will they never know that it is the beast in Revelation who makes himself drunk with the blood of saints, devours their flesh, makes war upon them, and overcomes them? He must have renounced reason and humanity, and must be transformed into a savage beast, who behaves toward Christians as the Church of Rome behaves towards us. Those French persecutors are so bad that they cannot be reproached. We cannot, if we wanted to, bespatter or throw dirt upon them, for they are already so defiled. It is impossible to create in the minds of others any idea of them that shall be base enough; and it is our shame, the stain of our country, and a dishonor to the name of any Englishman that in our country, which is naturally inclined to show pity and compassion to the miserable, there should be found any who wish well to so tyrannical a tyrant, and to a people so nourished and so fed with blood as his soldiers and creatures are. It is our judgment that we are so blinded, so stupefied, and thrown into so deep a sleep that we do not perceive our own blindness.

But I would be very sorry if I spoke to any such persons. I hope, and I believe, that there are none here so much under the curse of God, a curse all the more terrible since it is contrary to all that love of God, neighbor, and country that we ought to have. And if we are in any way cursed it is because we have had no more compassion for our brethren who have suffered such grievous things; because we have wept no more at the sight of their sorrows, but have still too many among us who are of the complexion of those spoken of in Amos 6:6. Men are generally unaffected with the miseries of others; they are like the priest and the Levite who left the poor, wounded person without any help; they do not fix their eyes or their minds on sad objects, for they find them to be very disagreeable.

5. Another occasion of weeping to good Christians is from both the duties of religion and the more than ordinary providences and dispensations of God that call them to it. There are several things which, though their consequences are very pleasant, yet are in themselves very sorrowful. Some of these I have already mentioned: the bitterness of repentance, being troubled at the afflictions of others, the duties of self-denial and mortification, crucifying the flesh with the affections and lusts thereof, dying daily, and keeping our hearts weaned from an inordinate affection for the enjoyments and comforts of the world.

All good Christians are to be in heaviness for a season, and to sow in tears. And to the things mentioned above may be added the calls we have to more public and solemn humiliations by the necessity of our own affairs, the judgments of God, and the pride, rage, and success of His and our enemies. And this is the duty to which we are now called. Let us take care that our days of fasting and prayers may be mingled with the sorrow of a true repentance and contrition so that God, who has been for us hitherto, may not be against us, and so that we may not smart under spiritual judgments, which, of all others, are most formidable and severe, according to Isaiah 22:12.

Thus good Christians have many just subjects of weeping; they weep to see themselves as in exile, and at a distance from their beloved country: they weep to find themselves compassed about with many infirmities and unbecoming passions that cause them to be engaged in continual war; they weep that they are exposed to so many furious assaults of the devil, and that they have so little strength wherewith to resist him; they weep when they consider that their good and gracious God is so greatly dishonored and forgotten in His own world.

From all that has been said, see, first, what need all good Christians have of faith and patience. They need faith to conclude that God does all very well in holiness and wisdom, though He allows the world and the church to groan under so many miseries and tribulations. They need patience to submit to what He appoints for their lot, and not in the least to repine or murmur at it. Without faith we shall be apt to stumble at these seeming disorders and the unequal distributions of His providence; without patience we shall be apt to struggle under the necessary cross, to be tired and say, "It is vain to wait upon the Lord."

We see, second, that good Christians have great reason to quietly leave the world, and to die when God is pleased to call them. It is a world of misery, of sorrows and vexation. We should not be fond of our chains, nor delight in our tears, nor embrace our griefs; but we should remember that we shall leave all these troublesome things behind us when we lie down in the quiet grave. For "there the wicked cease from troubling, and there the weary be at rest" (Job 3:17). Surely we do not esteem this strange land to be better than our Father's house! We do not think that the veil of tears is better than the joys of heaven. To that heaven, then, let us lift our weeping eyes; and with hope of that let us comfort our sad and mournful hearts. There let us hasten; there let us long to be; into that haven let us steer our distressed and weary souls. Let us breathe after that paradise that shall not be molested with the poisonous venom of the serpent, and where no thorns or briars grow. Let us not be found in a perpetual storm, nor be so foolish as to think our sighs are better than praises and hallelujahs. Let us hasten in our desires from this diseased world which, by its low situation, is apt to suffer an inundation of innumerable miseries, and prepare for that world where there is an eternal health and joy.

Chapter 25

The dreadful apprehensions a soul has that is under desertion, and in several respects how very sad and doleful its condition is, from the author's own experience

The next thing I design to insist upon is to show that the time of God's forsaking a soul is a very dark and mournful time. It is not only night, but a weeping, stormy night. It may be useful to you who have, it may be, lived hitherto in the beams and cheerful light of day to know what passes in this sorrowful and doleful night. And in this matter I will not borrow information from others, but will give you my own experience.

1. In this night the deserted soul is overwhelmed with continual thoughts of the holiness, majesty, and glory of the Lord; it does not think of Him with any manner of delight, as was the case with Asaph in Psalm 77:3: "I remembered God, and was troubled; I complained, and my spirit was overwhelmed." And in how deplorable a case is such a soul that cannot think of its God and its Creator but with grief and sorrow, that fixes upon nothing in Him but His terrible and severe attributes! In other cases, when a man is distressed on earth and beholds vexation and disquiet here, he can lift up his eyes towards heaven and see joy and comfort for him there; but in this woeful case, there is neither the light of the sun, the moon, or the stars for many days. The face of God is hidden and covered with a

dreadful cloud. Job 31:23: "Destruction from God was a terror to me, and by reason of His highness I could not endure."

2. The deserted soul in this mournful night looks upon God as its enemy, and as intending its hurt and ruin by the sharpness of His dispensations. And this makes the soul incapable of receiving any consolation from fellow creatures; for that soul will say to others, "Alas, if God is my enemy, as I apprehend Him to be, which of you can be my friend? I have a dreadful sound of His displeasure in my ears, and which of you can bring me any glad tidings? If His power, His irresistible power, is against me, who can keep off the killing blow! Job 19:6, 8: 'Know now that God hath overthrown me, and hath compassed me with His net. He hath fenced up my way that I cannot pass, and He hath set darkness in my paths.' And so verses 9–11, as well as Psalm 88:7: 'Thy wrath lieth hard upon me, and Thou hast afflicted me with all Thy waves.' "

If in such desertion God were apprehended to be upon a design of the future happiness and welfare of the soul, it would bear up with courage or with hope, but, having no such belief, it must sink and languish. The stroke that wounds us in such a case is the more painful, as it is edged with a sense of wrath. Psalm 102:9–10: "I have eaten ashes like bread, and mingled my drink with weeping, because of Thine indignation and Thy wrath, for Thou hast lifted me up and cast me down."

Thus does the weeping person vent his sorrows: "God never gives His people such a bitter cup but He mingles love and mercy with it. But, alas, I taste nothing but gall and wormwood, nothing but misery and vexation. He is with His people, but He has forsaken me. He has cast me into a fiery furnace where I am daily burned and scorched, and He is not with me there. He is unto me as a roaring lion, and who can turn away His powerful wrath? Ruth 1:20: 'The Almighty hath dealt very bitterly with me.' I have often heard that it is a terrible thing to fall into the hands of the living God. And now I find it to be so. All the wrath of men is nothing to His; one frown of His is more intolerable than all their rage and persecution. Job 16:12–13: 'I was at ease, but He hath broken me asunder. He hath also taken me by my neck and shaken me to pieces, and set me up for His mark. His archers compass me round about; He cleaveth my reins asunder, and doth not spare. He poureth out my gall upon the ground.' " (See also Job 10:16–17.)

Oh, what anguish, what desolation is caused in the soul by such thoughts as these! "I dare not," says the mourning person, "look up to heaven, for there I see how great a God I have against me. I dare not look into His Word, for there I see all His threats as so many barbed arrows to strike me to the heart. I dare not look into the grave, because there I am likely to have a doleful resurrection."

And what can a poor creature do who apprehends the Almighty to be His enemy? It is a common thing for people to say, "Why do you lament and mourn? You have many mercies left, many friends who pray for you and pity you." But, alas, what help is there in all of that if God Himself is gone! Nothing is then looked upon as a mercy. And as for the prayers of others, the distressed person will say, "They can do me no good unless I have faith, and I find that I have none at all. If I had faith, it would purify and cleanse my heart, but I do nothing but sin. Therefore God, since He is holy, must set Himself against me, His enemy."

3. In this doleful night, the soul has no evidence at all of its former grace. In this night, not only has the sun set, but not one star appears. Such a one looks upon himself as altogether devoid of the grace of God. He looks upon all his former duties as insincere or hypocritical; he feels his heart to be hardened at present, and concludes that it was never tender; he finds himself at present listless and indisposed, and concludes that he never had any true life or motion. He expresses his sorrows after this, or a similar manner: "I thought I had belonged to God, but now I find I am none of His. I thought I had been upright, but now I see that I was mistaken. The storm has come, and the house that I built upon the sand is now washed away. Those who are Christ's He enables to persevere to the end, but I am fallen from grace. I am an apostate, for if I had any share in the intercession of the great Redeemer, He would not leave me so sad and desolate.

"I thought that I had been planted in His vineyard, but now I am cut down as a barren tree. Oh, how greatly have I been deceived, who imagined myself to be an heir of heaven, and who am now seized with the pangs of hell! I see now that I was never right, never born again, never renewed by the Spirit, never changed from death to life. And, oh, what will become of me, who flattered my own soul to ruin! I thought myself safe when I was not, and well when I was diseased! To come to misery after I thought so long of happiness is a double misery. I am likely to be, after all my prayers, endeavors, and hopes, a reprobate and a castaway."

And such a soul concludes itself to be in a condition much more dangerous than those who never named the name of Christ, nor pretended to religion, because it reckons that their misery will be much more tolerable than its own. It judges itself to be a hypocrite, and then all the threats that are made against such persons overwhelm it every moment with inexpressible confusion. Thus the graces of the Spirit and the former fruits of holiness are not discerned in this sad and mournful night.

4. During this sadness, the soul cannot think of Christ with any comfort. Thus it argues: "He will be a Savior to none but those who believe. I have no faith, and therefore He will be no Savior to me. He who is to His servants as the Lamb of God will be to me as the Lion of the tribe of Judah. He who deals gently with them will tear me to pieces. I have heard of His sufferings and His death, but if His blood has not cleansed and purified me, I am likely to perish despite all that. I heard His voice and I disobeyed it. I heard His gospel and did not make use of it, and now even the glad tidings of salvation are not so to me. I did not know in the long day that I had the things that belonged to my peace, and now they are hidden from my eyes.

"Now I have to deal with the great and dreadful God Himself, and I have no one to plead my cause. Oh, how can I resist His power or bear His wrath? Christ indeed called me, but I did not open to Him; now He calls no more. He seems to be angry and enraged against me for my disobedience. And though I have sometimes cried, 'Have mercy on me, Thou Son of David,' He passes by and does not hear my cries. And, oh, what shall I do when He comes in the clouds of heaven, when I am to stand at His bar and be punished as an unbeliever! To others that will be a day of refreshment, but what will it be to me? The thoughts of it are now amazing."

Thus, by a sense of unbelief, the deserted soul is plunged in the waves and sees no way of escape. And by this unbelief it thinks of God as absolutely determined, and the thoughts of Him are as terrible as if there were no Mediator. The deserted soul is continually saying, "I have all my sins to answer for, and no one to undertake for me. I am condemned, and have no one to procure a pardon and salvation for me."

5. In this night the soul is full of terror. And how can it be otherwise when every thought of God and of Christ overwhelms it? Job 6:4: "For the arrows of the Almighty are within me, the poison whereof drinketh up my spirit; the terrors of God do set themselves in array against me." Such arrows that are shot by an almighty arm, with a great power and force, must, being so directed, pierce very deep; deep and painful must be the wounds that God makes. And then they are poisoned arrows too that are dipped in His wrath, inflame the wounds they make, and put the distressed person into pain and inexpressible anguish. Night is a time of terror, especially in commotions, uproars, and the like mischiefs (Psalm 91:5). And in this night it is much more so when a man's own conscience discharges a thousand accusations against him for his guilt; for then every sin gives a blow, and altogether, being set in array, they make a formidable force. And when God sets forth peculiar impressions of His wrath, and when they fall upon the naked soul with their scorching, burning drops, there is then not one quiet thought, nor one easy moment—all is amazement, confusion, and woe.

Lamentations 3:3: "Surely against me He is turned; He turneth His hand against me all the day."

A person who is thus distressed sits and muses on His misery, and would gladly find something that might be comfortable; but he cannot. What He first thinks of is tormenting; he changes that uneasy thought for another, and that one is as tormenting as the first. There is a circulation of flaming, disquieting thoughts, and such a person dwells as in a fiery furnace or as in a thicket of briars. Whichever way he turns himself, he is pained and wounded. All the terrible places of Scripture that are written against the wicked continually present themselves to his consideration, and he thinks that he shall most certainly have their portion.

Everything in nature that is frightful frightens him, since he still believes God to be against him. From all the terrible things imaginable he fetches something that still more afflicts him. And so he imagines: "Suppose I were to be sawn asunder, to be burned, to be buried alive or torn in pieces. What a sad thing that would be! And yet I am in a worse case than this, for I am now continually racked with guilt, and am likely to be in hell forever."

The terrors of the Lord we may indeed feel, but we cannot express them. They are so very terrible; they wound our most sensible and tender part; they cause our very souls to pine and languish away; they fix our minds on the contemplation of everything that is sad and doleful; and they fill us with confusion. As Heman says in Psalm 88:17, they are terrors that compass us round about. They seize upon every faculty and distress us in every part. To have God against us, His holiness to dazzle us, His power to overthrow us, His law to condemn us, and our consciences to accuse us—this is the sum of terrors!

6. Fear is another occasion of sorrow, and the night is usually a time of horror. We are then apt to be imposed upon with false as well as with real dangers. We can think of nothing but our misery, and the continual, unavoidable thinking of it makes us the more miserable (Job 13:21). These fears are as so many fetters from which we cannot fly; and when we think to shake them off, we put ourselves to more pain. "If I say, 'I will forget my complaint; I will leave off my heaviness and comfort myself,' I am afraid of all my sorrows. I know that Thou wilt not hold me innocent" (Job 9:27–28).

We are frightened with the greatness and majesty of God, with the glory of His being and the thunder of His power. We are frightened with the view of our innumerable sins, and with the dangers that attend them. The thoughts of heaven frighten us because we think we have lost that blessed place, and the thoughts of hell are no less frightful because we think we shall soon be there. The thoughts of life are frightful because it is with anguish and horror that we live. Nor can we bear the thoughts of death because we dare not die.

7. It is a night of weeping for deserted souls because they find no heart to pray, and no life in prayer. They fall upon their knees and cover the altar of the Lord with tears, but He does not seem to regard them. They beg and He gives them no relief; they cry and He does not answer, and this fills them with shame and grief (Lamentations 3:7–8). The thoughts of such poor people are in a continual hurry, and so are very full of wandering in the performance of their duty. Grief, by sad-

dening the spirits, destroys the freedom of our speech; for joy is the mother of eloquence and fluency. And when they would move up towards heaven, this sorrow dampens their vigor and makes them so that they cannot fly. And finding that they are still perplexed even after prayer, and still as uncomfortable as before, they are apt to throw it off and say, "It is vain to pray," as did Saul in 1 Samuel 28:15: "God is departed from me, and answereth me no more."

Sorrow is a very dull and sluggish thing. A man has no heart to go about any work when he is very sad. And this faintness occasions a new trouble. We are vexed when we do not pray, and when we would pray we cannot. Sorrows dampen our faith, our love, and our hope, and so spoil our duties; for, without these, they are without life and without acceptance. Sometimes our grief is so violent that it finds no vent; it strangles us and we are thereby overcome. "I am so troubled that I cannot speak" (Psalm 77:4).

It is with us in our desertions as with a man who gets a slight hurt. At first he walks up and down; but he does not look soon to prevent a growing problem, and the neglected wound begins to fester or gangrene, and brings him to a greater pain or loss. So it is with us many times in our spiritual sadness. When we are first troubled, we pray and pour out our souls before the Lord; but afterwards the waters of our grief drown our cries, and we are so overwhelmed that if we might have all the world we cannot pray, or at least we can find no enlargement, no life, no pleasure in our prayers. And God Himself seems to take no delight in them, and that makes us more sad (Psalm 22:1).

8. Such persons have no patience wherewith to bear

their evils. Oh, who is he who can bear the wrath of God? One thought of Him as a reconciled Father would sweeten the most heavy cross; but one view of Him as an Enemy causes all our strength to depart, and melts our very souls. In bodily evils the mind lends its assistance and furnishes the natural spirits with courage; but when the mind itself is weakened and troubled, what is it able to do? The wounded soul is most commonly fretful and impatient; the sight of heaven inspires our breasts with vital heat and makes us quiet and submissive under every dispensation; but the daily sight and fear of hell fills us with tumult and disorder. The language of deserted people, for the most part, is in groans, and in their prayers they chatter as a crane or a swallow, or mourn as a dove (Isaiah 38:14; Job 13:20–21).

9. They usually see no prospect of relief or deliverance, and that increases the sorrows of their doleful night. They are covered in the deep pit and see no way to fly from it (Job 9:27–28). They are wounded, and carry their wounds with them where they go; they are continually fixing their mournful eyes upon destruction and the grave (Job 7:7–8). They have indeed, now and then, some intermissions, but those are like the small breathers and refreshments of a person who is newly taken off the rack, only to be taken back to the rack again.

The tears of these poor, deserted people are not like the tears of Mary in the garden, for as soon as she began to weep she beheld her Lord. He quickly came to her help and changed her sorrows into consolations. His sweet voice, in a moment's time, ran through all the powers of her soul and made her heart leap with joy, scattering light upon it. But in this case He allows

His servants to be tossed for a long and doleful night before He is pleased to speak and to calm the storms, so that they are tightly besieged and have no relief at hand; they are as thirsty persons without water, hungry persons without bread. Psalm 142:4: "I looked on my right hand and beheld, but there was no man that would know me; refuge failed me."

10. This night of weeping is the more sorrowful because it is the time of Satan's cruelty. When our spirits are broken with long and painful afflictions, then this cowardly spirit sets upon us; he knows that he can easily perplex us when we are already thrown upon the ground. When the sun sets, then the beasts of the field creep abroad; when God has departed, then the devil comes. He comes and torments us with innumerable fears; he comes and triumphs over us, insults us, and says, "Where is your God now? What do you think of sin now? What has now become of all your hearing, your reading, and your many prayers? You thought to have escaped my power, and now I have you within my reach. Remember now that at such or such a time you sinned, and therefore God has forsaken you; you weep, and your tears are just, for you are miserable, and are likely to be with me forever."

Satan uses our sore afflictions to represent God to us as tyrannical, as one who will certainly destroy us. And it is our grief and our misery that we have so little in our desertions to answer him with. When we really believe that God has departed from us, what can we say? How this roaring lion most cruelly molests us when our glory and strength are gone! At other seasons we can oppose his malice and confidently say, "The Lord, that hath chosen Jerusalem, rebuke thee!"

Our enemy is indeed a knowing and a subtle spirit; he knows our weaknesses, sees our troubles, and urges even the very Scriptures and providences of God upon us to our disadvantage, and that with a marvelous importunity and diligence. He shoots at us with fiery darts that are extremely painful, and shoots them when we are under a sense of God's displeasure, which is like thrusting a red iron into a wound that is already very sore. It pleases the devil to hear us groan and to see us sad; and when we are already pressed down with our evils, he will be sure to throw more weight on us. Our groans are his music, and when we wallow in ashes, drown ourselves in tears, spread our hands for help, and roar till our throat is dry, he gluts his cruel heart with looking on our woes. It is the most pleasant sight to him to see God hiding Himself from His child, and to see that child broken with fears, torn in pieces with griefs, made a brother to dragons and a companion to owls, under restless anxieties and perpetual lamentations, feeble and sorely broken, his tongue cleaving to his jaw, his bowels boiling, his bones burned with heat, and his flesh consumed (see Richard Gilpin's *Treatise of Satan's Temptations* [published by Soli Deo Gloria]). He sets upon us after we have been long troubled and weary with our march in the doleful night. And, which is the sorrow of our sorrows, God may, for a long while, leave us in Satan's hands. And from his treatment of Job and Peter, we know what his temper is (Luke 22:31). This is the hour and power of darkness.

11. Sometimes this sorrow is mixed with deep despair. It is a tempestuous and stormy night. And, as Paul said in another case, all hope of their being saved is taken away. "I shall surely perish," says the mourning

soul. "I am damned and lost forever. I am already as if in hell, under inexpressible, insupportable pains and amazing fears. The Lord will be favorable no more. He has shut up His bowels and His tender mercies. He is gone, gone from me, and He is gone forever. No more shall I call Him 'Father'; no more shall I behold His shining face; no more shall I hear His kind and loving voice. He is my Judge and my Enemy, and I am afraid that He will be so forever. He has cast me off. He has forsaken me. He has condemned me, and I am lost forever. I am now likely to have my poor soul gathered with sinners and bloody men. I am now never likely to see that heaven where I once hoped to go. I see nothing but ruin, nothing but desolation, nothing but blackness of darkness." These unbelieving, despairing conclusions produce hard and strange thoughts of God, and an enmity to Him in our minds.

12. The deserted soul looks upon his present troubles as an introduction to more, and expects that these troubles are but the beginning of sorrows. Isaiah 38:13: "I reckoned till morning that, as a lion, so will He break all my bones; from day even to night wilt Thou make an end of me." How often we hear such persons saying, "Oh, what will become of me, should I die in such a state as I am now in! I am in such horror and amazement! Where will my guilty soul go then? Alas, I am in no way prepared to give up my accounts, and yet am likely every moment to be called away. If I cannot bear these pains and this wrath, what shall I do to bear an eternal hell! If I tremble so now, what shall I do when the blow is given and the final sentence passed! I have but one change to make, and it is likely to be a sad and woeful change, God knows! I dare neither live nor

die! Oh, what shall I do? Where shall I go? I must not stay, and I dare not depart. I am now sorely tormented, and I must forever and ever be so, and worse too! I now see that the gate is strait and the way is narrow, and that there are few indeed who will be saved. The shadows of the evening are stretched out upon me, and what shall I do if it proves to be an eternal night?"

As it is the glory of faith to show us future things as if they were actually present, and to give us joy from them so considered, so it is the torment of despair to make poor, distressed souls believe that they are as if in hell even while they are on earth, and that they are actually scorched with that wrath which is to come in greater measures.

13. From all these things follow strange discourses and expressions of sorrow. The distressed soul is forced to complain, to cry out, and to weep bitterly. Job 7:11: "Therefore I will not refrain my mouth; I will speak in the anguish of my spirit; I will complain in the bitterness of my soul." They speak without any manner of concern or fear, things that both vex themselves and make others tremble; they scarcely care what they say of God or themselves. "My soul is weary of my life; I will leave my complaint upon myself; I will speak in the bitterness of my soul" (Job 10:1). Nay, they frequently proceed to wish that they had never been born, knowing it is better not to exist at all than to be miserable (Job 3:3, 10:16–18). Nay, they may proceed so far as to wish even to be destroyed so that they may know the worst. Such is the sorrow of their hearts, and so violent is it. Job 6:26: "Do ye imagine to reprove words, and the speeches of one that is desperate, which are as wind?"

And there are two things that make their sorrows

more sorrowful. The first is comparing their state with that of others. The second is comparing their present state with their former state.

(1) It makes the deserted soul sad to consider the case of others to see with what peace and joy they live, with what hope and comfort, while they themselves are drowned in sorrows. "Others can sing the praises of God with delight while I am overwhelmed and my harp is hung upon the willows. Others can go into the solemn assemblies and hear His Word, but I am confined in my thick darkness and dare not go there. Others have the hope of heaven while I have the daily fear of hell. I am likely to see others enter into glory while I am shut out. Oh, what have my sins done! If I had not greatly sinned, I might have had as much quietness, comfort, and peace as they. I am now cut down for my unfruitfulness, and might have been serving God with as much cheerfulness, light, and hope as they do."

(2) It makes the deserted soul sad to compare its present state with its former one. To a person in misery, it is a great increase of that misery to have once been happy. It was to David an occasion of new tears when he remembered his former joys (Psalm 42:3–4). "Time was," says the poor soul, "when I thought of God with comfort, and when I thought of Him as my own God. To lose a God whom I once enjoyed is the loss of all my losses; of all my terrors, this is the most terrible. Time was when I could go and pray to Him and ease myself in prayer; but now I have no boldness, no hope, no success in prayer. I cannot call Him my Father any more. Time was when I could read the Bible, treasure up its promises, and survey the land of Canaan as my own in-

heritance; but now I dare not look into the Word lest I read my own condemnation there.

"The Sabbath was formerly to me as one of the days of heaven; but now it is also, as well as the rest, a sad and a mournful day. I formerly rejoiced in the name of Christ. 'I sat under his shadow' (Song of Solomon 2:3). I was in His eyes as one who found favor, but now my soul is like the Arabian desert, and I am scorched with burning heat.

"From how great a height I have fallen! How fair I was once for heaven and salvation, and now I am likely to come short of both! I was once flourishing in the courts of the Lord, and now all my fruit is blasted and withered away. His dew laid all night upon my branches, but now I am like the mountains of Gilboa: no rain falls upon me. Had I never heard of heaven, I could not have been as miserable as I now am. Had I never known God, the loss of Him would not have been as terrible as it is now likely to be. Job 29:2–3: 'Oh! That I were as in months past, as in the days when God preserved me; when His candle shined upon my head, and when, by His light, I walked through darkness!' "

These are some of the sorrows that deserted souls often meet with; and, indeed, they are but a small part of what they feel in this dark and stormy night.

Before I proceed any further, I shall answer two objections.

Chapter 26

Some objections answered, a further discussion of the doleful state of a deserted soul, and why it is that God is pleased to allow a very tempestuous and stormy night to come upon His servants in this world

OBJECTION 1. You make a great deal of noise and bother about desertions, and God's forsaking the soul. This is nothing but fancy or imagination, the whimsies and fumes of melancholy.

ANSWER. It is nothing new for us to hear such language from atheistic and profane people, from men who are covered with ignorance and sloth. I say "with ignorance" because they do not know the ways of God and His dispensations. I say "with sloth" because they will not search into the methods of His government. But were I to grant that it is imagination, it is no less tormenting because it is so, for a man who strongly imagines himself to be miserable is truly miserable. If a man thinks that he is unhappy, he is so while that thought remains. If these persons could give themselves leave to consider a little, they would find reason to suspect their own foolish objections. From what we read of him, who was more distressed with the sense of God's anger than David? Yet he was of a musical and a pleasant temper, of a ruddy and a sanguine constitution. Do these persons think that such a great prince as Job was led merely by humor and fancy when he complained so much of the arrows of the Almighty? Or that Heman, Asaph, and many others were men of no clear understanding? It is their ignorant pride that makes them talk so boldly of the judgments of God which they do not understand; but if their consciences are ever awakened with a sense of guilt, they'll find, in what I have now discoursed, something more terrible than fancy or imagination.

OBJECTION 2. You make a way to discourage men from all religion. If religion is such a mournful business, it is better to let it alone, and to rejoice and be merry, and to take our ease and our pleasures. Go to heaven by yourself, if you will; we'll join ourselves to more cheerful companions. We see those who are cheerful and brisk, who know no sorrow while they live, and who die in peace. We will unite ourselves to their assembly.

ANSWER. I desire such persons to consider that it is not our religion that is the cause of our sorrows, but our wanderings and deviations from it. If we were always obedient, we would have an eternal day. Our heavenly Father chastises us because we are undutiful. He does not delight in grieving the children of men; and even in these necessary corrections He carries on a profitable design for our future and final good.

It is true that this world is a vale of tears; this imperfect state that we are in on earth is a state of sorrow. But here is the excellency of religion: it will turn our present night into a brighter day, and all our sorrows into joy. If you slight God you may have joy for a while, but it is only a little while—and remember that your sorrows are yet to come. Remember that in this world Lazarus had evil things and the rich man had good things, but after death Lazarus was comforted and the other was tormented. Would you rather weep for a night or weep forever? Do not bless the wicked in your thoughts; their night is coming, and it will be a far longer and more doleful night. God will reckon with you who are now full of joy, for all your loud laughter and your scornful looks, for all your censure of religion and the satirical aspersions you throw upon it.

Now you may say, "We'll drink sorrow away; we'll not perplex our minds with sad, melancholy thoughts." But will death never come? Can you go with this jolly temper into the silent grave? Can you go jesting and laughing to the bar of the eternal God? What will come of all your mirth when you appear there, when you must hear your sentence and your final doom? What will come of you when the doom is past and the Judge will not be entreated, and when the door is shut? Where will you go? Where but to the place where there is weeping and wailing and gnashing of teeth! Let no man be discouraged at religion for its present sorrows and tribulations, but look beyond this night unto the coming day, a day full of light and joy.

But to proceed:

1. To lose the sense of God's favor is, of all other losses, the most dreadful loss. In other troubles the resolution and courage of a man will greatly diminish the sense of evil; but in this case none of that will avail. "A wounded spirit who can bear" (Proverbs 18:14)? God's departure from the soul is like the departure of the soul from the body. It is painful and very terrible, with only this difference: the poor, abandoned body, at the moment when it loses life, is incapable of pain, whereas the deserted soul is not only benighted, but vastly per-

plexed and in sore anguish and tribulation.

It is as when, after the setting of the sun, violent tempests and storms arise, which the darkness and horror of the night make all the more amazing. In a heart so forlorn, there is a flaming, tormenting sense of guilt and condemnation. Nothing is more delicate and tender than the soul; nothing is more capable of acute grief than the soul is.

In other losses something comfortable remains. If we lose our friends, we have a God who is unchangeable, and to whom we may repair for consolation. But in this case He Himself is apprehended to be gone. The loss of honor, the pain of diseases, the fury of persecution, the hatred and the rage of men, and even death itself are tolerable things compared to this. And though there is a tenderness in human nature, by which it must be somewhat sensible of these evils, yet there is an abundance of considerations that will wipe our tears away; in this mournful night there is nothing but anguish of conscience that draws up a process against itself as before the tribunal of God without hope of pardon of escape. The weight of mountains would not be a load as heavy as this; it is a night wherein we are kept waking with our danger, whether we will or not.

Wicked men, though they have as great a burden, yet are not sensible; they do not feel the bitterness of sin; they are like fishes bred in the sea, that do not taste the saltiness of the water. They are like swine that find something agreeable to their lower appetites even in that which is most nauseous to other creatures. When they sin, they do not feel the weight of it, for it is their nature to do amiss. Their iniquities are like waters that are not heavy in their own element. As intellectual joy is the most refined, pure and durable, so is the trouble of the mind, above all others, most troublesome. Job 6:2–3: "Oh, that my grief were thoroughly weighed, and my calamity laid in the balances together! For now it would be heavier than the sand of the sea; therefore my words are swallowed up."

2. Trouble of mind is usually attended with great pain of body too, and so a man is wounded and distressed in every part. "There is no soundness in my flesh because of Thine anger," said David. "The arrows of the Almighty are within me, the poison whereof drinketh up my spirit" (Job 6:4). Sorrow of heart contracts the natural spirits, making all their motions slow and feeble, and the poor, afflicted body usually declines and wastes away. Therefore, Heman said, "My soul is full of troubles, and my life draweth nigh unto the grave" (Psalm 88:3). In this inward distress, we see our strength decay and melt, even as wax before the fire; for sorrow, which is an ungrateful languor of the soul, darkens the spirits, obscures the judgment, blinds the memory to all pleasant things, clouds the lucid part of the mind, and causes the lamp of life to burn weakly.

In this troubled condition, the person cannot be without a countenance that is pale, wan, and dejected, like one who is seized with strong fear and consternation. All his motions are sluggish, and no sprightliness or activity remains. Proverbs 17:22: "A merry heart doeth good like a medicine, but a broken spirit drieth the bones." Hence come those frequent complaints in Scripture. "My moisture is turned into the drought of summer. I am like a bottle in the smoke; my soul cleaveth unto the dust; my face is foul with weeping, and on my eyelids is the shadow of death" (Psalm 32:4;

Psalm 119:83; Psalm 119:25; Job 16:16). Job 30:17–19: "My bones are pierced in me, in the night season, and my sinews take no rest; by the great force of my disease is my garment changed. He hath cast me into the mire, and I have become like dust and ashes."

Many times indeed the trouble of the soul begins from the weakness and indisposition of the body. Long affliction, without any prospect of remedy, in due time begins to distress the soul itself. David was a man often exercised with sickness and the rage of his enemies. And in almost all the instances we meet with in the Psalms, we may observe, as Dr. Gilpin notes in part 2 of his *Treatise of Satan's Temptations,* that the outward occasions of trouble brought him under an apprehension of the wrath of God for his sin (Psalm 6:1–6). All his griefs ran into this most terrible thought: God was his enemy. Little brooks lose themselves in a great river and change their name and nature. And it most frequently happens that when our pain is long, sharp, helpless, and unavoidable, we begin to question the sincerity of our relationship with God, though at its first assault we had few doubts or fears about it. Long weakness of body makes the soul more susceptible to trouble and uneasy thoughts.

I would write more on the troubles of a deserted soul, but I find them so excellently described by Dr. Gilpin in part 2 of his learned and experimental *Treatise of Satan's Temptations* that I must refer my reader to that work [published by Soli Deo Gloria]. I do not know of any other book that sets forth, with so much exactness and truth, these inward and spiritual afflictions.

I will now inquire why God allows such a night, so tempestuous and frightful, to come upon His servants.

He does it that His people may be conformed to Christ. As they are tempted and distressed, so was He; as it is with their souls a season of darkness, so it was also with His holy soul that was full of amazement under a sense of God's wrath—though He never despaired indeed, as many of His servants are apt to do under the violence of sorrow. Isaiah 53:3: [He was] a man of sorrows, and acquainted with grief." When He was so saddened for our sakes, it is reasonable to think that we should sometimes taste the bitter cup, and not always rejoice and be at ease. If God did not spare His only Son, why should we expect to feel nothing but what is very mild and gentle? Our Lord has told us that the world will rejoice, but we shall be sorrowful (see John 16:20–22). The sufferings of Christ were to give satisfaction to divine justice; ours are not to be looked upon with such an eye. By these terrors and desertions we learn to value and esteem the love of Christ, who was pleased to redeem us when it cost Him so very dearly, and who was pleased not to decline the field of battle, though it was not to be managed without vast labor and a mighty pain. And the apostle says, "Rejoice, inasmuch as ye are partakers of Christ's sufferings" (1 Peter 4:13).

He does it because our fall and our ruin came by pleasure. It was a delight, though a very short one, that made our forefather Adam apostatize; and it is equitable that we should be cured by something contrary to that which occasioned our disease, seeing that our joys are dangerous. He makes our grief and sorrows to be medicinal.

He does it because it is a very proper season wherein to be sorrowful. Among all the other excellent appointments of providence, this one is that there should be a time to weep (Ecclesiastes 3:4). There is in this weeping night nothing strange or uncouth. All our fathers have, in some respect, passed under a cloud, and a cloud that has dissolved in rain, and which has given the good pilgrims much trouble as they went along. 1 Peter 1:6: "Now for a season ye are in heaviness through manifold temptations." It is no more strange to see mourning in the church on earth than to see storms or snow in winter. Everything is beautiful in its season, and so is affliction. The night is useful to the world, though not as pleasant as the day. Our sickly state will not admit us to have nothing but what is satisfying to our palates; the wise God, therefore, many times, instead of very pleasant things confers the best upon us. We must allow the great Master of the family to maintain its order, prosperity, and welfare by His own methods, and to chastise us when and how and as long as He pleases; for His strokes, though very painful, yet are still very just. And it is in order to achieve some better thing that He designs for us that at the present we are made to grieve; for grief, as Dr. [Robert] Harris observes, is an imperfect passion, not made for itself but for some higher use, as are all the rest of the declining affections, such as hatred for love, fear for confidence, and so sorrow for joy, unto which it is subservient. Lancing and searing are not for themselves, but for ease and remedy. A bitter potion is not for sickness, though it may cause it for a time, but for health. In the same way, sorrow is made for joy, and joy is the end of sorrow. And God, we may be sure, will have His end.

He does it to show His own sovereignty both in afflicting and in comforting. He causes such a prince as Job to sit upon a dunghill, in anguish and trouble, while another sits in unclouded glory on the throne. He pulls down one and sets up another, and does whatsoever He will in heaven or earth. The withdrawing of His Spirit is an occasion of mourning for the soul, and one that He permits at various times; for though He does not deny what is absolutely necessary to the being of the Christian, yet He many times does not promise to give what would make it very comfortable. He, for wise reasons, allows the hearts of His people to be overwhelmed with sorrow when He could make them brim-full of joy, as in nature He lets the earth gape for thirst when He could immediately refresh it with seasonable flowers.

Who, in all this mysterious variety of His administrations, can say unto Him, "What art Thou doing?" Some countries are desert, barren and forsaken, burned up with scorching heat, and filled with beasts of prey; others are inhabited and fruitful, and greatly blessed, and He sees fit to have part of His dominions thus qualified. Some He draws with the sweet savor of His ointments, and they perceive nothing but what is gratifying and refreshing; but others He sorely terrifies with the greatness of His power, His holiness, and His majesty, and they never eat nor live with pleasure.

The Captain of our salvation causes some of His soldiers to meet with much more formidable dangers than others do: they have more sweat, fatigue, toil, and painful duty, though He will be sure to help them Himself when they are ready to give way. The manner of His dispensations to His servants is varied, both in life and at death. Some are chastened all the day long, and with sore pains upon their beds too, while others have no pain at all. Some go drooping to the grave, bowed down with God's displeasure, while His favor and His gracious eye make others go smiling there. Enoch and Elijah had a pleasant removal from the world; very short and very glorious was their passage hence. But most men groan a long while before they are called away, and then He does it to show His own power, so that when the wound appears to be desperate He can cure it with a word. When the night is most full of horror, He can bring the reviving day. When the storms are highest, He needs but say to the waves, to our doubts and our fears, "Be still," and immediately there is a calm.

What is such a God, so great and so good a God, not able to do! He who produced from a mere chaos this beautiful and pleasant world needs only to say to us in the middle of our doleful darkness, "Let there be light," and it shall be so. Job 4:18: "He maketh sore, and bindeth up. He woundeth, and His hands make whole." It is in acknowledgment of this sovereign ability it is that David prays in Psalm 51:8, "Make me to hear joy and gladness, that the bones which Thou hast broken may rejoice."

Why so? Had not Nathan told him that his sin was pardoned? Yes, but all the testimonies of men are nothing without the inward witness of the Holy Spirit. God has committed to men the administration of His Word, but reserves the Spirit to Himself, that Spirit which gives consolation to our hearts and peace to our consciences. When Mary and Martha were in sorrow for their brother's death, it is said in John 11:19 that many of the Jews came from Jerusalem to comfort them. But they received no comfort until Christ Himself had come there.

Chapter 27

Why it is that melancholy and troubled people love solitude, and why it is that serious persons are not as light and frothy in their conversations as others are. Some inferences deducible from the foregoing doctrine, and some advice to those who have never been deserted, and to such as complain that they are so

INFERENCE 1. Hence you see the reason why people in trouble love solitude. They are full of sorrow, and sorrow, if it has taken deep root, is naturally reserved and flies from all conversation. Grief is a thing that is very silent and private. Those people who are very talkative and clamorous in their sorrows are never very sorrowful.

Some are apt to wonder why melancholy people delight to be alone so much. I'll tell them the reason for it:

1. Because the disordered humors of their bodies alter their temper, their humors, and their inclinations, so that they are no longer the same as they used to be. Their very distemper is adverse to what is joyous and diverting. And they who wonder at them may as wisely wonder why they will be diseased, which they would not be if they knew how to help it. But the disease of melancholy is so obstinate, and so unknown to all but those who have it, that nothing but the power of God

can totally overthrow it. I know of no other cure for it.

2. Another reason is that people do not usually pay attention to what they say, nor believe them, but rather deride them, which they do not usually or cruelly do with those who are in other distempers. And no man ought to be blamed for avoiding society when it does not afford the common credit to his words that is due to the rest of men.

3. Another, and the principal reason why people in trouble and sadness choose to be alone, is that they generally apprehend themselves to be singled out as the marks of God's peculiar displeasure. Also, they are often a terror to themselves and a wonder to others because of their sharp afflictions. It even breaks their hearts to see how low they have fallen, and how oppressed, who were once as easy, as pleasant, and as full of hope as others are. Job 6:21: "Ye see my casting down, and are afraid." Psalm 71:7: "I am as a wonder unto many."

It is also usually unpleasant to others to be with them. Psalm 88:18: "Lover and friend hast Thou put far from me, and mine acquaintance into darkness." Though it was not so with the friends of Job, nevertheless to see a man whom they had once known to be happy to now be so miserable—one whom they had seen so very prosperous to be so very poor, in such sorry, forlorn circumstances, greatly affected them. He, poor man, was changed; they knew him not. Job 2:12–13: "And when they lifted up their eyes afar off, and knew him not, they lifted up their voice and wept; and they rent every one his mantle, and sprinkled dust upon their heads toward heaven. So they sat down with him upon the ground seven days and seven nights, and none spake a word unto him, for they saw that his grief was very great." The Old Testament represented one who was under spiritual and great afflictions as he who "sitteth alone and keepeth silence" (Lamentations 3:28).

INFERENCE 2. Hence we see the reason why the servants of God do not have such light and frothy spirits as others do. They do not indeed always mourn, but even when they rejoice it is with a serious and solid joy. Their own sins, the fear they have of sinning, and the concern they have for the sins of others cause them to walk softly. The many miseries to which they are inclined, and the many that they see the church of God groaning under, keep them from innumerable follies, from many lightnesses and vanities in conduct, which others do not regard. Frequently, though, when their countenances are grave, their hearts are full of the most lively joys.

INFERENCE 3. What a mean, sorry thing a Christian is, many times, in this world, as to his outward appearance. A mourner never makes as great a show as one in triumph does. His graces and his excellencies are, many times, like the ground in winter, covered with rain and storm, which make him to be greatly disregarded. Because Christ was a man of sorrows and acquainted with grief, therefore the Jews saw no beauty nor comeliness in Him that they should desire Him; they hid their faces from Him because He was stricken, smitten of God, and afflicted (Isaiah 53:3–4). The life of all believers is hidden with God in Christ (Colossians 3:3). That life is maintained with suitable nourishment formed by the gospel and preserved by the Spirit; but because of innumerable temptations and weaknesses, the glory of their grace is greatly eclipsed, hidden under a thousand crosses and infirmities, and does not yet appear in the clearest light.

A Christian in this world is like a king who travels *incognito* in a strange land. He is treated roughly by men who do not know the greatness of his birth and quality; he travels in the dress of a pilgrim; he is clothed with heaviness and has tears for his meat and drink. Or he is like the sun ascending to its meridian, which is obscured from our sight with many thick and watery clouds. Job 30:26–28: "When I looked for good, then evil came unto me; and when I waited for light, there came darkness. My bowels boiled and rested not; the days of affliction prevented me. I went mourning without the sun. I stood up and I cried in the congregation." Now the servants of God are going to the port of blessedness as Jonah went to the shore, covered with the waters of affliction. They seem, to a careless eye, like the seed that is buried in the ground, to be quite cast away; but they shall arise with new luster.

INFERENCE 4. This assures us that there is another, happier life after this one. "Blessed are they that mourn, for they shall be comforted" (Matthew 5:4). "He that goeth forth and weepeth . . . shall doubtless come again with rejoicing" (Psalm 126:6). This sorrow is the forerunner of abiding joys; these tears of holy persons are fruitful and proftable tears; and those souls that are now vexed with the sins of others, and their own, before long shall be sweetly refreshed. The night is long and doleful, but the morning comes that will cause them to forget all their former troubles. God puts their tears into His bottles, though it appears that they fall upon the earth unregarded and seem to be lost; but even then they fall into the lap of His providence which will make them bear fruit by His blessing, and to their eternal joy.

This little grain that is sown will return back again into their bosoms with measure, filled up and running over; the floods of tears that now surround them shall be turned into rivers of pleasure forevermore. "If in this life only we have hope in Christ, we are of all men most miserable" (1 Corinthians 15:19). Miserable indeed if we were obliged to bear so many crosses, to meet with so many dangers and such various calamities, and to have no reward; but thanks be to God, this is not our case. While we look upon this world, and upon the manifold evils that are here, we weep; but when we lift up our eyes to that pure, calm, and blessed world that is above, we may be cheerful and rejoice. Here we are tossed among rocks and shelves, with threatening waves and high winds; but there we have our rest. In this wilderness we are pursued with the roaring lions, annoyed with hunger, thirst, and other inconveniences; but we are all the while in our journey to the promised land. We shall be there shortly, and then we shall receive a blessed end to all our conflicts and difficulties.

INFERENCE 5. Seeing that there is such a weeping night for the servants of God, this verifies and confirms that maxim of the gospel that "strait is the gate, and narrow is the way, which leadeth unto life" (Matthew 7:14). We must go there through the very depths, and wade through many seas of griefs. All people find this journey to be difficult because of the frequent self-denials and mortifications to which they are obliged, because of the many sins that beset them and the many sufferings they must undergo; but deserted souls find it to be a narrow way indeed. To them it is covered with thorns and briars.

You whose mountain is still strong, whose hopes are yet unshaken, may think the road is easy. But if you ever come to be sorely tempted, to be afflicted with long and sharp trials; if you come to be greatly pained in your bodies and greatly troubled in your souls; if you are awakened with the sight of hell and the threats of the law, and are broken by the terrors of the Almighty—you will join your cries to ours and say that the way is very narrow indeed! Job, Heman, Asaph, David, and many others all found it to be so.

There is indeed a lion in the way, but that must not be used as an excuse for sloth, but rather as a motive to courage. We must use all the more caution, and be all the more watchful to avoid him. The sense of God's displeasure is as a hot furnace into which many of His children are thrown, though they shall come out unhurt. And when they do come forth, they shall be like gold. However, it is grievous to the sense when they must be saved so as by fire—when they must come to their crown by racks and torments, by anguish and tribulations, and to heaven by the very gates of hell.

I shall close this chapter with two exhortations: first, with respect to those with whom it is yet day, and who have never been forsaken by God; and, second, to such disconsolate souls with whom it is as yet a weeping and a mournful night.

1. If you have not been forsaken, and have always had the light of God's countenance shining on you, beware of the approaching night. As much as you can, prevent the declining of the day. I have shown you into

what a pit I and some others have fallen; take warning by our danger, and take heed, lest you also come into the same doleful case. If you have the smiles of your heavenly Father, if you have always been with Him, oh, do not provoke Him to turn those reviving smiles into killing frowns. Do not be secure or self-confident; do not be faithless, but believe and guard your faith; be watchful, for your enemy, the devil, goes about seeking whom he may devour (1 Peter 5:8). Work while it is day, for when this night comes I can assure you, by sad experience, that you cannot work. Pray now with fervor, for then you cannot pray; read now, and hear the Word of God, for then you will find no taste even in the Bread of Life. Beware of indifference and lukewarmness; beware of grieving the Spirit and of slighting His motions, for all these are the shadows of this doleful night. Your day is comfortable and your journey pleasant while the sun shines.

Oh, make haste to your eternal home, lest your feet stumble on the dark mountains. If you linger, wrath will overtake you, terrible and amazing wrath such as you cannot now believe, and such as you cannot bear. Credit the report that we bring you from the land of darkness, and do not go in the way that will lead you there. We have fallen among thieves and robbers, among temptations, dangers, and trials that have deprived us of all our comforts. Do not tread in a path where you will surely be set upon and greatly wounded if you do escape—even if you say, with Job 29:18, "I shall die in my nest, and multiply my days as the sand."

2. Do not severely judge or censure persons under spiritual trouble. It is night with them indeed, but they may live to see the morning come. God has overthrown

them, but He will build them up again; they are in darkness, but do not rejoice over them, for He will be a light unto them. Do not speak to the hurt of those whom He has wounded; do not look on with a lack of concern, or a secret pleasure, in the time of your brother's trouble. Job 30:11: "Because He hath loosed my cord and afflicted me, they have also let loose the bridle before me." Do not censure these mysterious dispensations of God and of His providence; stay till you see the beautiful structure that He will cause to rise from these ruins.

When they are tempted by the devil, do not, with Job's friends, insult them or increase their misery. It was a very great sin in those good men to aggravate his trouble by their rash discourses and by their sinister interpretations of it. God Himself decided the case for His servant Job and told his "friends" that they had not spoken of him the things that were right.

Do not be hasty to judge persons who are weeping, nay, even despairing for their sins. They are in bitterness, but such as God may speedily remove. He may change their wilderness into a paradise. He will perfect His power in their weakness, turning their evils into good and their darkness into a marvelous light. So stay till you see the end of the Lord.

He has taken men's comforts from them to improve them, and to restore those comforts to them upon better terms. He has removed their pots of water, but will, it may be, send them back full of wine. God is wont to bring most of His greatest ends about by seeming to look quite another way from what He has a special purpose to bring to pass. He seldom proceeds in a direct way to His ends, or in such a way as the creature would think stood most with reason to take. Rather, when His business lies in the east, He seems to take His journey full west. When He has a mind to build, He batters down; when His design is for light, His method and way is often through the greatest darkness.

Let the great example of Job forever repress our bold censures of afflicted and miserable people. Who would have thought that a man so distressed should ever have been delivered, that one who had so many pains should be cured! Who would have thought that one so poor, so derided, and so scorned by drunkards, little boys, and the meanest of the people should be honored and esteemed again! And yet all this happened to him, so that "his latter end was better than his beginning." He lived to see the funeral of his griefs and the resurrection of his comforts; the Lord who had afflicted him took off His heavy hand and turned again His captivity. He reestablished Job in all his former splendor, made him, for his short darkness, shine with a double glory, and gave him twice as much as he had before. For a year or two of trouble, God gave Job many pleasant, long years of joy till he was "old and full of days," till he was satisfied with living and calmly desired to die.

The scope of the book of Job is, as Bishop {Symon] Patrick says, to establish the great article of providence, and thereby to preserve us from error in thinking that God's knowledge is like our knowledge, or that His intention, providence, and government are like ours. This foundation being laid, nothing will seem hard to a man, whatsoever happens; nor will he fall into dubious thoughts concerning God, such as whether He knows what has befallen us or not, and whether He takes any care of us. Rather, he will be inflamed more vehemently with the love of God; as the end of the book says, "Wherefore I abhor myself and repent in dust and ashes" (Job 42:6). Our wise men say that those who act out of love will rejoice in chastisements (see James 5:11).

To you with whom it is still night, I shall only add these few words. Though I have myself come to the quiet shore, yet I sympathize with you who are yet laboring in the deep. You are afflicted and tossed with tempests, but, as in Isaiah 54:10–11, " 'The mountains shall depart, and the hills be removed, but My kindness shall not depart from thee, neither shall the covenant of My peace be removed,' saith the Lord that hath mercy on thee. 'Oh, thou afflicted, tossed with tempests and not comforted, behold, I will lay thy stones with fair colors, and lay thy foundations with sapphires.' "

I know you think it is a long night, and so it is, but it is not eternal; the day will break and the shadows flee away. Your wise Physician is preparing cordials for your hearts and balsam for your wounds. Let Him have your desires; to Him address your prayers; with your weaker arms be yet reaching after Him. You are scorched with wrath, but He will be a refreshment in your heat; you are in darkness, but He is the Sun of righteousness who will chase all the clouds away. Fly to this city of refuge; pant for this Fountain of living waters. And while you are condemned in your own thoughts, look to this Advocate and Mediator, and He will plead your case.

The wrath that burns you may be as hot as hell, but His blood will extinguish the tormenting flame. The devil may be too strong for you; therefore beg for help from this Jesus who has overcome him, and who will teach you to get the victory. He takes pleasure in helping those who have no helper; and when there is no one to deliver you, His own arm will bring salvation. "He hath borne our grief, and with His stripes we are healed." And trusting in His satisfaction, you may freely implore the mercy of His Father, nay, even appeal to His justice; for He will not have two payments for the same debt. You may say, "Thou hast promised to pardon sin for the sake of Thy well-beloved Son; let it be unto me according to Thy Word."

You may in vain complain of your troubles to those who have never felt the like; they may grieve you more by their harsh expressions, but remember that when you go to one who is experienced, you go to one who has tasted of the same bitter cup, to one who was Himself forsaken of God for a season, and who knows how it is with you in the like case. Remember that those who come to Him, He will in no wise cast out.

Chapter 28

The great joy that fills a soul when the favor of God returns to it after it has been long in darkness

"Joy cometh in the morning" (Psalm 30:5). Having shown in several chapters what a mournful night it is for a deserted soul when God is withdrawn, and what happens then, it is now time to hasten to what is more pleasant and reviving, according to the order of divine providence, which appoints that where there has been weeping in the night there should be joy in the morning. Hence we may observe that the return of God's favor to a soul is matter of great joy to it; or these words may denote the readiness of divine consolations.

Three things are the usual occasions of joy, all of which are present in this case: (1) the remembrance of some danger that we have lately escaped, (2) the possession of a present good, and (3) the solid expectation of some future happiness.

1. The remembrance of a past danger occasions a more lively sense of joy. As past joys renew our grief and make our sorrows more sorrowful, so the griefs that are past give us a sweeter and better taste of joy. After long sickness and acute pain, it is very pleasant to be at ease; it is pleasant to rest when we have been tired all the day with hard labor. The laurels of a soldier flourish with a purer green when they have been obtained with a mighty difficulty; the danger of the combat brightens the glory of the succeeding triumph. The mariner is

grateful to stand upon firm land, and from there to behold the waves in which he was likely to have drowned.

One who has been long in chains rejoices to find himself at liberty. It is very pleasant to a man who has long been thirsty to be refreshed with the fountain of living waters. It renders the joy more accomplished and satisfying when refreshment comes after long and grievous miseries. After long despair, the least beam of hope is more reviving. A man who has lost his way all night has cause to rejoice at the sight of day.

The faith of new converts is full of joy when they compare their former danger and their present safety, their former darkness and the shining light that guides their paths. In the same way, souls who have been in great anguish and tribulation for sin, who have apprehended themselves to be cast out of the presence of the Lord, find it very pleasant to behold His face again. It is pleasant to those who, by reason of their sore affliction, have been companions to owls and dragons, to come into religious assemblies and, instead of voicing solitary groans and tears, to join with the multitudes of those who keep that holy day. The soul is then like the returning prodigal in that it finds itself in the arms and embraces of a loving Father and well treated, when it looked (as it might justly do) for rebukes and wrath.

Thunder, lightning, and storms make us appreciate the calm and pleasant weather more. It is pleasant after a long absence to meet a friend again. We find a joy sparkling in our eyes and in our breasts at the sight of those whom we have not seen for many sad and doleful years, and whom we have longed to see. Our pleasure is heightened when a blessing arrives that was unexpected. The mercy that fills us with the biggest joy is the one which is extremely suitable to us, and which we did not expect to receive. The crown sat easier upon David's head after he had so often thought that he was going to fall into the hands of Saul. Life has a better taste when there has been only one step between us and death.

With what transports does a kind mother see her son coming home whom she gave over for lost and dead! What a cheerful reuniting Jacob had with his son after he had so long thought that he had been torn to pieces! As soon as he came near, he fell upon his neck, and there the revived soul of the poor old man was ready with excess of pleasure to melt away. He never thought to have seen Joseph, his dear Joseph, any more. He was sorrowful for his apprehended death, even going down to the grave; and the news of his son's welfare made him feel young and live again. Hearing it, the spirit of Jacob revived, and Israel said, "It is enough; Joseph my son is yet alive. I will go and see him before I die" (Genesis 45:28).

The Jews, given liberty to return from Babylon, were so surprised with the favor of their sudden deliverance and the greatness of the mercy that they could hardly believe it was true. It seemed to be the mere effect of imagination which, during the interruption of our normal thoughts, by sleep puts various deceits upon us. Psalm 126:1: "When the Lord turned again the captivity of Zion, we were like them that dream." They were delivered in an illustrious and surprising manner, and it is thus expressed for three reasons:

First, a man does not foresee what he dreams of. A man who is apt to enjoy sound and refreshing sleep does not know whether he will dream or not.

Second, it arrived without any pain to those who were delivered, just as when we dream we are in repose and in no trouble. And this heightens both the glory of a deliverance and the love of the delivered when the person delivered takes no care about it.

Third, this deliverance was above all that they could hope for. We dream of things that we do not see when we are awake. Such are the chimeras which our imagination forms but our senses do not notice.

The return of comfort to a soul that was even expiring in grief and sadness is like the raising of Lazarus to his mourning sisters. They thought that if the Lord had been there he would not have died, but they did not in the least think that he would be raised again. Reviewing our former miseries increases the sense of our present happiness. The light that the grace of the gospel brought into the world, and that dissipated the obscurities that compassed it about, made the apostles full of admiration when they thought of their former ignorance and error, and of the light and knowledge that God had given them. Ever are they wondering at the riches of His grace who, instead of the corruption in which they were plunged, gave them sanctification, joy, and hope.

What a surprise it was to the poor shepherds who were in the field, watching their flock by night, to see an angel and the glory of the Lord shining round about them, to see such a glory when they anticipated nothing of the sort, nor did they expect so great a grace. But it is usual with God to bestow the most eminent favors when men are not looking for them. Christ came to seek sinners when they did not think of Him, and when their minds were filled with other objects; as a result they were afraid, for great objects, when they present themselves suddenly to us, usually give us much astonishment. The reason is that our spirits on these occasions do not have the liberty to use their forces, and they are most frequently dissipated, and that dissipation causes fear. When a soul has long had in itself the sentence of condemnation, a pardon from God is very comforting. Our former darkness increases our present comfort, as shadows set off the light.

2. Joy arises from the possession of a present good. Thus the presence of God is unspeakably sweet to a soul from which He was once departed.

First, it now thinks upon Him as being reconciled. As our sadness came by unbelief, so our joy comes by faith. When the soul was in anguish, every thought of God was terrible and amazing; but now nothing is as refreshing, as desirable, or as satisfying as to think of Him. Psalm 94:19: "In the multitude of my thoughts within me, Thy comforts delight my soul."

Now the poor sinner does not look upon Him as an enemy, but as a Father. No more does he see in His hand a flaming sword, but a scepter of grace. He hears no more God's angry voice, but His gentle, comfortable calls and invitations. Isaiah 66:13–14: "As one whom his mother comforteth, so will I comfort you, and ye shall be comforted; and when ye see this, your heart shall rejoice, and your bones shall flourish like an herb."

Oh, what a joy it is to the soul to find God there with it, to behold the wonders of His pardoning mercy, and to see that all its unbelief, all its impatience, all its murmurings in its wilderness condition shall not finally obstruct its journey to the land of promise. To be pardoned when it thought itself to be actually perishing in its guilt aggravates the mercy of escape.

It is true that God loves His people even when He is angry with them. He designs their good by the sharpest and most severe strokes. And when He withdraws it is so that they may give a better welcome to Him at His return. When our lower region is most cloudy, the sun is still full of light; but it is pleasant to us to see the clouds vanish and the sky clear, and to be refreshed with His enlivening beams again.

God is indeed the same forever. Our distresses, fears, and troubles do not alter His kindness. These several variations in us make no change in Him, any more than the various alterations in the air imply a diversity in the sun, which is one and the same itself though the changes are multiplied here below. But paternal wrath is wrath still, and God's love is what we ought to earnestly desire, and at the manifestation of which we should greatly rejoice.

A Mr. Peacock, when was under great distress of conscience said, "Oh, God, reconcile me to Thee, that I may taste one dram of Thy grace, by which my miserable soul may receive comfort!" Such was his longing after Him. And afterwards, when the storm began to cease, he was put in mind of God's mercy to him and said, "Oh, the sea is not so full of water, nor the sun of light, as God is of goodness. His mercy is ten thousand times more!" This good man had longed for only a drop of consolation before, and God had given him full draughts of it. Thus far are the ways of God above our ways, and His thoughts above ours.

In our sore trials we think of God as a frowning Judge, but when we are delivered we see Him to be our best Friend. We see that He is really kind to us of whom we were so afraid. Who can express the joy of having Him be at peace with us? There is a heaven in the smiles of a reconciled God.

Imagine a person who is condemned to death for his crimes and who, at the same time that he prepares to undergo it, sees a herald from the king bringing his pardon in his hand. And when the herald stops the execution by crying, "Mercy, mercy to this miserable man," with what transports of joy does the poor malefactor see this messenger and hear these tidings!

Such, and so pleasant, is the joy that a deserted Christian finds after he had heard the sentence of ruin and saw it near, when the law condemned him and his conscience echoed to the voice of the law, to find that he is absolved, the sentence is reversed, and the sins that made him afraid are blotted out. Then it is that the mourning soul dares to look up to God as being no more at war with him, nor is it afraid of the thunder of His power. Then that soul is refreshed with His sweet and amiable attributes; then the disorders and the pangs that it felt within are vanished and all is quiet; then it dwells not as in the shadow of death, nor as on the borders of an eternal grief.

Second, as the deserted soul by faith obtains a possession of Christ, so it is full of joy. And Christ is both the object and the author of it. He has purchased it by His own blood, and has borne our griefs so that we might not mourn forever. It is a constant, inexhaustible source of joy to the believer to be possessed by this Savior, who is the brightness of the glory and the express image of the Father. He is His word, His wisdom, His love, His good will, and the treasury of His graces, in whom His fullness dwells. This divine Savior is our light that chases away the darkness of our night, and He dries our eyes with His gracious hand. He is that glorious sun that arises with healing in His wings, who not only cheers our hearts but cures our wounds, dispels the night, and makes the voice of sighing expire at the first dawning of the day. He is the tree of life, the celestial manna that gives us immortality (see Jean Daille on Philippians 4:4). This is our David who defeats our enemies, our Solomon who establishes among us a sweet and inviolable peace.

Our Savior expiates our crimes and gives our mind rest. He saves us from the wrath to come. He delivers us from our sins, from hell, and from our slavish fears, and causes us at length, in our darkest and most tempestuous nights, to hear His voice saying, "It is I, be not afraid." We are first saddened by unbelief, and faith then revives us; and this faith is attended with joy and peace.

When the poor, deserted soul begins to apprehend its interest in Christ, all its apprehensions are changed, and that soul says, "Heretofore, in my terrible anguish, I thought that He was my sure enemy, that I had no portion in His blood nor any share in His intercession. I thought that, since I was under unbelief, so I should be vastly more miserable than those who never heard of Him, more miserable than heathens and pagans and all the rest of men to whom the gospel never came. I then thought, and was fully persuaded, that I should not hear of Him any more with comfort. I then thought that I would see Him coming in the clouds to my terror, that I should be placed at His left hand and, from there, be commanded to depart. But now He has come in a way of mercy and of love. He has pleaded for me when I had nothing to say for myself, and His Word has calmed the storms that made me so very afraid. He cast an eye of love upon me when I expected nothing but His frowns. Now I can go and pray in His encouraging name, and now I have hope when I pray. His satisfaction and His intercession are both the constant fountains of my joy."

Third, this joy that comes after a night of sad and mournful desertion is the work of the blessed Spirit, who is called by way of eminence "the Comforter." Peace is one of the fruits of the Spirit. He causes us to close with Christ and to embrace the promises. He assists our weakness and teaches us to pray. He convinces us of sin, and lays us low that He might raise us up again. He humbles and purifies us, and fills our hearts with lasting and abiding joys.

This joy is not the product of a natural temper, but a disposition that has its origin in heaven and leads us there. It is not the pleasant motion of our natural spirits to which it owes its birth, but as our grief was in our souls, so the joy is in the same. As our consciences were disquieted, so it is in them that God works a stillness and repose.

Fourth, this joy revives our graces. In this mournful night we were quite blasted with the violence and fury of the storm. We were like the ground in winter, destitute and forlorn; no fruit appeared. But the manifestation of God's favor is to us as the return of spring. Song of Solomon 2:11–13: "For lo the winter is past, the rain is over and gone. The flowers appear on the earth, the time of the singing of birds is come, and the voice of the turtle is heard in our land. The fig tree putteth forth her green figs, and the vines with the tender grape give a good smell." That solitary season is now gone, wherein nothing but doubts, fears, despondency, and accusations overwhelmed the soul. The floods that kept it under are dried, and there is now a cheerful and pleasant alteration. The clouds have vanished and the sky is bright; a new world and a new face of things now appear. A return to our prior mercies is like Noah's entrance into the world after it had been cleansed and washed by the deluge.

God's favor makes our tears like the gentle dew of night which, with the warming, kindly beams of the sun, makes the plants and herbs, the gardens and the flowers look fresher and greener. When God departs, our weakness to what is good increases; we have no power left, but the joy of the Lord is our strength (Nehemiah 8:10). This is like the return of health and good digestion to one who has long been sick; it causes a new ferment and motion in the blood, and enables all our actions to be accompanied with more life and vigor. Men under strange fears and amazement are incapable of service; and when we are deserted, that is what we feel. When we apprehend ourselves to be castaways we offer the bread of mourners, if we offer any at all; but none of our sacrifices are with joy and gladness. A man whose bones are broken cannot go about his work; and when our spirits are wounded, if we work at all, we do it but lamely. We may halt a little, but we cannot run in the way of God's commands. Our sorrows make us serious and thoughtful, but it is joy that makes us active. It is the oil of gladness that causes our wheels to move and makes us advance forward, like the chariots of Amminadab. One who is hungry or thirsty uses only feeble endeavors compared to what he does who is newly refreshed.

Fifth, this joy that comes in the morning, after a night of weeping, is very pleasant to the soul as it is then delivered from the insults and triumphs of the devil. In that doleful night, that evil spirit continually terrifies and frightens us; but when the morning comes, he who dreads the light flies away. Then it is in some measure with us as it was with our Savior in the wilderness: when the devil left Him, angels came and ministered unto Him—though there is a vast disparity between Him and us. He conquered and was in no way the worse for it, but we come bleeding from the field of battle. Our souls are defiled with Satan's temptations, and the wounds we receive in our conflicts now and then hurt us, and yield us remembrances of our sin by their pain and smart perhaps even to our dying day. However, it is a joy to us to think that though we were beset on every side, yet we have escaped as a bird out of the snare of the fowler. "The snare is broken and we are escaped" (Psalm 124:7). God has brought our souls out of the deep dungeon, and he who was our jailer did not have enough power to keep us there. And our deliverance is so strange and miraculous that our going out is like Peter's in Acts 12:9: "He went out, and wist not that it was true which was done by the angel, but thought he saw a vision." It was wonderful to Peter, who had looked for a sudden execution on the next day, to come to his praying friends in safety; and so it is to us, who thought ourselves a while ago doomed to die.

The devil has winnowed us, and, oh, that we could say that our chaff is gone! This archer has sorely shot at us, but, thanks be to God, he has not obtained his design, which was our total ruin. We have been in a very fiery furnace. Oh, that it were with us as with the three children who came out and were not hurt at all. We have been in a den of lions, in a howling wilderness, but we have not perished there. It is a pleasure to us that we now have something to answer to the great accuser of the brethren; that we can now, by faith in our great Captain, ward off his blows and quench his fiery darts.

Sixth, this joy that comes in the morning after desertion is from the propriety that we have in God, and in the promises of the gospel. David says in the last verse of Psalm 42, He is "the health of my countenance, and my God." It is pleasant to know that God is good, but more pleasant when we can taste His goodness, and when we can say with the blessed virgin in Luke 1:46–48, "My soul doth magnify the Lord, and my spirit hath rejoiced in God my Savior, for He hath regarded the low estate of His handmaiden." It is pleasant to hear of Christ, but more pleasant by far when we, with old Simeon, embrace Him in our arms and say with the church, "I am my beloved's, and He is mine."

Then the soul will be cheered with perpetual delight, saying, "Having God, I have enough. Enter into thy rest, O my soul, for the Lord hath dealt bountifully with thee." When the soul can reflect on and think of Him as its own portion, then the sorrows and darkness of the night are gone, for it has God, who is all light, and with Him is no darkness at all. And to see the light and to possess the light are the same thing.

There is, as one has observed, a reflected and a direct light. I see palaces, mountains, towns, fields, and trees with a reflected light; and hence it is that I see them without possessing them. But I see the light of the sun and the stars by direct rays; and in seeing them I possess them. For to rejoice in the light of the sun and to possess it are the same thing. We now see God indeed by a reflected light which comes to us from the creatures, and hence it is that all those who see Him do not possess Him. But in heaven God will be seen without veils or reflections. His light will be a direct light which will fill us throughout.

It was a comfort to the patriarchs and holy men of old to have the hope of Christ's appearance. They saw His day afar off and they rejoiced; but how much more is it to that soul which has actually seen Him come, and not only spreading His beams to remove the general darkness of the world, but shining with a peculiar light and heat into itself. It is peculiarity that endears things to us; our own friends, our own relations, our own joys are the most pleasant.

It is not from Christ's being singly considered as a Mediator that we derive this comfort, but from the reflection that we are able to find our happiness in Him. It is that which creates the sweetest motions in our hearts. Before we have this relationship, there may be a calmness of spirit and lesser degrees of complacency, expressing themselves in love, hope, and desire; but it is the actual possession of a good as our own that is the parent of a real joy. The Christian may find some comfort in beholding the incarnation of our Savior's sufferings and the promise of His second coming, but when the soul can say, "He died and rose again for me," this gives it a very lively satisfaction, and makes it say, as in Habakkuk 3:17–18, "Although the fig tree shall not blossom, neither shall fruit be in the vines; the labor of the olive shall fail, and the fields yield no meat; the flock shall be cut off from the fold, and there be no herd in the stalls, yet I will rejoice in the LORD, I will joy in the God of my salvation."

Chapter 29

The further properties of the joy that comes to a soul after long desertion: it is irresistible, though usually gradual; it revives the body and the natural spirits; it fills the late mourner with the hope of glory, and causes him to express his delight to others. From all this we may justly admire the wisdom of divine providence

Seventh, this joy is irresistible. As all the darkness of the night cannot hinder the approach of the welcome day, so neither can all our doubts and fears, nor all the horrors of the night hinder the beams of God's favor when He is pleased to shine upon us. Job 34:29: "When He giveth quietness, who then can make trouble?" Notwithstanding all the directions and helps that our ministers or friends give us in our trouble, we refuse to be comforted; but when He speaks the Word, we must obey. He creates the fruit of the lips, namely peace; and we can no more resist His almighty power than the first chaos could withstand His command when, in the language of a God, He spoke and said, "Let there be light." Our escape from our spiritual troubles bears some proportion to the resurrection of our Lord from the dead. As that was not owing to any ordinary or created power, neither is ours, but to a power that is celestial and divine. It was not the effect of the power of God in the ways of nature—such as is the rising of the sun, the return of the seasons, or the fruitfulness of the earth—

but the effect of a power altogether infinite and supernatural; it is not according to the usual laws of nature or the course of ordinary providence.

Eighth, this joy is usually gradual, and not all at once. I say usually, for sometimes persons in great distress and agonies of soul have been suddenly relieved in their darkest night, and in the deepest dungeon a great light has shone upon them, so that those who have one hour cried out that they were damned and lost have, the next hour, triumphed in the hope of glory. From the fear of hell they have come to a glorious view of heaven, to their own exceeding comfort and the comfort of all who heard them.

But, though God may do what He pleases, this is not His ordinary way. As the night comes and the sun goes down by degrees, so the morning comes and the sun rises by the same degrees. In the same way, it rarely happens that people fall into great distress of conscience suddenly, but rather some lesser afflictions make way for greater strokes. And so seldom are any comforted immediately, but rather their comfort comes like the break of day: there are some faint streaks of light, some little supports, and quiet hopes before the sun arises. In this, God accommodates Himself to the weakness of our nature; for a sudden passage from a great affliction to a great joy is a thing which our tender nature is hardly capable of bearing. Usually, the consciences of those who have long been terrified and afflicted begin to be calm, as the humors of the body that have been disordered return to their ancient course; for so long as the spirits and the blood are disordered, so long the soul will be unavoidably in some unpleasant agitation.

Ninth, this joy has a pleasant influence on the body, and revives the body as well as the mind. They fall sick and droop together, and they recover and rejoice together. When God is our God, it causes health in our countenances as well as pleasure in our hearts. And though I know that an abundance of poor people have been long amazed with the fear of God's wrath, and have feeble, sickly bodies to the day of death, yet this calmness and peace of mind greatly mitigates their pains, and pours honey and sweetness into the most bitter cup. For what is it that makes affliction, in trouble of mind, so intolerable but that the afflicted person looks upon it as the beginning of sorrows, as a few drops before a more dreadful storm, and as the introduction to hell and woe? But when the sting of guilt is removed and sin is pardoned, the yoke fits very easily on their shoulders which used to gall them before. Proverbs 15:13: "A merry heart maketh a cheerful countenance."

Joy, as well as grief, cannot be dissembled if it is real and very strong. Joy in the heart is like the rain at the root of the grass: that grass will, after being moistened to the bottom, appear much more green and flourishing. Proverbs 17:22: "A merry heart doeth good like a medicine." Even that cheerfulness which arises from natural and ordinary causes is very healthy, and adds much to the strength and vigor of the body; much more, then, will that joy promote it which is founded on the Word of God and the hope of His acceptance. No question but that David had this in mind when he said, in Psalm 51:8, "Make me to hear joy and gladness, that the bones which Thou hast broken may rejoice." Or Psalm 35:10: "All my bones shall say, 'Lord, who is like unto Thee, which deliverest the poor from him that is too strong for him, and the needy from him that spoileth him!"

No troubles waste our natural spirits more than our inward griefs and fears; no joys refresh and make them more sprightly than the joys of our souls. Job 33:24–26: God "is gracious unto him, and saith, 'Deliver him from going down to the pit. I have found a ransom. His flesh shall be fresher than a child's; he shall return to the days of his youth.' He shall pray unto God, and He will be favorable unto him; and he shall see His face with joy." Those who have written of long life, and the means to obtain it, advise us to keep our minds always full of splended and illustrious objects, of histories and the contemplations of nature, and the like; but the best medicine is a quiet conscience. And though all our religion will not, indeed, save us from sickness, yet it will enable us to bear it, and will keep us from being too concerned and overwhelmed with the manifold and unavoidable calamities of this mortal life. This is joy, indeed, that will recreate our souls and our bodies too; it will prepare the one for its passage to glory and the other for its lying in the grave. Thus our soul, which is our glory, shall rejoice, and our flesh shall also rest in hope (Psalm 16:9). And both at length, as they have mourned, so will rejoice together, and that forevermore. For when God is pleased to speak, and to help us in both our bodies and our souls, it is multiplied salvation, and many thousand cures in one.

3. The third general point [following point 2 from the previous chapter] is that joy arises from the hope of some future good; and this good must be both very agreeable to the soul and very certain. For if it is not so,

there cannot be other than a weak and trembling joy. There is a great pleasure in the expectation of what is to come, if it is great, lasting, and attainable. Now to one who has the returning sense of God's favor, it is very pleasant to look for that hour or day—or rather for that cheerful eternity—when he shall have the same reviving smiles of his heavenly Father in a brighter and more conspicuous manner; when not only the night of weeping is gone, but that morning has come which shall shine more and more to a perfect day.

And thus will the comforted person say: "If the taste that I now have of God is so sweet, oh, what will the full enjoyment of Him be! If in this strange land I am entertained as with the bread of angels, what feasts will refresh me when I am home, when I am past the storms and beyond the grave, and when sins and tears shall give me no further molestation!"

The first fruits make such people long for the full harvest. And thus it is that the apostle says, We "rejoice in the hope of the glory of God" (Romans 5:2). This made the church say, "Make haste, O my beloved, and be thou like a roe, or to a young hart upon the mountains of spices" (Song of Solomon 8:14). Expectation of any main event is a great advantage to a wise heart. If the fiery chariot had fetched away Elijah unlooked for, we would have doubted the favor of his transportation.

4. This morning-joy will express itself. As our grief causes us to groan and sigh, so this joy makes us, in an open, pleasant way, manifest our gladness. The reviving sense of God's favor so fills our heart that we cannot, without dishonor to Him and prejudice to ourselves, conceal or stifle it. When we apprehend ourselves to be

happy, we take a peculiar pleasure in communicating to others the news of that happiness, and are much more pleased by such a communcation. This joy is always attended with an expression of the mercies of our Deliverer, so that we cannot but say to our brethren, "Come and behold what God has wrought for me! Behold what salvation His own arm has accomplished!" So we read in Psalm 51:12–13: "Restore unto me the joy of Thy salvation, and uphold me with Thy free Spirit; then will I teach transgressors Thy ways, and sinners shall be converted unto Thee." In other words, "Then I shall be able to tell them that Thy ways, however rugged they seem to be for a while, yet are at length even and pleasant ways, and that they lead to life and happiness; and, beholding the beams of Thy love that make me so pleasant and so cheerful, they shall, by such a sight, be encouraged also to true religion." To the same purpose is Psalm 16:9: "My heart is glad, and my glory rejoiceth." David's inward joy was not able to contain itself.

We testify to our pleasure on lesser occasions, even at the gratification of our senses, such as when our ear is filled with harmonious melody, our eye is fixed upon admirable and beauteous objects, or our smell is recreated with agreeable odors. Our taste is pleased by the delicacy and rareness of provisions, and much more will our soul show its delight when its faculties, which are of a more exquisite constitution, meet with things that are in all respects agreeable and pleasant to them—and in God they meet with all of those. With His light our understanding is refreshed, and so is our will with His goodness and His love.

Thus Psalm 126:1–2: "When the Lord turned again the captivity of Zion, then was our mouth filled with laughter, and our tongue with singing." It was a sign that their hearts were very full of joy, as the mouth and the tongue poured it out in such great abundance. Nay, their neighbors could not but take notice of it: "They said among the heathen, 'The Lord hath done great things for them,' " far beyond the methods of an ordinary providence. Their liberty was strange and miraculous, and surpassed all imaginable reasons; and, behold, as people take delight to mull a pleasant thing over and over again, they echo the heathens' observation in Psalm 126:3: "The Lord hath done great things for us, whereof we are glad."

Others knew only by report that God had been so good to them, but they knew it by sweet experience. In the delivered people it was, indeed, an inward jubilation with a loud cry and a song of triumph. When God is withdrawn, we are forced to speak in the anguish and bitterness of our souls; when He returns, the return is so pleasant that we cannot hold our tongues. In our troubles there is latent grief, so sinking and so very sad that no words can express it; so in the good hope of God's acceptance there is a sweetness that cannot be declared. "Ye rejoice with joy unspeakable and full of glory" (1 Peter 1:8).

We dare not give a particular relation of our grievous sufferings lest we discourage many poor people who are apt enough of themselves to sink and be discouraged. Or, if we would, we cannot, for they are so very terrible. Similarly, the sight of God after a long darkness fills us with wonder and with pleasing astonishment; we feel that we are delighted, but we cannot fully tell what it is to be so; and sometimes we are in such transporting joys that, like the blessed apostle when he had a view of paradise, whether we are in the body or out of it we scarcely know. The poor soul is so transported that it is in every way surrounded with delight: "Will God dwell in such a heart as mine, that has been so full of murmurings and unbelief! Will He pardon and accept me? Shall I, who was doomed to die in my own sad thoughts, have the hope of glory? And, instead of my slavish fears from the dread of hell, shall I have the sight of heaven? Shall I be His favorite, of whim I had such hard and unbecoming thoughts? Oh, what grace is this! How unlooked for! How undeserved! And yet how suitable! Is this the manner of men, O Lord God? Is this Thy kind usage of a poor sinner, and of so great a sinner as I have been? This is grace indeed! This is all free love and mercy! How can this be passed over in silence?"

Such a person, who escaped after such apprehensions of so near a danger, is like the lame man who was healed in Acts 3:8–10: "He, leaping up, stood and walked, and entered into the temple, walking and leaping and praising God. And all the people saw him walking and praising God, and they were filled with wonder and amazement at that which had happened unto him."

Inward anguish causes the distressed many times to roar out vehemently, so heavy is the load that presses them; on the contrary, when the fear of wrath is removed, they rejoice with shouting and a loud voice, like those who conquer or who finish their harvesting. When a man is under inward anguish and tribulation, he looks upon himself as a beacon fired on a hill, to give warning to others and to show them the danger of sin; so, when he comes to peace and hope again, he wishes that he might be placed as if on a mountain, and enabled to trumpet out to all the world the riches of the grace of God, so that as none may presume when they see his misery, so none may despair when they see his safety, and his escape from that misery.

Uses

INFERENCE 1. From all that has been said, see the wisdom and the beauty of divine providence. As in the world there is a comfortable succession of night and day, so, as for our mourning, after the sorrows of the night, the joy of the morning comes. This night comes, and this morning dawns, when it is most proper for it to do so. "He hath made everything beautiful in His time" (Ecclesiastes 3:11). The storms, rain, and cold of winter are as beneficial to the universe as the summer's heat. We, from our self-love, judge God either with more admiring or less becoming thoughts, as He deals well or ill with us; but it is not particular churches nor particular persons whom God regards only, but His whole creation. His providences to us contribute to the good of that. We do not know to what uses God will put us, but it ought somehow to support us to think that, in whatever state we are in, we are serving His design. However pressing and violent our dangers and tribulations are, He can save us, even by methods contrary to those which our reason apprehends. By throwing us down He can make us more established, and by seeming to destroy us He can promote our welfare. He can make unlikely things advance His purpose.

It is often darker just before the break of day; the going back of the sun on the dial of Ahaz was to be a sign of Hezekiah's longer life (Isaiah 38:8). Therefore, if you will allow me a small digression, it is a very evil thing for men to censure the providence of God because of the present miseries He allows His servants to be afflicted with. There are many who think it a piece of zealous loyalty not to blame their superiors for the higher matters of government which are above their reach, and yet they dare to arraign at their own bar the supreme Ruler of the world if what He does is not according to the model of their fancies or suitable to their imaginations, or because, while others are gratified, their humors are crossed and disappointed. They do not consider that the difference and variety of circumstances among particular men are necessary to the general and public good.

To censure God and reflect upon His conduct is as if a country clown, who never traveled beyond the smoke of his own cottage, should condemn the proclamation of a king or the votes of a parliament when he does not know the great reasons of state that these actions depend upon. But, as St. Basil observes, when men are first crossed in their worldly affairs, they begin for lack of patience to doubt whether God indeed regards the things of this world, whether He takes notice of particular men. When they see no end of their miseries, but one evil continually follows another, they are blasphemously apt to think there is no God.

God can bring affliction to test and manifest the graces of His people. The stars, which are a chief part of the glory of the world, are most illustrious and visible when the day is gone. And then God makes the sun rise again, which displays new objects to us. The rods of

God are many times very sharp, but at last we shall find that they were dipped in honey and managed with love.

The conduct of divine providence is always wise and good, but very often mysterious and unfathomable, and in nothing more so than in His bringing an abundance of His servants to heaven by the very gates of hell, and in allowing Satan to buffet and vex them so that they may triumph over him in the latter end. He makes them to be in great perplexities so that the sweet wonders of His deliverance may the more appear. "We went through fire and through water; but Thou broughtest us out into a wealthy place" (Psalm 66:12). Thus He preserved Moses in a cradle of bulrushes, and would not allow the great infant to perish, though he was in manifest danger either to be carried away by the force of water, or to be devoured by crocodiles, with which that river abounded.

Noah was preserved by the ark, not by any art in navigation, but by the government and conduct of God Himself. He hastens deliverance many times when it seems to be at the remotest distance. In the evening it shall be light, in a season when it was not to be expected. In all His works of nature and of grace, He makes things that seem contrary to His designs to further His design. Thus, some observe, the earth hangs upon nothing in the midst of the fluid air, though it is the heaviest of all the elements. God renders it fruitful for the production of all necessary things, though it is of itself cold and dry. So the sea, which is situated above the earth, and seems to threaten it with new deluges, yet is kept in its own channel; for after it has been raised even to the clouds in threatening waves, its fury dies again into a calm and observes the bounds that

God has set for it.

Thus our Lord Jesus also works. By being tempted, He conquered the tempter; by dying, He subdued death. At the sending of the Spirit, first the house shook and trembled, and then it was filled with the glory of the Lord—first, deep sorrows; then, mighty joys. John, in Revelation 14:2, "heard a voice as the voice of many waters, and as the voice of a great thunder." And then he heard "the voice of harpers harping with their harps, and they sang a new song before the throne."

A due consideration of the providence of God will keep us from the absurd opinion of the heathens, who believed that the deity envied the felicity of men, and that he who was most prosperous was near to a sudden overthrow. Even the learned men among them were so apprehensive of this idea that they dared not acknowledge their own ordinary blessings without an excuse. You can see instances of this in Dr. Meric Casaulson's *The Original Cause of Temporal Evils* [1645]. Upon this account, Augustus, in whose days the Savior of the world was born, once a year turned himself into a beggar and received alms, as much as the common people would give him. He mistrusted his own felicity.

The heathens had but parcels of the Scripture, and those were too greatly adulterated by tradition; it is no wonder that they made a contrary use of it. By sad experience they found the effects of Adam's fall and God's resulting curse; they were not well informed of all the particulars, since the devil was busy with them as he was with Eve, promoting a misapprehension of God, as if He were envious. Upon due consideration, though, what seemed to be envy and malignity, in the judgment of blind and corrupt nature, will appear as mercy, being used by God as a profitable medicine or antidote against the greatest and most dangerous infection of the soul. For crosses and afflictions in this world are not effects of envy in the supreme Dispenser of all things, but they are rather arguments of His goodness and providence. "All things shall work together for good to them that love God" (Romans 8:28). Sickness and health, poverty and riches, anguish, fear, and horror—all shall contribute to their salvation. And in the most fiery furnaces, in the most painful troubles, they shall find the refreshments of His grace.

His providences work together; they are in concert, and are not to be taken apart, like a composition of various ingredients. For there are some that, if taken alone, might kill the patient; but when they are joined with others, which by their contrary qualities temper their excess, they do marvelous things, being "counterpoisonous" to each other. God, many times, lets our darkness stay long so that we may know what a pleasant thing it is to see the light.

Chapter 30

The different ends that God has in the afflictions of the good and the wicked, and what reason we have to be reconciled to His providence. We must be satisfied that God carries us to heaven in His own way and method

INFERENCE 2. This shows us the different ends that God has in the afflictions of the good and the wicked. To the one they are medicinal, to the other they are penal; to the one they are in love, to the other they are in wrath; to the one they are the shadows of an eternal night, and to the other they are the forerunners of the morning. Often God's people are thrown down by their fears, by Satan, and the world; but as often they may say, "Rejoice not against me, O my enemy." They may be dejected, but they may say with David, "O my soul, hope still in God." Afflictions are common to the good and bad alike, as the entrance to the sea was to the Israelites and the Egyptians; but the Israelites, led by a cloud and a pillar of fire, were enlightened and assured, and passed in safety, praising God as they came out. But to the Egyptians this cloud that separated them was full of darkness, and they drowned in the waves while the others stood upon the dry land.

So God comforts His people by the light of His Word and the support of hope from His holy promises, whereas the wicked are finally swallowed up by sadness and despair. The righteous fall and rise again, but the feet of the wicked stumble on the dark mountains and never rise again.

The Chaldeans formerly measured their natural day differently from the Israelites: they put their day first and the night afterwards. But the Israelites, on the contrary, ordered their day according to the order that was observed in the creation; for in the beginning darkness was upon the face of the deep, and of every one of the six days it is said, "The evening and morning made the first day." So the times of the world and those of the church are disposed differently; for the world begins hers by the day of temporal prosperity, and finishes it by a night of darkness and anguish that is eternal. But the church begins hers by the night of adversity, which she suffers for a while, and ends them by a day of consolation which she shall have forever.

The prophet, in this psalm, begins with the anger of God, but ends with His favor. In olden times, when the people entered into the tabernacle, they first saw unpleasant things, such as the knives of the sacrificers, the blood of victims, and the fire that burned upon the altar and consumed the offerings; but when they passed a little farther, there were the holy place, the candlestick of gold, the shewbread, and the altar of God, on which they offered perfumes—and last there were the holy of holies, the ark of the covenant, and the mercy seat and the cherubim, which was called the face of God.

INFERENCE 3. This may serve to reconcile you to God's providence. The night of trouble does not allow you to see the beauty of the church; but though she is black, she is comely still. He who makes His sun shine upon the unthankful and the evil will not always cover

Himself with clouds from His own people. His common care has provided for the pleasure of His creatures: fruit to delight their tastes; flowers of various colors to delight their eyes and sense of smell; rivers, trees, meadows, and groves, and all the variety to be found in nature, to recreate and entertain them. And if all this accommodation is made for rebels, He will not fail to entertain His subjects with joys of a better kind. Joy is sown for the righteous, and it will arise in the time of harvest—and that time will shortly come.

If God has done so much to gratify the senses of His creatures with suitable satisfaction, the souls of His people, who are more noble, shall not be disappointed with such as are celestial and divine; for joy is that which, with a sweet allure, attracts the heart of man. God regards the distressed and has a peculiar pity for those who are in the greatest trouble, as mothers tend, with a peculiar care, the weakest child (see the sermons of Thomas Manton on 2 Thessalonians 2:17).

The world indeed admires, flatters, and waits upon those on whom the sun shines, and who are in a prosperous condition. As rivers run into the sea where there is no need of water, so the world heaps its friendships and kindnesses on those who least need them, and forsakes the disgraced, the poor, and those who are in want. But when God's servants are in the greatest troubles, He encourages them by His name, which is "the Father of mercies, and the God of all consolations." He is most mindful of them, visits them most, and gives them the most of His comforting presence when they are most afflicted. 2 Corinthians 1:4: "He comforteth us in all our tribulations." He will not give His people a constant ease. They shall not be excused from the common inconveniences of the fall—from sickness or death—but He is willing to be their portion. In all conditions He is their own God. They shall labor, but they shall have rest; they shall fight, but He will crown their heads with victory. They shall sow in tears, but reap in joy. The waves and the floods that now overwhelm them shall be turned into rivers of pleasure forevermore.

USE OF EXHORTATION. The use is contained in the following particulars:

1. Be very well satisfied that God carries you to heaven in the way that He thinks most proper. It would indeed be a very desirable thing to be at ease, to travel with His light about us; but if we must go through darkness, danger, and calamity to heaven, let us be satisfied that His will is done, though we go there weeping and groaning. Perhaps you think that he does not deserve the name of Christian who will not allow God to guide him down any path as long as it leads you to salvation; but, alas, how few there are who are satisfied with His methods!

When His candle shines upon our tabernacle, we are well enough pleased, but when He begins to correct and chasten us for a long season, then we murmur and repine; and when we meet with difficulties, tears, and troubles one upon another, then we think He is a hard master. This is our common case, and our common folly. We can all make the prayer of Jabez our own: "Oh, that Thou wouldest bless me indeed, and enlarge my coast, and that Thine hand might be with me, and that Thou wouldest keep me from evil, that it may not grieve me" (1 Chronicles 4:10). But how few can say heartily with our blessed Lord, "If the cup must not pass, Thy will be done"? He could bring you to heaven without a tear or a sigh, but, if not, who can resist His order or blame His providence? He led the children of Israel forty years wandering to and fro in a great and a terrible wilderness, wherein were fiery serpents and scorpions, and drought and no water (Deuteronomy 8:15), when He could have led them quickly to the land of Canaan.

You must not think to come to heaven without many a sad thought and many tears; through the valley of Baca you must travel on your way to the mount of God. The ark that had Noah in it did not immediately rest; it was not in one day that the great waters abated or fell into their old channels. Your passage to glory may be safe though it is very troublesome. The rods that seem to be the most painful may be the most necessary to you; for though the Israelites met with various troubles, yet "He led them forth by the right way, that they might go to a city of habitation" (Psalm 107:7).

It may be that you shall be shipwrecked into the haven, and, though you may be saved, yet it shall be as if by fire. Through many a sharp cross, through many a bitter tribulation, and in the fire, your comforts and your ease may suffer loss for a time, but it shall be made up again. Afflictions ruin none who belong to God, and many a Christian shall say at last, "I would have perished, if I had not perished. I would have been undone forever if I had not been afflicted."

Out of the ruins of our flesh God raises the glorious structure of the new creature, and from the destruction of our earthly comforts He causes heavenly joys to spring. Let us not find fault with God's providence, for it will turn our water into wine, our tears of grief into the most pleasant joys. As at the marriage of Cana, we will have the best at last. Our afflictions will increase our grace, and we shall, before long, mount up from the wilderness of this world, fraught with myrrh and frankincense and all the spices of the merchants.

Let us not find fault if we meet with the waters of Marah in our journey to the land of promise (see Bishop Joseph Hall on "The Marriage in Cana" in his *Works*). Thirst and bitterness are the portion of pilgrims; it is enough for us that we shall have rest at last, though we must not expect that the providence of God should go out of its ordinary course for us. Let us confide in His goodness, His faithfulness and loving-kindness, His Word and promise. These make up the quiet harbor into which we must put our trembling souls; these are the consolations that will make our bitter waters sweet. Submit therefore to God; to Him pour out your hearts, though you are long afflicted with one wave upon another.

Chapter 31

The conclusion of the whole treatise, with directions to such as have been formerly in the darkness of a sorrowful night, and now enjoy the light of day

Let us, with whom it was once night, make great use of that morning-joy that now shines upon us, and that briefly in these particulars:

1. Let us be continual admirers of God's grace and mercy to us. He has protected us with His goodness when He saw nothing in us but impatience and unbelief; when we were like Jonah in the belly of hell, His compassions yearned over us, and His power brought us safely to land. What did we do to hasten His deliverance or obtain His mercy? If He had not come to our relief until He saw something in us to invite Him, we would never have been relieved. No more did we contribute to our restoration than we do to the rising of the sun or the approach of day. We were like dry bones, without motion and without strength (Ezekiel 37:1).

We said that we were cut off and our hope was gone; and then He caused breath to enter into us and we lived. Who is a God like our God, who pardons iniquity, transgression, and sin; who does not retain His anger forever; who is slow to wrath and delights in mercy; who has been displeased with us for a moment, but gives us hope of His everlasting kindness? Oh, what love is due from us to Christ, who has pleaded for us when we ourselves had nothing to say; who has brought us out of a den of lions, and from the jaws of the roaring lion! In Henry Jesse's book entitled *The Riches of Grace Displayed in the Life of Mrs. Sarah Wright,* he quotes Mrs. Wright as saying, "I have obtained mercy, who thought my time of mercy past forever. I have hope of heaven, who thought I was already damned by unbelief. I said many a time, 'There is no hope in thine end,' and I thought I saw it. I was so desperate that I cared not what became of me. Oft was I at the very brink of death and hell, even at the very gates of both, and then Christ shut them. I was as Daniel in the lions' den, and He stopped the mouth of those lions and delivered me. The goodness of God is unsearchable; how great is the excellency of His majesty that yet He would look upon such a one as I! That He has given me peace who was full of terror, and who walked continually as amidst fire and brimstone!"

2. Let us walk humbly, and be full of cautious fear, that we do not offend a God who is so terrible, and that we do not grieve a Benefactor who is so good. Let us walk softly all our days, remembering that there was but a step between us and hell. Oh, let us put our mouths in the dust; let us loathe and abhor ourselves for the manifold iniquities that we were guilty of during the darkness of the night. And now that the morning has come, and such a morning as we never hoped to see, let us walk as children of the day, so that, having come out of the furnace, we may be as gold that is refined.

3. Though we rejoice, yet we must rejoice with trembling. I say with trembling, lest another night so black, so frightful, and so dismal come upon us. Let our obedience be more lively, and as the tender grass springing out of the earth by clear shining after rain. But let

us remember that our joy is not yet perfect, though it is as the light of the morning when the sun rises. It is not a morning without clouds (2 Samuel 23:4). The sun will be clouded with many fogs and mists, for it is yet but a morning sun; it will shine with greater glory in its height when the noonday and our complete salvation come.

The devil who has tempted us will assault us again; let us watch so that his designs may not take effect, for it may be that he has but left us for a season. Alas! Our unbelief and our other sins are not yet wholly dead. Let us rejoice that the face of God now shines upon us; but let us tremble to think what would become of us should it be hidden again. Let us rejoice that we have good hope through grace, but let us tremble lest despair and the pains of hell should take hold of us again. The fear that we have of future suffering somewhat now diminishes the brightness of our joy, though we ought not to live under the perpetual bondage of such fears, but to trust in God and hope that He will be our guide even unto death.

We are brought indeed out of the miry pit and the deep clay, yet we cannot but tremble at our foregoing misery. We are like a person who, after a shipwreck, has, with great difficulty, gotten safely to land upon a plank of wood; he finds himself in a safe place and rejoices in it. Nevertheless, the noise of the waves and the great agitation that he was so lately in make him tremble. He remains for a good while astonished at his former danger and his present safety.

Let us not have a trembling of distrust, but of vigilance and holy care—not to doubt the promises of God, but to keep down our own pride and carnal security. Let us pray that as He has set our feet upon a rock, so He would establish our goings. As we remember how low we have fallen, into what depths, and under what calamities, we have constant cause to be afraid. Psalm 149:6: "Let the high praises of God be in their mouths, and a two-edged sword in their hands." Let us be as those soldiers who, though they have newly gotten the victory over their enemies and rejoice for it, yet, amidst all their acclamations, stand on guard lest the remainder of those who are unsubdued should rally their scattered forces and attack them again to their disadvantage.

We must be very active in the service of our God. We must begin to travel while the morning lasts, and while we have day before us.

4. Our mouths must be full of praise to Him who has delivered us. Shall we not praise Him, to whom we vowed praises when we were in trouble? Shall we not praise Him, who alone has wrought salvation for us? None but He could help us, and He has done it. Magnificently He has delivered us, far above all our hopes. Oh, how much more pleasant is it to you and me to call Him "Father" than to fear Him as a Judge! How much more pleasant is it to celebrate His praises than to mourn over His departure, and to tune our harps after our captivity than to have them hanging on the willows!

Oh, let us praise Him, for He deserves our praise; let us praise Him, for He has remembered us in our low estate; let us praise Him, for His terrors, His rebukes, and His frowns are gone (Psalm 116:1–2; Psalm 37:6). The lightning and thunder, the horror and the darkness of the tempestuous night are over, and a cheerful and calm day now revives us. Let us praise Him, for He is infinitely excellent; let us praise Him, for He expects our praise. Psalm 116:1–3, 5: "I love the Lord, because He hath heard my voice and my supplications. Because He hath inclined His ear unto me, therefore will I call upon Him as long as I live; the sorrows of death compassed me, and the pains of hell gat hold upon me. I found trouble and sorrow. Gracious is the Lord, and righteous, yea, our God is merciful." Psalm 27:6: "Now shall mine head be lifted up above mine enemies round about me. Therefore will I offer in His tabernacle sacrifices of joy. I will sing, yea, I will sing praises unto the Lord." Did we ever hope to see the light of God again? Did we ever hope to think of heaven as our own portion, and of Christ as our own Savior? Did we ever hope that we should be thus at ease, and thus joyful, as we now are? God is our helper. God is our refuge and our stronghold; blessed be the name of the Lord.

5. Let us call upon our brethren and our friends to help us praise the Lord (see Psalm 145:2–3, 8–9, 14). As for myself, I make these requests: Bless the Lord, O house of Aaron and Levi. Bless Him, you ministers of the gospel who prayed for me in my trouble, and have had your prayers granted. Bless the Lord, O house of Israel, and all you people everywhere who sympathized with me, and kindly remembered me in my desolate condition. Bless Him, you old men, that you have gotten so far towards the haven without being thrown into the waves, or without being endangered by the rocks as I have been. Bless Him that you have not met with such violent temptations and great sorrows as I have met with, though I set out long after you did. Bless the Lord,

you young men, that you have not been weakened along the way with sore affliction, and with the terrors of the Lord, under which I groaned for so long. Bless Him, everyone, both small and great, against whom He does not proceed in such smart and severe providences, and in such long and sharp afflictions. Bless Him that you see before your eyes, and to help your faith, a person lately brought from the borders of the grave and of hell—one for whom you were concerned, and for whom you prayed; one who still needs and begs for your prayers, that he may never come to such a sad and doleful night again.

It is a common custom to congratulate our friends upon their recovery from sickness, or when they return from some foreign land; but nothing more deserves our common thanks than when a person has come from under the sense of God's displeasure to a sense of His favor and love again. Thus it was with Job in Job 42:11: "Then came there unto him all his brethren, and all his sisters, and all they that had been of his acquaintance before, and did eat bread with him in his house; and they bemoaned him, and comforted him over all the evil that the Lord had brought upon him." The psalmist, in Psalm 66:16, has a design to excite others to praise God with him: "Come and hear, all ye that fear God, and I will declare what He hath done for my soul." Or as the father of the prodigal said to his older son, who repined at the kindness that the father gave the younger son upon his returning home, "It was meet that we should make merry and be glad, for this thy brother was dead and is alive again, and was lost and is found" (Luke 15:32).

It is the design of God that the great and eminent

deliverances which He gives to some of His servants should be noticed by all the rest, so that, as they usually bring along with them a common benefit, so He should have a common return of praise. Psalm 66:8–9: "O bless our God, ye people, and make the voice of His praise to be heard, which holdeth our soul in life, and suffereth not our feet to be moved." Joining with others who have been in great distress, and who have escaped, is to answer the obligation we are under with regard to that precept to rejoice with those who rejoice. It is an encouragement to those who are yet in trouble. Psalm 130:7: "Let Israel hope in the Lord, for with the Lord there is mercy, and with Him is plenteous redemption." And to those who are yet at ease, we may say, as Paul did to Felix, that we wish they were such as we are, in some respects, that is, excepting our bonds, our anguish and tribulation; we with that they also had such experiences of the goodness and mercy of God.

6. Let us always wait and hope for that eternal felicity which will at length dawn upon all the people of God in the great morning of the resurrections. At their entrance into heaven there will be joy indeed. There is no night there; it is a place that is continually blessed with a bright and shining day. It is true that, as in nature the nights are not equal, those of the winter are much longer than those of the summer; but however long they are, they are always followed by the light of day. So whatever diversity there is among the afflictions of the faithful—to one they are much longer than to another—yet they shall have an end. Jacob wrestled with the angel all night, but in the morning he got the victory.

I confess that sinners in this world have their pleasures, but these are so beset with thorns, so attended with fears and pains, so short and so vanishing, that they do not deserve the name of pleasures. But in heaven, the sun that rises in the morning of our new glory will never set again; those pleasures are not like those of sin, lasting only for a season, but are forevermore. There our now-imperfect joy will be complete and full. It will be satisfying and eternal too. We shall feel the love of God in so sweet and transporting a manner that we shall never doubt whether He loves us or not. We shall always behold our Father's face. He will look on us with delight, and we shall look on Him with praise and joy.

This world, because of its lowness, is subject to inundations and miseries, and innumerable vicissitudes of pain and grief; but that high and glorious world is the place of triumph and victory. Then we shall see our sin, which made us weep, be totally defeated; then we shall see that devil who tempted us be trodden under our feet, and never able to tempt us any more. Let us often remember that saying of our Lord in John 16:21–22: "A woman, when she is in travail, hath sorrow because her hour is come. But as soon as she is delivered of the child, she remembereth no more the anguish, for joy that a man is born into the world. And ye now therefore have sorrow. But I will see you again, and your heart shall rejoice, and your joy shall no man taketh from you."

Oh, what a glorious morning that will be that has no cloud to obscure its light, and will never be followed with a sad or gloomy night! As our sufferings did here abound, our consolations then will much more abound. We shall forget all our labor and all our trouble when we see to what a glorious kingdom we are born, though that birth was by pangs and torment. Our joy will be like the joy of harvest: it will requite us well for all our care and toil. Our hopes here are like the first streaks of light in the sky that show the coming of the day, but our possession of blessedness will be as the sun in the fullness of His glory. That delight will indeed be the Sabbath of our thoughts, and the sweet and perpetual calmness of our minds, that will never be in horror and anguish any more.

Precious and admirable are those tears that end so well, and which prepare us for so good a state. Who would not choose thus to weep that he may rejoice forever? Lift up your eyes to the Jerusalem above, the city of the living God, you mourners and prisoners of hope, for it is the city of peace. Revelation 21:3–4: "Behold, the tabernacle of God is with men, and He will dwell with them, and they shall be His people, and God Himself shall be with them, and be their God. And God shall wipe away all tears from their eyes; and there shall be no more death, neither sorrow nor crying, neither shall there be any more pain, for the former things are passed away."